Food and Animal Welfare

Contemporary Food Studies: Economy, Culture and Politics

Series Editors: David Goodman and Michael K. Goodman

ISSN: 2058-1807

This interdisciplinary series represents a significant step toward unifying the study, teaching and research of food studies across the social sciences. The series features authoritative appraisals of core themes, debates and emerging research, written by leading scholars in the field. Each title offers a jargon-free introduction to upper-level undergraduate and postgraduate students in the social sciences and humanities.

Food and Animal Welfare

Henry Buller &
Emma Roe

BLOOMSBURY ACADEMIC
LONDON • NEW YORK • OXFORD • NEW DELHI • SYDNEY

BLOOMSBURY ACADEMIC
Bloomsbury Publishing Plc
50 Bedford Square, London, WC1B 3DP, UK

BLOOMSBURY, BLOOMSBURY ACADEMIC and the Diana logo are trademarks of
Bloomsbury Publishing Plc

First published in Great Britain 2018

Cover design: Adriana Brioso
Cover image: Domestic fowl (Gallus gallus f. domestica), free range white young laying hens.
(© blickwinkel / Alamy)

A catalogue record for this book is available from the British Library.

Library of Congress Cataloging-in-Publication Data
Names: Buller, Henry, author. | Roe, Emma, author.
Title: Food and animal welfare / Henry Buller & Emma Roe.
Description: London ; New York : Bloomsbury Academic, 2018. | Includes bibliographical
references and index. Identifiers: LCCN 2017046918| ISBN 9780857855787 (hpod) | ISBN
9780857857071 (pbk.)
Subjects: LCSH: Food animals–Moral and ethical aspects. | Animal welfare. | Food-supply–
Moral and ethical aspects.
Classification: LCC HV4757 .B85 2018 | DDC 179/.3–dc23 LC record available at https://lccn.
loc.gov/2017046918.

ISBN: HB: 978-0-8578-5578-7
          PB: 978-0-8578-5707-1
          ePDF: 978-0-8578-5737-8
          ePub: 978-0-8578-5694-4

Series: Contemporary Food Studies: Economy, Culture and Politics

Typeset by Integra Software Services Pvt. Ltd.
Printed and bound in Great Britain

To find out more about our authors and books visit www.bloomsbury.com and sign up for our
newsletters.

Contents

List of Figures

List of Charts

List of Tables

Acknowledgements

Much of the material for this book has come from the authors' experience in, and contribution to, a number of research projects undertaken over the last decade or so. First and foremost among these has been the EU FP6-funded Welfare Quality project, which ran from 2004 to 2009 under the leadership of Harry Blokhuis. Out of that large collaborative research project came more specific pieces of work both in the UK and in Hungary upon which we have drawn for much of the book, but particularly Chapter 5. Other sources of research funding that have contributed to the empirical work underlying this book include the ESRC-funded 'Understanding Human Behaviour through Human/ Animal Interaction' project (2009–2010, RES-355-25-0015), the University of Southampton Research Fund (2009) in Chapter 3, the British Academy funded 'Negotiating Post-Mao Natures: A recent history of NGO involvement in improving farm animal husbandry in China' (2007–2008, SG-45237) in Chapter 6, and AHRC-funded 'Protein Pressures and the Utopian Fair' (2016) and AHRC-funded 'Man Food: Exploring men's opportunities for "becoming an ecological citizen" through protein-related food practices' (2017–2018, AH/P009611/1) in Chapter 7.

Through these various projects and other work, we have had the privilege of working with a large number of people (academics, scientists, activists, carepersons, farmers, veterinarians, policy-makers, consumers, etc.) as well as bodies and organizations committed to improving the lives of farmed animals. Among them, we would like to expressly thank (in no particular order) Mara Miele, Harry Blokhuis, Marc Higgin, Adrian Evans, Terry Marsden, the late Jon Murdoch, Unni Kjaernes, Christine Cesar, David Main, Andy Butterworth, Becky Whay and colleagues at Bristol Vet School, Linda Keeling and colleagues at the SLU in Uppsala, Ruth Layton, Ashleigh Bright, Roland Bonney, the late Christopher Wathes, Steve Hinchliffe, John Bradshaw, Paul Hurley, Beth Greenhough and John Law, FAWC, UFAW. We also thank our friends, colleagues and students at the Departments of Geography at Exeter and Southampton; our families including Mary Rose Roe for sharing her life-long fascination with animals and their daily experiences; and Carl Roe, a village shop keeper, who inspired academic interest in food retailing, supply and growing. Finally, we would want to thank each other for a long-standing scientific collaboration and friendship that is as energetic and stimulating today as it ever was.

We dedicate this book to the next generation of protein eaters, including Lewis, Elliot and Amélie.

Introduction: Food and Animal Welfare

We largely take farm animals' lives (and deaths) for granted when we eat them and their products. For most of us, meat, egg and dairy consumption has become so distinct – geographically, morally, aesthetically – from livestock production that the animal 'disappears'. The very vocabulary of food often denies its animalian origin, principally to protect our own sensibilities either as carnivores or as co-animals (Twigg, 1979; Goldenberg, 2001; Evans and Miele, 2012). Packaging, presentation and labelling intentionally obscure the animal corporeality and liveliness behind the product (Vialles, 1994). Animals, if they are represented, often take an abstract and idealized form, close enough to suggest authenticity but distant enough to absolve responsibility. The worlds of consumption and production seem further apart than ever. They have become, in Goodman's (2002: 272) words, 'autonomous, "purified" categories of social life, sites only skeletally connected through the act of purchase'. If historically, domestic farm animals were considered subsidiary members of the human community (Thomas, 1983), towards the end of the nineteenth century it was already clear that 'the gulf was now very much wider between human needs on the one hand and human sensibilities on the other' (Thomas, 1983: 191). The industrialization and intensification of animal husbandry, coupled with the increasingly cheaper cost of animal products, a rapidly expanding urban consumer market and new retail and processing technologies, have all contributed to a process that distances animals from animal products while at the same time de-animalizing the latter (Guzman and Kjaernes, 1998; Buller, 2012). 'Most Americans', write Singer and Mason (2008: 37), 'know little of how their eggs are produced'. Regular annual surveys by the organization LEAF show surprisingly and consistently high proportions of young Britons unaware, for example, that bacon comes from pigs or milk from cows (LEAF, 2015). Of course, such distanciation serves the animal production sector well. As Shukin

(2009: 21) puts it: 'Rather than undermining the hegemony of market life, the contradictions of animal rendering are productive so long as they are discursively managed under the separate domains of culture and economy'. In terms of the broader universe of human–animal relations, consumers meanwhile both have their 'critters' *and* eat them.

The central argument of this original book, written by two social scientists/ geographers with a strong scientific and ethical commitment to bringing a social science understanding to farm animal care and welfare, is that concern for the welfare of farm animals (whether that concern is interpersonal, scientific, moral, gastronomic, aesthetic, social or economic or indeed a combination of these) constitutes a significant and vital linkage between the processes and the acts of consumption and production. Those links can be explicit or implicit, overt or hidden. They are rendered visible, or obscured, for a range of reasons, running from ethical engagement and anthropomorphic excess to economization, purposeful market segmentation and profitability. In drawing attention, first, to the corporeal materiality of animals as future food as well as to the feelings and psychological experiences of farmed animals and, second, to the practices of care, responsibility and attention afforded those animals by those who work alongside them, we argue that concern for the welfare of farmed animals fosters an inter-species communion of relationality and interdependence within the food chain that, whether we like it or not, implicates us more directly in the lives of those we eat and in the quality and value of those lives. Yet those interdependencies are mediated in a variety of different ways by different actors for different ends. Untangling such mediations is our goal.

Since the 1970s, farm animal welfare has emerged as a major consideration in the rules and standards governing animal production across a wide range of countries and global regions. In October 2016, the United Nations Committee on World Food Security published its 'Proposed draft recommendations on sustainable agricultural development for food security and nutrition, including the role of livestock' (United Nations, 2016). Recommendation 'D' of Article VIII, entitled *Animal health and welfare*, reads:

> Improve animal welfare delivering on the five freedoms and related OIE standards and principles, including through capacity building programs, and supporting voluntary actions in the livestock sector to improve animal welfare. (United Nations, 2016: 2)

Animal welfare concerns are having an increasingly important impact upon the way animals are farmed, transported and slaughtered, upon the structures, institutions and regulations that accompany these processes and upon the individual practices of husbandry and care. Animal welfare concerns affect how animal products are prepared, selected, identified, sold and consumed. In many parts of the world, animal welfare is a significant factor in the segmentation of product markets and an increasingly important ethical concern in consumer choice. Finally, it is, we must hope, improving the lives of those animals that are farmed.

Those lives should be 'worth living' (FAWC, 2009). Recent food scares in the UK and Europe, such as Foot and Mouth, bovine spongiform encephalopathy or BSE and bird flu, the emergence of more ethical forms of food consumption, even the topical engagement of celebrity chefs, have all contributed to the growing profile of this issue, one to which the retailers and food manufacturers, as well as producers and consumers, are increasingly responding. In this way, how a farm animal lives, the quality of its life and the materialization of that quality become critical elements in linking together issues of food production and food consumption.

Animal welfare permeates the entirety of the food chain, transcending the traditional divisions between production and consumption, between farm and fork, from the animal body that is 'created' and cared for to the carcass that is rendered and the steak that is eaten. Yet this permeation is only partially acknowledged. In many ways it is hidden, differentially and selectively made visible at diverse stages in the food chain, for a variety of reasons. As the science of animal welfare as a distinctive branch of veterinary science, applied ethology and animal biology has developed, so too have the (bio)-politics and the ethics of animal farming and animal care, opening the necessity, we maintain, for a more critical social science investigation of animal welfare, its practice, its science, its commodification and its governance (Bock and Buller, 2013). New regulatory and institutional frameworks have developed and new political and economic actors have emerged. Despite this, the constitution of animal welfare, its definition, its practice and its ethical resonances within the food chain are not fixed. They are, we argue, differentially constructed, mobilized, negotiated and practised at varied points and through multiple processes. It is here that a social science perspective has a distinct and, we would argue, critical contribution to make to the study of farm animal welfare and its negotiated place within the food chain.

This book proposes an original and multiple examination of these various actions to consider the integrative (and disintegrative) nature of farm animal welfare as an analytical frame and lens for studying the geographies, economies, cultures, practices and politics of the food sector. Drawing in part upon recent empirical research undertaken by the authors themselves over the last decade or so, both individually and together, it offers a unique look at those farm animal lives – how they are cared for, how that care becomes defined and assessed as welfare, how this impacts upon and becomes part of what defines product value and quality, how it moves through the food chain (from property of a life to property of a product) and is marketed, sold and eventually consumed. We are interested in this volume to explore how concern for the welfare of farm animals is translated into strategies and practices of care and to use Haraway's (2008: 71) ingenious turn of phrase, 'response-ability', both on farm and beyond into the supply chain to include processors, retailers and consumers. We seek to explore, through case studies, how local cultural politics and practices within and across national boundaries shape the practice and feasibility of various welfare and care strategies. In short, our central objective in this book is to explore how the welfare of individual animal lives, differentially defined by cultural values, by objective science and by the shared corporealities of animal and keeper, becomes assembled, transited and redefined as it is mobilized through the food chain from site of production to site of consumption. Our argument is that consideration for the welfare of the animal, whether scientific, ethical or simply pecuniary, is a variable relational achievement, differentially constructed and differentially expressed but which nevertheless offers a crucial connectivity (whether explicit or concealed) between production and consumption.

To do this, we draw upon a range of cognate conceptual and theoretical positions. Our analysis is located within both contemporary food studies (Goodman, 1999, 2001) and the maturing domain of animal studies (Buller, 2014). Recent writing on post-humanism (Wolfe, 2010) and more-than-human worlds (Whatmore, 2006; Bastian et al., 2017) inform this investigation as does the work of Callon (1998) and others on commodification and economization. We draw in particular upon scholars such as Haraway (2008), Despret (2006), Porcher (2016) and Puig de la Bellacasa (2017) all of whom, in various ways, interrogate how shared and caring relationships between humans and (in our case, captive) animals matter, or might matter. 'That mattering', writes Haraway (2008: 70), 'is always inside connections that demand and enable response, not bare calculation or ranking'. 'Response', she goes on, 'of course grows with the capacity to respond, that is, responsibility', and a little later on in the same passage: 'animals in all their worlds, are response-able in the same sense as people are; that is responsibility is a relationship crafted in intra-action through which entities, subjects and objects, come into being' (2008: 71). We seek in this book to explore and trace that 'responsibility' as it is differentially manifested (and given value) throughout the food chain. Because animal welfare is a curious blend of naturalist animal science and human ethics, values and behaviour (Fraser, 1999; Sandoe et al., 2003), we draw too upon science and technology studies in this volume, interrogating the science and qualification of animal welfare, both negative and positive, within the contested biopolitics where the supply of animal lives and the demands of human markets interact (Shukin, 2009).

Of course, farmed animals are consumed and their bodies and body processes exploited by human kind all over the world. In this book, however, our geographical and sociocultural coverage is, perhaps inevitably, limited largely, but not exclusively, to the Global North and, in particular, to Europe. Certainly, our own predominantly UK perspective on farm animal welfare, its definition and conceptualization, its societal impact and its economic role within food supply chains lead perhaps to a major emphasis in the analysis being placed upon highly industrialized and commercialized animal agricultural systems feeding into centralized and corporate retail sectors where consumer demands are regarded as both powerful and diverse. As a result, other formations of husbandry, processing and commercialization, along with other culturally specific interpretations of animal welfare and human societal concern for it, are not so systematically addressed here. Our only justification for this, apart from the fact that it unavoidably reflects our own personal trajectories, is that increasingly it is this broadly generalizable 'northern' industrial model (rather than simply geographical provenance) that is responsible for the majority of animal products (particularly, poultry, pigs and eggs) available for human consumption across the world.

Throughout the book, we combine critical and reflective review and analysis with data and observation drawn from our own empirical, policy-related and ethnographic work. Our recent and ongoing collaborations with farm animal welfare scientists, applied ethologists, veterinarians, policy-makers and others in the UK, France, Sweden, the USA, Hungary and China have both inspired and contributed to the current volume. We have drawn heavily on this and other research, from our joint involvement in the European Union (EU)-funded Welfare Quality project (Buller and Roe, 2008, 2010) and in collaborative work on the commodification of poultry welfare (Buller and Roe, 2013), to individually undertaken research on farms (Buller, 2012; Roe and Greenhough, 2014), in slaughterhouses (Roe 2010; Buller 2016), within veterinary practices (Buller, 2015b), in animal laboratories (Greenhough and Roe, 2011; 2017) and both alongside and within academic research institutions and policy-advisory bodies.

In addition to more conventional styles of review and analysis, we have incorporated into the book in a number of places narrative and observational accounts of specific encounters with farmers, animal carers and animal welfare researchers both in the UK and elsewhere (notably China). These we present as distinct and intentional departures from the style of the rest of the book in the hope that they provide concrete and in-depth examples of how specific forms and practices of animal care and welfare assessment become enrolled into processes of food chain qualification and commodification. In all of this, we offer a unique and original social science perspective, one that we argue is much needed, on the transitioning and transformative place, practice and policy of animal welfare throughout the food system.

The book comprises seven chapters. In the first of these we bring together two, until now, relatively distinct areas of scholarship that are seldom conceptualized together other than in a singularly instrumentalist fashion: food studies and animal studies. We begin by situating the study of farm animals and farm animal welfare within contemporary food studies literature, defining such study as occupying a complex place within this now substantive scholarship, yet one particularly open to an integrative interdisciplinary analytical perspective. We then trace the emergence of farm animals and their welfare as a relatively new theme in recent social science, and explore the intellectual lineage of current scientific engagements with animals, non-human bodies and human–animal care relations, particularly through human–animal studies and animal geographies. Our argument in this opening chapter is that the welfare of farm animals – as a component of animal subjectivity, an element of objectified product quality and a factor in consumer choice – pervades the entire food chain offering the possibility for a more analytically coherent perspective on the hitherto distinctive worlds of production and those of consumption.

The second chapter explores in some depth how formal concern for the welfare of farmed animals has emerged over the last half century in the Global North, and particularly in Europe and the USA, and how it is currently expressed and articulated through three distinct forms of engagement. The first of these is scientific engagement, and we trace the manner in which the welfare of farmed animals becomes a distinct and calculable object of a distinctive science and scientific epistemology, one that has, in its fifty or so years of existence, shifted significantly from an early mechanistic and essentially productivist approach to one that is arguably, and in part at least, far more qualitative and individualistic today. The scientific measurability of welfare has, however, rendered it more visible, prompting the development of our second and third engagements. On the one hand, there has been an emergent ethical engagement with the welfare of farm animals. Here, we chart the ethical concern for the welfare of farm animals that has been a keen component of late twentieth-century social engagement leading, most commonly, to selective consumer preference. On the other hand, the measurability and calculation of levels of positive and negative welfare have permitted the enrolment of farm animal welfare into differential expressions of product quality and the segmentation of animal product markets. Drawing, in part, on the work of Callon, we explore, in this final part of the chapter, how welfare has become established as 'economic'.

In Chapter 3, we take our first step back from the broader more synthetic analysis of categories and trends in the relationship between farm animal welfare and the food system offered in Chapter 2 to present a more specific and detailed examination of distinct on-farm practices, where care is performed and enacted at the inter-individual human–animal level. Taking Mol et al.'s (2010) insistence on care as practice (a practice that, in the case of livestock farming, can no longer be seen as a simple alternative to technology), and Puig de la Bellacasa's (2017: 5) notion of care as a 'concrete work of maintenance', we explore the differing dimensions of labour, affect and ethics that contribute, at least in part, to the welfare of individual farm animals (both as knowledge/ science and as practice), even in those moments where, as Puig de la Bellacasa (2017) points out, one or more of these might be withheld or absent. Employing a more distinctive narrative style, this third chapter draws upon observational and ethnographic fieldwork research undertaken by Roe in 2009 on the work of farm animal carers. It explores closely the demands and practices of caring for animals within the economy of food production with a view to establishing care as a form of inter-species *naturesociety* practice that becomes embodied within the welfare of the animal's life and ultimately the 'quality' of the animal product. The chapter also discusses the topic of making an animal killable through empirical observations of when and how killing takes place on the farm for those animals that don't make it into the formal human food supply chain. The chapter closes by exploring the individual challenges for those tasked with making decisions or actually performing the kill.

The fourth chapter turns away from the farm and from lived animal lives to focus more directly on the food product, and the mechanisms by which the materialized matter of welfare (Roe, 2010) becomes commodified, marketed and ultimately consumed as a component of product 'quality'. We show how the welfare of farmed animals is increasingly used as a means of differentiating products and segmenting markets within food retailing through a series of what Callon et al. (2007) refer to as 'market devices' such as certification, assurance, auditing and labelling. In this chapter, which borrows much from work we have done on the construction and placing of farm animal welfare within the food processing and retailing sectors (Roe and Higgin, 2008; Buller and Roe, 2010, 2012; Buller, 2013a, b), we trace four 'frames' (responsibilization, segmentation, assurance and labelling) demarcating the mechanisms by which welfare 'claims' are made, marketized, governed and enacted through different stages of the food processing and retailing chain.

The fifth and sixth chapters expand the scope of the book by extending our analysis of welfare in the human food chain to the exploration of different national contexts and experience. We are interested here in investigating how the growth of broad societal concern for farm animal welfare, how the maturity of animal welfare science and how the advent of an increasingly far-reaching governance regime (which is both regulation- and market-led), all increasingly prevalent in Western European and North American states, impact upon the food chain organization and production–consumption relations within other states where there has been little traditional engagement in these areas. Hence, Chapter 5 examines differences across Europe in how the retail market for higher animal welfare–friendly food products has operated, with particular attention to Hungary's capacity, as a relatively new EU Member State, to address farm animal welfare, and the EU regulatory and policy regime to which it has signed up as a condition of entry. In Chapter 6, we return to the more in-depth ethnographic and narrative style employed in Chapter 3. Using extracts from field notebooks and interview transcripts from ethnographic research undertaken by one of the current book's authors (Roe) in 2007–8, this chapter looks in detail at the emergence of farm animal welfare in China during the period 2007–8 and the key role played by international animal welfare organizations in driving the Chinese welfare agenda.

In the final chapter, we come back to our starting question: how, through the processes of food production and consumption, and, to what degree, can we actively engage with the lives (and with actively improving the lives) of those farmed animals upon whom we largely (rightly or wrongly) depend for food and other commodities. What we are looking for in this final section are contemporary and novel mechanisms of ethical connectivity between the consumer of, for example, meat and eggs and the lived lives of cattle and hens; mechanisms that reach across the distinctions between the human–animal proximities of production and the human–animal distances of consumption, between welfare as lived non-human animal experience and welfare as 'value added', between the intimate practices of caring for and detached practices of caring about. For the moment at least, there is little real alternative to animal farming as a means of meeting the protein requirements of our ever-expanding humanity, though there are suggested alternative animals that might be more appropriately farmed. Our perhaps naive hope is that, even within the inevitably asymmetrical bio-political-capital agencies of inter-species animal farming, there are better ways of overcoming the inherent and normative objectification through which non-human animal lives become human food products. Part of that process must include a reimagining of our interdependencies and what we ultimately share with non-human animals.

Chapter 1

Food and the Animal

It matters which worlds world worlds. It matters who eats whom and how. It is a material question for cosmopolitical critters. (Haraway, 2015: xiv)

Humans have always eaten other animals. Although vegetarianism and veganism are historically far more prevalent than traditional narratives of human food practices might suggest, and even define the pre-fall dining practices of humanity (Eisenman, 2013), the killing and eating of non-human animals is often held to be a foundational ontological act. It is their very edibility that distinguishes them, and therefore us, in the hubristic and self-serving classification of the universe we call our own. One consequence of this long-standing edibility has been that human history is inexorably intertwined with animal history (Fitzgerald, 2010; Bourke, 2011) even though the latter remains largely invisible (Fudge, 2002). The result is a co-evolved relationship. All eating is relational as species co-evolve with the other species they eat (Pollan, 2009). However, human omnivorousness has not only adapted and responded to the physical and biological availability of different foodstuffs and nutrients, animal or otherwise; it has gone a lot further. First through animal domestication and, far more recently, through the emergence of the modern high-meat protein Western diet (and the intensive livestock systems required to supply it), food has become far more than simple nutrition and agriculture far more than simple nutrient supply. Our relationship to food and food animals has, over the last 150 years, undergone a very profound change (Pollan, 2006). There are many dimensions to this both quantitatively and qualitatively but one in particular draws our attention. In 1997, the European Union Amsterdam Treaty's Protocol on Animal Welfare formally recognized animals as 'sentient beings' and required Member States to 'pay full regard to the welfare requirements of animals'. This was later adopted as a more legally powerful Article in the 2009 Lisbon Treaty. Although limited in its legal reach only to European Union Member States, this formal acknowledgement of sentience is both an acceptance of what many people involved directly and indirectly in the lives of animals have believed for a long time and an indicator of the growing societal and scientific concern for the way in which animals, and in particular farmed animals, are treated within animal farming systems. At one level, this cultural shift in how we understand and relate to animals, particularly the animals we eat, has generated a market in foodstuffs where there is concern for the subjective experience of the animal life lived, before being slaughtered to be eaten or while producing eggs or dairy products for human consumption. At another level, intensive animal production and indeed the very consumption of meat and other animal products are coming under increasing challenge on ethical, health, distributional and environmental grounds even as, globally, the number of animals farmed and meat consumption itself continue to increase vertiginously.

The emergence of these concerns has largely coincided with a new academic and scientific interest in both animals and food. Food studies and animal studies are now established interdisciplinary fields within the broader social sciences. Yet, as these have grown and developed over the last twenty or so years, we are struck by the relatively limited engagement of both with the various issues associated with farm animals, their welfare and their products. Our aim therefore in this chapter is first to trace and explore the reoccurring absences and reluctant presences of farm animals within both these banner specializations and their parent disciplines. We argue that although sociology, geography and other cognate social sciences have, to a point, come to embrace animal and food studies as distinctive and innovative areas of scholarship, farm animals specifically remain, as so often, either at the periphery of all this or otherwise enrolled in a very distinctive set of engagements and activism. Yet, we maintain, farm animals offer a unique material and a conceptual link not only between human and non-human but also between the processes and relations of production and consumption. The chapter then goes on to explore and introduce some of the key conceptual ideas that underpin those linkages, notably labour, matter, ethics and, finally, welfare.

Food and animal becomings: Narratives

Disciplines and sub-disciplines abound in the social sciences. Postmodernism, and its challenge to the intellectual and scientific edifices and orderings of modernism, has helped to stimulate a veritable flourishing of new scientific 'objects', 'subjects' and epistemologies. Writing in 1988, the geographer Michael Dear refers to the 'maze of diverse interests' and 'extreme eclecticism' that characterizes what he feels is the 'crisis' or growing 'disarray' of his discipline. Identifying over fifty 'topical proficiencies' in geography, Dear sees in this multiplicity a dangerous fragmentation. A similar critique, this time of the social sciences in general, is offered by Van Langenhove (OECD, 2003: 46) who laments the division of the 'established disciplines' into 'many competing (or even mutually ignoring) theoretical and/or methodological schools'.

Among these divisions and fragmentations, both 'animals' and 'food' have newly emerged as sub-disciplinary preoccupations or foci in their own right within (and, on occasion, across) a number of cognate 'established' subjects – sociology, geography in particular but also anthropology, psychology, ethnography, politics, political economics and so on. The fact that neither appeared in Dear's lists of Association of American Geographers (AAG) Speciality Groups hints that these are relatively recent specializations, at least in geography. Indeed, although today we might recognize a rapidly expanding corpus of social science scholarship under the banners 'Animal Studies' or 'Food Studies', both food and animals have long been neglected by the more mainstream preoccupations of their ontologically cautious disciplines.

For Beardsworth and Keil (1997), the long-standing absence of food and eating from the more mainstream body of sociological enquiry remains a puzzle. The human food chain, they argue, is the 'core sub-system of the social system as a whole, the very foundation of human social organization' (1997: 2; see also Levi-Strauss, 1964). Yet, despite a rich tradition in agrarian and rural studies, food, with its evident sociocultural attributes and significances, remained for sociologists and geographers largely a cultural artefact of limited explanatory power and thereby scientific interest. Atkins and Bowler (2001), citing Mennell et al. (1992), suggest that its simple familiarity and its mundanity prevented food from entering the Anglo-Saxon social science lexicon (though they acknowledge its importance in French and Italian academic traditions). Jackson (2013) refers to the accusation that food studies were seen as 'scholarship lite' not so very long ago.

If food was, for a long time, largely 'invisible' to the (human) social sciences, the same is even more so for animals (Noske, 1997). Placing her hopes in environmental sociology, Tovey (2003: 196) writes:

> Environmental sociology tends to absorb animals into 'wild nature', with virtually nothing to say about the huge numbers that exist of domestic, service or functional animals (food animals, experimental animals in scientific laboratories, working animals in circuses, transportation or elsewhere); and it tends to recognise animals only in the form of populations or generic types, without individual character, knowledge, subjectivity or experience.

'To read most sociological texts', she goes on, 'one might never know that society is populated by non-human as well as human animals' (Tovey, 2003:

197). Elsewhere (Buller, 2013b, 2014, 2015a), we have explored the emergence of 'animal geography' as a distinct area of scholarship and there now exist a significant number of texts on the emergence of animal studies across a number of disciplinary perspectives (e.g. Wolch and Emel, 1998; Franklin, 1999; Philo and Wilbert, 2000; Haraway, 2008; Peggs, 2012; Weil, 2012). This is not the place to retrace the distinctive histories of animal and food studies. We are more interested in their intertwining and potential relatedness for both inform the current study. There are a number of points we wish to make here.

First, contemporary food studies and animal studies both start from the premise of a fundamental epistemological redefinition of the status of their relative objects of study. As Winter (2003) illustrates, food used to be seen within the academy principally as the raw material or product of agriculture. Similarly, animals, whether wild or domesticated, were frequently evoked as the markers of a distributional geography of either environmental or human agency (Philo and Wilbert, 2000; Buller, 2014). Both animals (particularly farm animals) and food easily disappeared within a newly forged political economy of agriculture that in its 1980s heyday offered both macro-analysis of agro-food globalization, following the collapse of the post-war food regime (Marsden et al., 1986), and micro-analysis of agro-food labour divisions but, in Busch and Juska's (1997: 689) words, told us 'little about its specifics'. What has ultimately liberated food and animals from this conceptual myopia has been a growing frustration with, first, the inattention paid by instrumental political economy analysis to cultural difference and cultural meaning, particularly as it impacted upon the complex networks that ultimately linked global agro-food systems (or indeed global wildlife trading, Whatmore and Thorne, 1997) to localities, food consumers and individuals – human or otherwise (Marsden et al., 1996). Second, and at roughly the same time, a growing post-humanist interrogation of the dualist ontology of 'nature' and 'culture' that had been so seemingly foundational to modernity (Latour, 1993) and was well rooted in agro-food studies (Goodman, 2002: 182), began to implicitly challenge the way in which such studies ignored the relational materialities and socialities of the 'natural', whether they were ecosystems, animals, food matter or bodies – human or otherwise (Fitzsimmons, 1989). What was required was 'a new analytical engagement with the materiality of nature; that is an ontologically real and active, lively presence' (Goodman, 2002: 183). Up until this point, 'nature' (in which we might also place animals) had been, in agro-food research, something to be mastered, something subsumed or appropriated into the metabolic relations of the agricultural processes under solely human agency (Goodman, 2002). Farm animals, as the machines of productivity, were exemplary in this regard.

Both food studies (Cox, 2012) and animal studies (Whatmore, 2006) draw from the so-called 'cultural turn' of the social sciences in the 1990s. This brought a new understanding of the multiple cultural and semiotic referentials that both defined food and animals and differentially enrolled them into the complex networks that comprised social life. Acknowledging the shift in attention away from the formerly dominant political economy of food production towards the socio-materialism of food consumption (Ashley et. al., 2004), Goodman and Dupuis (2002: 5) write:

> The current interest in food consumption and its politics is informed by the earlier 'turn' to culture and the cultural in post-structuralist and post-modernist social theory which contested the dominant optic of production relations, workplace politics and associated conceptualizations of power.

Similarly, Philo and Wolch (1998: 107) speak of a new 'cultural animal geography' which 'reflects upon situations where people and animals coexist in particular sites and territories', leading to an interrogation of the different cultural meanings, and socio-spatial practices, that emanate from such classifications as 'wild', 'unclean', 'domestic' and 'charismatic' (Philo, 1995; Hvorka, 2008). However such anthropocentric and constructivist cultural referentials, while they laid bare the complexities and ambiguities of multiple human–animal relations, ultimately did little to alter the epistemological status of 'the animal' or the supremacy of 'human' culture. For that, a further rotation in the social sciences has been necessary, one referred to as the 'post-human' (Wolfe, 2010), the 'non-human' (Grusin, 2015) or the 'animal(s)' turn (Wheeler and Williams, 2012). Inspired by post-structuralist and post-humanist contestation of the ontological invincibility and exceptionalism of the human and the human subject and its consequences, coupled with a methodological endeavour to get beyond the text and language (the 'counter-linguistic turn', Weil, 2010), as well as by a new ethical sensibility for the more-than-human, contemporary animal studies have, in decentring the human, effectively recast the animal and animals as subjects not only 'of a life' but of an equal or, at very least, contributory relational status in our understanding of, and being in, the world (e.g. Haraway, 2003; Jerolmak, 2009; Nimmo, 2011). Whether such conceptual and metaphysical strides within the (multispecies) academy have had any impact upon the foreshortened lives of farm animals is a point to which we return in this volume's conclusion.

Second, and partly as a result of the common stimulus of post-structural critique, contemporary food and animal studies share a certain preoccupation with alterity and with it, a febrile engagement with ethics. Food studies have certainly been intellectually invigorated over the last twenty or so years by an interest in alternative food systems (Maye et al., 2007), an interest that brings together the politics of quality, the social control over processes of production, valorization and commercialization, consumer reflexivity, food knowledge, alternative food networks and fairer trade (Goodman et al., 2012). Although this new food politics has been largely confined to operating in the gaps within the mainstream industrial agro-food sector, it nevertheless offers a far-reaching critique of that sector, exposing its unsustainability and uneven distributional impact. In doing so, these alternative food networks bridge the hitherto abyssal divide between the worlds of food production and those of food consumption through an active politics of reconnectivity, something that has been welcomed in British farming policy:

> The key objective of public policy should be to reconnect our food and farming industry: to reconnect farming with its market and the rest of the food chain; to reconnect the food chain and the countryside; and to reconnect consumers with what they eat and how it is produced. (Policy Commission on the Future of Farming and Food, 2002: 6)

Starting with an emphasis on the potential social power of consumers and their representatives, and acknowledging the twin processes of 'marketization' and 'commodification' (Caliskan and Callon, 2009) by which markets are enrolled in social practice, 'alternative' food networks extend their transformative reach deep into food provisioning and global trade circuits (Goodman et al., 2012). In many countries, organic, fair trade and free range have now become familiar not only as labels in higher range specialist outputs but also as production systems serving mainstream retail outlets. As we shall demonstrate later on in this volume, farm animal welfare has become part of the new ethical repertoire of consumer-driven food concerns, at least in some parts of the world.

The alterity inherent in contemporary animal studies has a similar potential for far-reaching impact. As we have seen, such studies implicitly or explicitly challenge human exceptionalism, the singular relevance of human agency and the broader ethos of unequivocal anthropocentrism. 'We have an intellectual responsibility', write Wolch and Emel (1998: xi) in one of the first texts of *Animal Geographies*, 'as well as an ethical duty to consider the lives of animals closely'. A significant number of those engaged in animal studies specifically seek, through their scholarship and activism, profound and lasting changes in the way humans treat animals. When it comes to food animals and their treatment in industrial livestock production systems, animal studies and food studies may variously come together over a common agenda linking food identity politics, consumer concern for ethical supply chains and animal freedoms.

'Critical animal studies' (CAS) more specifically draws on anarchist political theory, feminism, intersectionality, critical race studies, post-humanism and activist political engagement (Best et al., 2007; Twine, 2010; Taylor and Twine, 2014; White, 2015). CAS are explicit in their 'normative commitment to the removal of all forms of animal abuse', which include the killing and eating of animals, as well as their embrace of emancipatory and 'engaged theory' as means of achieving social change (Taylor and Twine, 2014: 6). As such, CAS take issue with what Twine (2010: 21) calls, rightly or wrongly, the 'docile ethics' and the residual humanism (Wolfe, 2010) of much human–animal scholarship. Others go further by declaiming what they see as the comfortable alignment and complicity of animal studies with animal testing, animal agriculture and vivisection. CAS have little place for welfarism in animal husbandry (Cole, 2011).

Notwithstanding their independent trajectories, food studies and animal studies share certain communalities in radical approaches to their subject matter, in their relatively subversive placing within the disciplinary homelands and in their transformative agendas, both scientific and political. We have felt it useful to highlight some of these. Of course, for a great many humans and for a great many non-humans, animals are also food. While the watchword of the biannual meetings of the British Animal Studies Network might well be *we don't eat our subject matter*, animals are known to us principally by their edibility (or otherwise). It is to this that we now turn.

Animals becoming food: Entanglements

Given the communalities identified above, the absence of food animals from contemporary food geography is striking. Food geography writing largely begins with the product. In his widely cited and, in many ways, groundbreaking paper *Follow the Thing: Papaya*, Cook (2004: 643) starts his account in the following way: 'Once they're picked, they start to die. Twisted off the stem.' Such an approach, we have argued elsewhere (Roe, 2006: 106–7), 'shows little concern for agricultural nature and its constituent metabolic relations'. The 'inter-species metabolisms and exotic corporealities' (Goodman, 2001: 196) from which food – and particularly food of animal origin – comes are somehow excluded from these food narratives, always at risk of fetishizing the commodity (Goodman et al., 2012). Food and flesh are disassociated in a manner that fails to account for non-human life (whether animal or plant) as anything other than actual or potential product. Yet, animals, both materially (Atkins, 2011) and symbolically (Douglas, 1970), permeate our food systems, whether we eat them or not.

Animal capital flows everywhere through the institutions and enterprises of contemporary global capitalism (Shukin, 2009; Emel and Neo, 2015). 'When a cow is just a cow, McDonalds becomes possible', writes Steeves (1999: 2).

Not surprisingly then, the emergent field of human–animal studies (including animal geography) has also shown a certain reluctance to engage with farm animals (Buller, 2015a), where the incontestable imbalances inherent in such an instrumental relationship fly in the face of would-be post-human symmetries. Pet animals, wild animals and, though to a lesser extent, zoo animals make up by far and away the bulk of the existing animal studies menagerie. However, farmed animals are not entirely absent from the animal studies canon. They appear most often as units of production (Symes and Marsden, 1985) or commodities within food chains or networks (Stassart and Whatmore, 2003; Watts, 2000; Wilkie, 2005; Jackson et al., 2006; Shukin, 2009; Emel and Neo, 2015). Elsewhere, they have been evoked as carriers of zoonotic diseases (Enticott, 2001; Donaldson and Wood, 2004); or as genetically manufactured by modern, intensive breeding techniques (Morris and Holloway, 2008). Exceptionally, some authors have sought to identify and explore the lived experiences of animals themselves such as the work of Holloway (2007) and Risan (2005) who study bovine subjectivities through their complex interactions with human beings and technologies. Few, however, have looked explicitly at the transgression from living animal to meat (though see Roe, 2010 Miele and Rucinska, 2015; Buller, 2016).

A major component of contemporary human–animal studies is nonetheless explicitly critical of livestock farming – in terms of the general ethical context of eating animals (Fudge, 2010), in terms of the treatment of farm animals within (particularly industrialized) production systems (Gillespie and Collard, 2015) and in terms of the contribution of animal studies to a broader intersectional critique (Twine, 2010; Nocella et al., 2014). Yet, as we have argued elsewhere (Buller, 2013c), such entirely defendable positions may nonetheless obfuscate the mundane theatres and daily performances of care as well as mutual, and by no means entirely negative, assembly. Farm animals share the work environments and living places of many humans in what are often intimate and caring forms of coexistence. As Emel and Neo (2015: 360) acknowledge: 'We are already in cohabitation and under co-obligation to the others in this entanglement'. The question for animal studies might be less how to simply get rid of farm animals but rather, as Haraway asks, 'how to honour the entangled labour of humans and animals together' (2008: 80). This has been our cue in this current work though we extend that entanglement of labour (and care) to include the entangled materialities and 'fleshy kinship' of animal bodies as they become food. Adams (2000: 14) talks of the 'absence' behind every meal of meat, the absence of the animal 'whose place the meat takes'. Exploring ways to acknowledge, and perhaps to act upon, the animal presence in the 'stuff' of what we cat is a fundamental objective of this book.

Entangled labour

The industrialization of the livestock farming sector over the last fifty or so years has driven a double disappearance. On the one hand, farm animals have gradually been removed from our sight, progressively enclosed in all-year-round mass housing units where a single broiler shed in the UK might contain 30,000 birds for the brief six weeks of their life, while we ourselves become increasingly concentrated in towns and cities. For many people, their only engagement with a chicken comes at the supermarket. On the other hand, and in step with the industrialization and intensification of the livestock sector, full-time farmers and farm labourers have similarly disappeared in an industry that measures its modernization by falls in farmer–animal ratio. As the number of dairy cows in Europe (EU 28) rises to 23.47 million (a 1.2 per cent rise between 2012 and 2013), the number of dairy farms fell by 6.2 per cent over the same period (AHDB, 2017). The 'entangled labour' of humans and animals is becoming increasingly mediated through technology and machinery where physical presence is replaced by distant observation and, under the banner of sustainable intensification and precision farming, by animal self-regulation. As massed farmed animals or birds become the transitory, and increasingly low-value, 'crops' of an enhanced and excessive biology, the opportunities for entanglement become limited. While a dairy or beef farmer might invest time and attention in contact with animals of repetitive or long-term value, the numbers and shortened lives of many animals and birds on farm for fattening might preclude realistic co-response-ability.

In her book *Livestock, Deadstock*, to which we return later, Wilkie (2010) explores the pragmatic nature of producer–livestock interaction. She argues that non-monetary values play an important role in husbandry relations as farm animals, unlike other market commodities, are both sentient and sociable (see also Holloway, 2002). What counts for them should be important (Buller, 2012). Porcher (2002), in one of a series of studies of human–animal relations in livestock farming, identifies a wide range of parameters of affection that underlie such relations, yet are threatened by increasingly intensive production methods. In Chapter 3, we explore in greater depth the nature and expression of care as a component of welfare in farmer–animal relations. Here, we are interested in these entanglements of labour.

I'm working wi [sic] them every day. People work with people every day and they're their work colleagues. I work with the animals. (commercial stockman, quoted in Wilkie, 2010: 131)

For Porcher (2006), the interactive and interdependent nature of human and animal labour within animal farming systems has been profoundly ignored or misunderstood both within the academy (in sociology and in animal welfare science) and in the process of agricultural modernization.

> The big unknown in scientific construction of the 'well-being of livestock animals' has been the question of work. The highly particular position of animals in this specific work world is nonetheless what founds the relation between the animals and livestock farmers and forms the basis of production systems. Treatment and handling of livestock animals – in other words, animal living conditions – are a component of work organization, an arrangement that involves humans and animals in the same system. (2006: 57–58)

Shared work and labour, she argues, are critical to understanding human–animal relations on the farm. Work is not a solely human activity, just as farm animals do not suffer on their own (Porcher, 2011). Cows invest their intelligence into the activity of work and, what is more, collaborate and cooperate with each other in doing so, leading to the emergence of what she refers to as a 'collective intelligence' (Porcher, 2011). But it can also lead to collective suffering, physically, mentally and morally, similarly shared by both animals and humans. From this notion of shared work, Porcher constructs a moral position based upon shared experience, shared labour, shared friendship and pleasure as well as shared suffering between farmer and animal (2002, 2006). Admitting a certain Marxist romanticism (Porcher, 2011) for a livestock industry founded truly on localist principles of 'husbandry' and the freedom of work rather than the instrumentalism of 'production', she maintains that contemporary industrial animal systems offer little hope for honour; certainly not Witmore's (2015: 240) bovine city, a concentrated animal feeding operation (or CAFO) of some 58,000 cattle which he describes as 'an industrial assemblage of urban infrastructures, machinic manipulators, pharmaceutical companies and a knowledge economy that divides up the undividable'.

Entangled matter

Farmed animals exist either as potential food (post-slaughter, through their bodies) or as food itself (through their body products, such as eggs or milk). Their potential to become food shapes how they enter the world, as the productivity (whether measured in potential carcass weight, milk volumes or egg numbers) of their maternal and paternal parentage will have been carefully taken into account. Once born, the medicalization and manipulation of these food animals' bodies will adapt them to a life spent, most commonly, in high-density animal housing within specific age or gender groups of their species. The quality and volumes of food they are given and the level of 'exercise' or natural behaviour they are permitted become integral components in a production process that seeks fast and efficient growth and high levels of productivity, passing rapidly to the achievement of appropriate slaughter weight.

Ultimately, living animal tissue or flesh becomes meat and is consumed, becoming in turn the nutrients (or waste products) of other living bodies, human or otherwise. Other bodily by-products from farmed animals, deemed unfit for human consumption, feed human-companion animals. Although multiple semiotic and representational mechanisms are in place to distance the living animal from the 'dead' product (and thereby separate its consumption from its production), there is labour too in the material entanglements that comprise the different processes through which animals are assembled into food.

Returning to the words of Haraway cited at the start of this chapter – 'It matters which worlds world worlds. It matters who eats whom and how. It is a material question for cosmopolitical critters' (Haraway, 2015: xiv) – we wish to pause a moment on this 'material question'. Recent work in both (agro-food) geography and animal studies, informed by post-human and new materialist theorists such as Bennett (2001) and Barad (2007), brings matter to the fore, from 'the matter of nature' (Fitzsimmons, 1989) to matter as turbulent, interrogative and excessive (Anderson and Wylie, 2009). In this vein, Coole and Frost (2010: 2) write that 'foregrounding material factors and reconfiguring our very understanding of matter are prerequisites for any plausible account of coexistence and its conditions'. But this is not entirely 'dead' matter. It is matter for which affect – the capacity to affect and be affected – is 'part and parcel, not an additive component, of bodies' materiality' (Chen, 2012: 5); it is 'agentive, not a fixed essence or property of things' (Barad, 2007: 137) but 'produced and productive, generated and generative' (ibid.: 137).

Later Barad asserts that 'matter itself is always already open to, or rather entangled with the "Other"' (ibid.: 393). Matter, and in the context of this book the matter that is animal body, 'animates cultural life' (Chen, 2012: 2). In this way, a farmed animal's life, and its welfare, becomes differentially embedded, through various discursive and material practices, into a final food product. Some product ranges might draw specific attention to the broad environment and conditions of that life ('free range', 'grass-fed') though few, as we shall demonstrate, refer specifically to the quality of individual animal lives. Nevertheless, to borrow Stassart and Whatmore's (2003: 449) phrasing, the stuff of food can become 'a ready messenger of connectedness and affectivity' across the 'growing distance between the spaces of production and consumption and [...] the enduring metabolic intimacies between human and nonhuman bodies'. Although Stassart and Whatmore's (2003) study of a Belgian beef cooperative and its products focuses more particularly upon networks that metabolize 'risk' in the food chain, they draw out three elements of this vital 'connectedness and affectivity' that are useful here. First, they identify the significance of what they call 'spokesproducts' (the 'flagship product') in 'fleshing out the middle ground between production and consumption' and substantiating trust in the network. Second, they emphasize the polyvalent and multiple agencies, practices and sites that constitute the network not in a predetermined way but in a provisional and open-ended way. Finally, they pick out the 'heterogeneous intermediaries' (trademarks, product specifications, operating procedures and product quality) that hold the network together. Of all three, they write:

> Privileging neither production nor consumption, this metabolic mode of ordering populates the middle ground, translating between the knowledge practices of animal husbandry and their body subjects on the farm and those of food consumption and their body products on the plate. (Stassart and Whatmore, 2003: 460)

While we might think of meat as metabolic matter, this is matter that has mattered and perhaps should matter still. That mattering is made to matter within food chains, we maintain, whether as a component of product quality or as some kind of ethical relationship between consumer and consumed, through a materialization of sentience.

Entangled ethics

It is difficult to think or write about farmed animals and their eventual consumption without addressing, either explicitly or implicitly, issues of ethics. While we do not wish to rehearse the well-known arguments for and against livestock farming and the killing of farmed animals, we want to argue here that the new emphasis on materiality, coupled with a wider acknowledgement of sentience in farmed animals, evokes an original approach to ethics, one based on 'the coextensive materiality of human, non-human and natural subjects' (Iovino, 2012: 64.) While Bennett (2002: 112) sees materiality as 'a rubric that tends to horizontalize the relations between humans, biota and abiota', thereby helping us to overcome the distance between the human and the non-human, we want to argue for a distinctive materiality of the animate, the flourishing, the living or the having lived. In Bennett's (2009) cornucopia of detritus, she notes an 'unblemished dead rat' as if recognizing the more affective biotic power of decay's blemishing. She is repelled by the dead rat but not by the stick of wood that lies next to it. This 'unblemished dead rat' is certainly a different 'thing' to a living, breathing, scurrying rat, but being unblemished, it still has the power to repel as a rat, with all the material, semiotic and affective presence that a rat evokes. To paraphrase Harman, who acknowledges the 'difficult problem posed by animals', and substituting Bennett's rat for his 'animal': 'behind the unblemished dead rat is the rat itself marked by an excess deeper than the fact that it is, at the time, dead' (2010: 191). Isn't this a different order of vitality and vibrancy – one that demands our attention? For to be an animal is to be attentive, to be receptive, to pay attention, to be interested and to interest: 'If someone would ask me what an animal is', said Deleuze (1988), 'I would answer "a being on the lookout". It is a being fundamentally on the lookout'.

Derrida famously rails against the violence in humanity's use of the singular 'animal' to define all non-human animalian existence but we are also wary of a flat ontology that levels the 'worldless' with the 'poor of world'. Elsewhere (Roe, 2010), we have shown how, following Whatmore (1997), non-humans of all kinds attain an ethical significance in the relations they form with humans. Such a 'relational ethic' is generated through the assembly of multiple materialities, matterings (Barad, 2007), affects, meanings and practices between the human and the non-human.

Farm animals are, for the most part, members of sentient species. They, like us, have the capacity for feelings and (self)awareness. While there is considerable debate over the extent of that sentience (Broom, 2014), its definability and detection (Dawkins, 2012) and the nature of our response to it (Bekoff, 2006), it has been widely accepted scientifically and legally enshrined in a growing number of countries, including those of the European Union. Within the broader context of human–non-human animal relations, the sentience of farm animals, their capacities not only to suffer but also to experience pleasure, their self-hood and their subjectivity, all endow them with the status of becoming matters of concern (Latour, 2004: 256–7), which, we might suggest, is more helpful, than mere materiality in generating our own responsibilities with regard to animals. Does a belief in animal sentience infer consequentially greater ethical engagement and responsibility? Certainly, when it comes to concern for the interests of individual others, sentience, for Singer (1995), should replace simply being human as the basis for unique moral consideration. More controversially for some, he suggests (after Bentham) that without sentience, or the possibility of sentience, there is no capacity for suffering and therefore no basis for moral concern and the consideration of individual interests. But this is a well-engaged and well-documented debate that we do not want to enter here. The point we wish to make is that our growing understanding of the sentient capacities of the living farmed animal (and its resultant experiences, behaviours and awarenesses), the relationships that exist, and are nurtured, between the sentient carer and sentient cared-for and, finally, the more distant sympathies and empathies that enjoin attentive food consumer and food animal all contribute to the generation of significant, and increasingly widely acknowledged ethical responsibilities.

Yet, and here we introduce a concept that we return to later in this book, there are also material expressions of that sentience that enliven the food chain. We do not accept that the transition from living animal to carcass for human consumption is a nullification of that original sentience. Indeed various components of the animal's sentient life, its lived life – such as pre-slaughter stress and aggressive behaviours brought on by confined housing systems in pigs to well-developed muscle tissue from an active, outdoor life in cattle – can significantly affect the taste, texture and quality of the eventual product endowing it with additional and enduring 'meanings and materialities of sentience' (Roe, 2010: 276).

Here, then, we refer to the idea of 'sentient materialities' (Roe, 2010) which we hold to be particularly useful because it allows us to chart the forming and performance of ethical relations across the living animal–animal product and production–consumption divisions within the food chain. It also lends itself to a consideration of praxis – or as Iovino (2012: 64) puts it, 'a shift of the hub of ethical relationality from principles to practices'. In this way, the experiential practices of life as a food animal are inscribed into the materiality of its products and/or its bodily flesh as meat. We might thus begin to think of the animal-based foodstuffs that we consume as sentient materialities, which, we argue later on in this book, opens up new conceptual and ethical bridges between human and non-human.

On welfare

This book is about farm animal welfare and the manner in which different constructions and practices of welfare influence both the production and the consumption of animal-derived food, acting as a relational link between human and animal. Animal welfare is a complex issue, neither entirely absolute nor wholly relative. Welfare is an animal state but one that is, in farming systems, heavily dependent upon human practice. Individual animals may benefit from positive welfare states or suffer from poor or negative welfare states. Welfare ranges across a number of factors, from the ability of an animal to 'cope' physiologically and psychologically with its environment (Broom, 1991) to a dynamic assembly involving variously the 'needs', the 'freedoms', the 'preferences', the 'naturalness' and the 'wants' of individual animals (Fraser, 2003, 2008a; Lund et al., 2006).

Socially accepted notions of beneficial welfare conditions may vary enormously across different social and cultural communities and their ethical as well as their economic values, across different animal species, across different contexts of human–animal interaction and across different environmental conditions. They may also vary significantly with respect to more scientific or empirically derived assessments of beneficial (or poor) animal welfare. As we demonstrate in Chapter 2, welfare science itself has very distinctive approaches to the definition and measurement of welfare. Finally, assessing, determining and maintaining acceptable levels of welfare (both positive and negative) among farm animals have, inevitably and by definition, to fit with the economic imperatives of agro-food production though, of course, both may change in relation to each other.

It is perhaps, at this juncture, worth *distinguishing* animal welfare from animal cruelty and animal rights. Animal welfare considerations sit somewhat uneasily between the two. On the one hand, welfarism largely accepts the supremacy of human rights over non-human rights and the utilitarian (and for some biological) justification of producing, killing and eating animals as long as this is undertaken in a manner judged to be humane (with minimal suffering), respectful and caring. On the other hand, cruelty, as intentional and unnecessary or avoidable harm, is wholly rejected as morally unacceptable. Of course, the devil is in the detail; what constitutes humane, respectful and caring husbandry or slaughter and who decides? What harms are considered unavoidable or necessary within production systems? How might the welfare of the individual animal be weighted against the welfare of the group and so on.

In practice, farm animal welfare rests on a shifting combination (or a compromise) of scientific, juridical, ethical and affective referentials. As Fraser (1999) demonstrates, achieving a common goal through this is often highly problematic. Increasingly, the actors involved in seeking or achieving these compromises multiply as consumers, citizens, NGOs, retailers, processors, professional bodies, regulatory authorities, religious groups, governments (national and international), producers, stockpersons, animal carers, veterinarians, scientists and others all bring their own positions, evidence and beliefs to the complex and multiple issue of farm animal welfare.

Chapter 2

Worthy Lives

Nous devons la justice aux hommes, et la grâce et la bénignité aux autres créatures qui en peuvent être capables. Il y a quelque commerce entre elles et nous, et quelque obligation mutuelle. (Montaigne, De la Cruauté, 435)[1]

Section 14 of the UK Food Safety Act (1990) states that 'Any person who sells to the purchaser's prejudice any food which is not of the nature or substance or quality demanded by the purchaser shall be guilty of an offence' (HMSO, 1990: 12). The phrase 'nature or substance or quality demanded' is a long-standing one, appearing in successive food control legislation over much of the latter half of the twentieth century. The UK government's explanation of these three key terms (Food Standards Agency, 2009) identifies 'nature' as the genuineness of thing itself (haddock is not cod, margarine is not butter, horse meat is not beef), 'substance' as uncontaminated composition (an earwig in a bottle of milk, as discovered by a Colchester consumer in 1996, is not consistent with the 'substance demanded', Department of Food Law, University of Reading, 1996) and 'quality' as conformity to accepted, legislative as well as reasonably expected standards (e.g. a stale loaf or food displaying some other form of deterioration from its expected state).

To what extent is the welfare of farm animals 'demanded by the purchaser', whether they be the final consumers or retailers, food processors, wholesalers, food services and so on? Is the welfare and life conditions of farm animals a constituent of the 'nature', 'substance' and/or 'quality' of food products and, if so, how is this articulated and operationalized and by whom? In this chapter, drawing on both social science and veterinary science literature, we consider the 'commerce', as Montaigne would have it, between humans and farm animals, through an investigation of farm animal welfare as a contemporary societal concern within 'Western' societies of the Global North and trace the complex and interwoven trajectories of science, ethical practice and farm

---

[1] We owe justice to men and grace and kindness to those other creatures that are capable of it. There is a commerce between them and us and a mutual obligation.

animal care within the framework of the broader commercial environment of food production. In doing so, we acknowledge and investigate three distinct, but related, referentials for engagement with farm animal welfare. The first of these is *empirical*. A distinctive animal welfare science emerged largely over the last forty years around the principle that farm animals, as sentient beings, are able to feel pain and to suffer, both physically and mentally, as a result of husbandry practices and conditions. Critical to that principle is not only that the feelings and sufferings of farm animals matter to them but also that they can be scientifically identified and empirically measured as can their impacts upon farm productivity. The second referential is *ethical*. For many in society, concern for the welfare of farm animals draws upon an ethical commitment for the well-being of fellow sentient creatures and a desire to minimize (unnecessary) suffering during their often short lives. This is a concern for life and living, a bio-political investment in cross-species sensibility, anthropomorphic conviviality and the engaged deontological ethic of care. It might be professional, a commitment to a way of working; it might be intellectual and rational, the product of a thought-through, but nevertheless distant, concern; it might be embodied and experiential, the practice and consequence of shared lives, spaces and affects. The final referential is *economic*. At the end of the day, lying alongside any human(e) concerns society or individuals may have, animal husbandry in all its various forms exists to yield marketable products whose nature, substance and quality constitute value for food chain actors and consumables for end users. It is significant then that animal welfare concerns, having largely emerged in the 1960s as a critique of contemporary livestock practices, have, over the last twenty or so years, become a highly commodifiable element within the food sector. This, as we have asserted elsewhere (Buller and Roe, 2013), has major implications for the meaning, practice and operationalization of animal welfare for all within the food supply chains. Drawing partly on the work of Callon and others (Caliskan and Callon, 2009, 2010), we explore how the welfare of farm animals – as beings occupying what is perhaps a unique position within the web of social, material and economic relations – becomes constituted as 'economic' within contemporary animal production. Such an approach we maintain, in keeping with the problematic of this book series, confounds the more simplistic representational dualism of supply/demand, producer/consumer analysis and allows us to trace the active performance of welfare (Callon, 1998) as an ongoing element in the 'nature', 'substance' and 'quality' of food.

Today, farm animals' lives have a value beyond that traditionally represented solely by the locomotive or metabolic power they may embody. Not being economists, we do not ask how this new value can be specified in monetary terms. This is a complex question at the best of times (see Bailey Norwood and Lusk, 2011). Moreover, as the Farm Animal Welfare Committee argues (2011: 7), the connection of humans to animal welfare is 'a complicated relationship which is only in small part reflected in markets or by prices'. Our concern here is to trace the growth of welfare as value, in scientific, ethical and economic terms. Farm animals and their lives are 'valuable' to different degrees and across different contexts. The Farm Animal Welfare Council (2009) states that all farm animals should have a 'life worth living':

> The intention of British policy should be that an animal kept in full compliance with the law should have a life worth living. This minimum should apply uniformly to all farm animals, regardless of their species or husbandry. (FAWC, 2009: 19)

How that 'worth' is defined and achieved is the subject of this chapter.

Empirical engagement

For the welfare of farm animals to become mobilized as a 'value', that value has to be creatable, identifiable, distinguishable and calculable. To a large extent, this has been the central role of animal welfare science, a relatively new sub-discipline that emerged perhaps paradoxically from the industrialization and intensification of animal husbandry in the post-war era and brings together veterinary science, animal science and applied ethology. Veterinary medicine, from its gradual professionalization in the UK, starting at the end of the eighteenth century with the formation of the Royal Veterinary College (in 1791) to its institutionalization with the 1948 Veterinary Surgeons Act, became closely associated with raising the profitability and efficiency of a rapidly industrializing post-war food and farming sector. Animal health, body productivity and functioning, reproductability and the capacity to cope with the spaces, procedures, interventions, mutilations, vaccinations and other material, environmental and somatic components of modern husbandry, became the watchwords of a veterinary sector very much aligned with livestock farming through its productivist objectives and scientific method. As Woods (2013) has pointed out, the veterinary 'client' here was the farmer and the broader livestock industry, rather than the individual farmed animal. A profession-centred ethics dominated. 'Veterinarians', she argues (2013: 15), 'continued to equate the ethical care of animals with veterinary care'. Behind the closed doors of increasingly artificialized indoor husbandry units, driven by an expanding retail and consumer demand and facilitated by what Jasanoff (2004) and others have identified in other contexts as the post-war 'social contract' between science and technology on the one hand, and the State on the other, veterinary and animal science combined to create a formidable livestock sector in the UK and elsewhere into which individual animals and their individual welfare arguably all but disappeared.

> We don't think of hogs as animals, not in the same way as cats and dogs and deer and squirrels. We say 'pork units'. What they are Bob, is 'pork units' – a crop like corn or beans. ('*Ribeye Clark*' in Proulx, 2002: 302)

Yet, the appearance of 'welfare', as a concept and condition of farm animals and as a mechanism for productivity, also heralds a critical shift in science, in humanist ethics and in governance practice. Indeed, one might be tempted to say that as welfare science pushes the boundaries of sentience and mental capacity even further from the human, it marks a critical shift to a potentially more radical bio-politics (Wolfe, 2013).

Late eighteenth- and nineteenth-century Europe saw the gradual appearance of legislation governing cruelty towards animals (Thomas, 1984). Its principal obstacle was the long-standing and widely accepted position that farm animals were merely property and could be treated however their 'owner' might wish; no legal distinction being made between animate and inanimate possessions (Radford, 2001). When nascent anti-cruelty legislation began to appear in the UK (e.g. the Martin Act of 1822 and the Pearse Act of 1835), it largely ignored farmed animals to focus predominantly upon performing animals (such as bears and cockerels) and pets (dogs, cats, monkeys) under a reformist zeal that had more to do with human societal control than animal freedoms. Nevertheless, things were changing (Ritvo, 1987). Radford (2001) argues that nineteenth-century concern for the conditions of animals, including farmed animals, in England came about as part of a broader and emergent middle-class sensitivity towards children (notably, child labour), slavery, factory conditions, the poor, prisons and so on. Here was a bourgeoisie on a mission:

> A major transformation occurred around the turn of the nineteenth century as a country which had been strongly associated with sports involving cruelty to animals such as bull-baiting and cock-fighting, came increasingly to define itself – led by Evangelicals and middle-class reformers – by opposition to such cruelty. It would seem, however, that it was not simply that cruelty to animals became newly defined as particularly un-English, but that it became defined as particularly English – or rather, particularly bourgeois-English – to witness, with condemnation and sympathy, the spectacle of cruelty to animals [...] The

mistreatment of animals becomes charged with new energies as the object of a national discourse. (Kreilkamp, 2005: 92)

From a Foucauldian perspective, the mounting involvement of the State in regulating such activities defined the new bio-political disciplining of both docile humans (Foucault, 1979) and even more docile animals (Novek, 2005) though it wasn't just the State. This growing social movement for the protection of animals, represented, for example, by the Royal Society for the Protection of Cruelty for Animals (RSPCA), created in 1824, also exemplified this developing conscience and, again in Foucauldian terms, the potential for a more radical form of governance. The result is a growing raft of legislation, covering an expanding range of domesticated animals, culminating, first, in the 1849 Prevention of Cruelty to Animals Act and, later, in 1911, in the Protection of Animals Act. This latter made it an offence, in a public place:

> to beat, kick, ill-treat, override, overdrive, overload, torture, infuriate or terrify any domestic or captive animal, or wantonly or unreasonably to do or omit to do any act which cause such an animal unnecessary suffering. (Radford, 2001: 87)

In their wantonness, such acts as are listed by the 1911 Act lie outside the realms of what is considered socially and morally acceptable treatment of animals. These are by definition exceptional and excessive acts of cruelty creating incidences of deplorable suffering in what might otherwise be considered relatively benign methods of animal husbandry. However, as animal husbandry changed during the twentieth century through State-facilitated intensification, concern and attention shifted from deliberate acts of cruelty to the more generic condition of farmed animals, increasingly housed in battery and high-density artificialized environments. The scientific and technical innovations that drove intensive animal husbandry now created a new domain of concern and policy intervention (Woods, 2011). Standards (whether moral or sociotechnical) for how animals were kept on farm were, in effect, non-existent. Yet, the traditional terminology of 'cruelty' was deemed inappropriate.

> By contrast, welfare – derived from an Old English term meaning to 'fare well' – had more positive connotations relating to the capacity to thrive, grow and produce. (Woods, 2011: 18)

Although we are wary of ascribing a paradigm shift in the conceptualization of animal welfare to a single popular publication, there is little doubt that Ruth

Harrison's seminal book *Animal Machines*, published in the UK in 1964, set in motion a series of political, institutional and scientific responses that, in tune with the times, led to a fundamental shift in the scientific understanding of farm animal welfare and paved the way for its marketability. Described as 'the torch that lit the flame of the farm animal welfare movement ' (Webster, 2013: 8), *Animal Machines* offered a powerful and well-documented critique of the negative impact of modern husbandry techniques on the lives of animals and the ethical paradoxes inherent in the differential treatment of food animals from companion animals. The book opens with the following words:

> I am going to discuss a new type of farming, of production line methods applied to the rearing of animals, of animals living out their lives in darkness and immobility without a sight of the sun, of a generation of men who see in the animal they rear only its conversion factor into human food. (Harrison, 1964: 35)

With chapters given over to broiler chickens, poultry packing stations (slaughterhouses), battery birds and veal calves, and including a 'pictorial summary' made up of some twenty-four black-and-white images principally of animals within intensive production systems, Harrison's book sought to draw public attention not to specific acts of ill-treatment on farms but to the systematic cruelty and degradation of the animal, as she saw it, within 'factory farming' as a whole. Placing a particular emphasis on the nature of indoor housing systems, the artificiality of the environment, the density and confinement of animals and their subsequent health, welfare and behavioural problems (from anaemia and lameness to tail biting and cannibalism), all of which generate the need for further scientific and technological interventions and manipulations (such as beak trimming, castration and prophylactic medicine use), Harrison offered a remarkably informed, and in many ways, devastating critique of how science and economic profitability replaced 'stockmanship' and 'affection' (both her words) in farmer–animal relations, leading to poorer and less healthy animal lives and (for Harrison is no abolitionist) poorer, less healthy and potentially 'dangerous' human food. Crucially then, Harrison's book argued that intensively farmed animals were effectively denied a life by husbandry practices that were inherently and unavoidably cruel in the pursuit of intensive production and cheap food products (Sayer, 2013).

The response of the livestock sector to the book and the publicity it attracted were perhaps predictable. Adopting productivity as the only valid indicator of an animal's well-being, farmers argued that a productive animal was inherently healthy, thriving and coping well with its confinement (Woods, 2011; Sayer,

2013), an argument later put to the Brambell Committee (Brambell, 1965: 19). Furthermore, as Sayer (2013) points out, the food industry sought to place some of the blame for industrial farming techniques on the inattentive and unselective consumer concerned more with buying cheaply than buying healthily. The impact of the book on the veterinary profession and veterinary science was, however, significant. At one level, Harrison is rather equivocal in her reference to vets.

> What do veterinary surgeons think of all this? Are they willing and able to keep a check on the industry? Do they have an oath like the Hippocratic oath compelling them to help all animals, or have they become merely the administrators of yet more drugs? (Harrison, 1964: 37)

And a little later

> Veterinary surgeons must shudder when they enter the sheds where these animals are kept; all the basic concepts of health are so flagrantly broken. (151)

In the final pages of the book, Harrison asks that 'we' are 'assured that no cruelty is involved in intensive rearing' (203) having previously acknowledged the widespread 'reluctance to define cruelty in relation to animals reared and killed for meat' (175). In order to ensure that intensive rearing does not involve 'cruelty', not only does cruelty (and its corollary, suffering – itself implying good and bad welfare states) need to be established and scientifically defined but the real and potential impact or contribution of intensive methods on that welfare has to be determined. Reviewing the impact of Harrison's book in 2013, Webster (2013: 7) remarks: 'there was little welfare science in the book. For the good reason that there was very little welfare science around at the time'. Thus, one immediate consequence of the book was to set in motion the establishment of the UK Government's Brambell Committee charged with examining 'the conditions in which livestock are kept under systems of intensive husbandry and to advise whether standards ought to be set in the interests of their welfare, and if so what they should be' (Brambell, 1965: 1). Defining welfare as a term that 'embraces both the physical and mental well-being of the animal', the Brambell Committee maintained, rather radically at the time, that 'any attempt to evaluate welfare therefore must take into account the scientific evidence available concerning the feelings of animals that can be described from their structure and functions and also from their behaviour' (1965: 9). In this, the Committee implicitly and explicitly took issue with the prevailing view – one that underscored the principles of 'factory farming' (a term used extensively by Harrison) – that animal welfare could be simplistically equated with productivity.

More specifically, the Committee identified a number of unacceptable husbandry practices. The mutilations regularly undertaken on farmed animals to help them cope with intensive conditions were rejected by the Committee as impermissible on welfare grounds. It was similarly unconvinced by the argument that with ample food and freedom from predators, birds in battery cages have little need to express 'normal' movement or behaviour. Pervading the Committee's report, however, is the acknowledgement that little evidence existed about exactly how much space a broiler should have, how much water a pig might need access to and how much room a farrowing sow might need.

Although neither Harrison's book nor the Brambell Report invented contemporary farm animal welfare, they collectively redefined it as something substantively different from 'cruelty' (Woods, 2011) and kick-started significant and lasting developments in animal governance, in animal science and in animal ethics. With regard to the former, the Brambell Report, while recognizing the economic need to retain, even extend, intensive livestock farming, nevertheless concluded that existing legislation was far from adequate to effectively protect the welfare of farmed animals. The subsequent post-Brambell legislation (the 1968 Agriculture [Miscellaneous Provisions] Act) introduced government powers to set mandatory welfare standards for livestock systems, enabled the establishment of a government advisory committee on animal welfare and allowed for farm inspections by the State Veterinary Service; the bio-political reach of the State now extended to, at least some, non-humans. The Brambell Report also laid down a major epistemological challenge for both 'science' and 'society': how to scientifically and objectively identify and account for the feelings and well-being (both physical and mental) of farm animals that were meaningful for the animals and morally valuable for human society. Finally, Brambell inspired a new ethical basis for the consideration of farm animal lives, one based upon the concept of 'freedoms'. The Committee's report (1965: 13) included the following principle:

> An animal should at least have sufficient *freedom* of movement to be able without difficulty, to turn round, groom itself, get up, lie down and stretch its limbs (our emphasis).

The newly established Farm Animal Welfare Council (now Committee) took this forward by publishing in 1979 as guiding principles for the forthcoming animal welfare codes, what have become universally known as the 'five freedoms'. In their original iteration (FAWC, 1979), FAWC sought merely to ensure that the welfare codes provided farm animals with:

1. freedom from thirst, hunger and malnutrition

2. appropriate comfort and shelter

3. prevention, or rapid diagnosis and treatment, of injury and disease

4. freedom to display most normal patterns of behaviour

5. freedom from fear

They were later restated, preceded by the bolder assertion that 'an animal's welfare, whether on farm, in transit, at market or at a place of slaughter should be considered in terms of *"five freedoms"*. These freedoms define ideal states rather than standards for acceptable welfare' (FAWC undated, emphasis in original). The freedoms themselves became:

- freedom from hunger and thirst, by ready access to water and a diet to main-tain health and vigour

- freedom from discomfort, by providing an appropriate environment

- freedom from pain, injury and disease, by prevention or rapid diagnosis and treatment

- freedom to express normal behaviour, by providing sufficient space, proper facilities and appropriate company of the animal's own kind

- freedom from fear and distress, by ensuring conditions and treatment, which avoid mental suffering

Much has been written on the 'five freedoms' (Webster, 1994, 1998, 2016; FAWC, 2009; McCulloch, 2013) and governments across the world have readily endorsed them and their 'memorable simplicity' (Mellor, 2016a: 1). Although they have provided a universalist humane touchstone for animal welfare – Webster (1998: 263) refers to them as a 'platonic ideal state, unachievable but a worthy paradigm' – their focus on mitigating negative welfare conditions (freedom from hunger, thirst, fear, etc.), rather than enhancing positive welfare states reflects, in part, the nature of welfare science at the time of their formulation yet has since prompted recent criticism. Mellor (2016a), for example, has advocated the replacement of 'freedoms' by 'provisions', which address both the enhancement of positive welfare states and the minimization of negative experiences. FAWC itself (2009) has drawn attention to the frequent confusion in interpretation of the fourth 'freedom' which explicitly refers to 'normal' rather than 'natural' behaviour, arguing that 'natural' behaviour is a particularly complex and elusive notion in animals that have, for many generations, lived in, and adapted to, 'unnatural' conditions. Others argue that the 'five freedoms' take an overly anthropocentric and ethical view of suffering. Korte et al. (2007), for example, maintain that fear has 'fitness value' for animals and is normal in appropriate situations. To require 'freedom from fear' as a blanket requirement is both unfeasible and a largely anthropocentric construct. Similarly, they argue, pain can also be construed as a 'natural defence mechanism', one consistent in certain circumstances with the expression of 'normal behaviour'.

Implicit in the eventual five freedoms and the original Brambell Report were a series of questions for which, at the time, there was no real substantive answer: how much water, what sort of diet, what sort of shelter, when are they healthy, what degree of comfort, what form of expression, what degree of fear and distress, what type of behaviour, how much space, what mental suffering constituted good or poor welfare, what do animals want? Hence animal welfare science emerged as a distinct sub-discipline in the 1970s in order, first, to provide empirical evidence for the idea that farm animals can suffer, both mentally and physically, from the conditions and practices of husbandry and, with this evidence, offer solutions for improvement in husbandry practice and, second, though this came later on, to show that purposeful and positive mental experiences could be gained from good husbandry management (Veissier et al., 2008). To achieve both, however, welfare science, as a form of engagement, has had to struggle, and continues to do so to this day, with four major conceptual challenges: empiricism (and its limits), anthropomorphism, the notion of animal sentience and, finally, 'naturalness'.

Empiricism and the challenge of veterinary 'evidence'

Farm animal welfare science (which includes both veterinary science and the science of applied ethology) has also had to come to terms with the problematic ethical charge that it has been unescapably complicit, by its very existence, in sanctioning forms of animal keeping and husbandry that many find abhorrent. The Brambell Report of 1965 disapproved of any form of animal confinement that 'frustrates most of the major activities which make up its natural behaviour' (1965: 13). Yet many intensive egg-laying, broiler, intensive dairy and pig production systems might be said to still do just that, and have been doing so for many years post-Brambell (e.g. Wiepkema et al., 1983; Lyons et al., 1995; Da Silva, 2006; Von Keyserlingk et al., 2009; Lay et al., 2011). For some commentators (e.g. Porcher, 2002, 2011; Lymbery, 2014), welfare science, with its mission to 'put the animal first', has rarely questioned or challenged enough the rationale or premise of intensive livestock farming and the forms of confinement that are seen as necessary for it. On the contrary, welfare science has, for the most part, legitimated intensive systems by providing standards and tolerance levels that are rarely at odds with standard industry practice – often either out of an awareness of the likely impact of any substantial change on the economic viability of the production systems concerned or due to the lack of an effective higher welfare alternative. When, principally (and exceptionally) for welfare reasons, tethers and close-confinement stalls for breeding sows were banned in the UK, the national pig industry suffered substantial economic decline (House of Commons, Environment, Food and Rural Affairs Committee, 2008) from which it has only recently recovered. On the other hand, the reluctance of some welfare bodies to unequivocally support the full implementation of the ban on beak trimming in egg-laying hens (FAWC, 2007) is due, in part, to a concern that, within high-density houses, birds will full beaks will be able to inflict significant damage on each other. Yet, as Singer (2008: viii) points out, in the face of the inevitable expansion – at least in the medium term – of intensive livestock systems, actively working to improve the welfare of animals within those systems is of far greater value and importance than seeking (and failing) to persuade the majority of meat-eaters to abandon animal products and thereby farm animals altogether. Animal welfare science, and its practitioners, is, in Singer's words (2008: ix), 'finding ingenious ways of enabling the animals themselves to tell us what they want and thereby showing that the science of animal behaviour supports the critics of factory farming and not its defenders'.

The empiricist challenge for the emergent animal welfare science was to be able to derive the experimental means to demonstrate the mental and physical states, needs and, ultimately, wants of farm animals and the manner in which each of these is affected or frustrated by husbandry practice, equipment or housing design. As Broom (2011) remarks, the influential evidence of poor welfare provided by Brambell and his committee did not always stand up well to scrutiny. Drawing variously upon biology, veterinary science and (applied) ethology, animal welfare science set out to show that welfare, from good to poor, is 'measurable and hence is a scientific concept' (Broom, 2011: 127). This was both an experimental and an observational science. The negative physiological and behavioural impacts of (what are still often relatively common) parameters and interventions such as confinement, overcrowding, reproductive intensification, lack of daylight, intrusive and painful mutilations (such as tail docking, castration and beak trimming), inhumane culling methods, highly targeted feed regimes and accelerated growth on body health and productivity could be ascertained through physiological research and testing. The effect of overcrowding or, say, tail docking on animal behaviour could be observed in experimental sites.

In its early days, and partly reflecting its ethological heritage, animal welfare science was concerned primarily with the basic health and biological functioning of animals within livestock farming systems (e.g. Broom, 1968). As animal welfare science has moved on from the understanding of how animals 'cope' – or don't cope – with the environments and practices of intensive production, to the understanding of what matters to them in terms of needs and wants and the achievement of more positive emotive and psychological states, the methodologies have become more challenging. Preference testing, where animals 'choose' a given outcome from a range of alternatives, their choice being confirmed by how hard they are prepared to work (or suffer, temporarily) to achieve it, has become an accepted method for going beyond mere welfare consequences (Davies et al., 2015; Nicol, 2015). Getting specifically at farm animal 'emotions' has been even more difficult, though the pioneering approach of qualitative behavioural assessment, developed in particular by Wemelsfelder (2007), has demonstrated how more qualitative approaches to welfare can achieve empirical scientific validity in their own right. A third approach to welfare (see Chart 2.1), one advocated by Rollin (1993) among others, has been through the notion of naturality and natural behaviour (e.g. Wood-Gush and Vestergaard, 1989; Spinka, 2006). Focusing on an animal's 'natural' (genetic) behaviour or nature (otherwise known as *telos*), Rollin advocates a welfare that addresses the nurturing and fulfilment of the animals' natures which we return to later in this chapter.

The emphasis on scientific legitimacy (Broom, 1988) is important and revealing. 'The scientific study of animal welfare is emphasised so that decisions

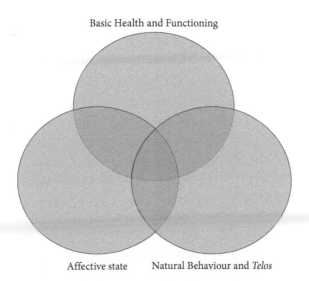

Chart 2.1 The three concepts of farm animal welfare. Source: Adapted from Fraser (2008a).

are made on factual rather than emotional grounds' (Broom, 1991: 4174). Aware that growing welfare considerations might put pressure upon otherwise accepted intensive husbandry practices, welfare scientists need to provide strong and unequivocal evidence of their claims. Evidence and measurement have always been critical issues for animal welfare science (Mason and Mendl, 1993) and there are still significant areas of contention over the evidential bases for claims over animal suffering (Bermond, 1997) and sentience (Dawkins, 2012; Key, 2016). In 2014, FAWC reported that 'farm animal welfare remains an area of considerable evidential complexity and confusion' (FAWC, 2014: 8). For Dawkins (2006), evidence is often the 'hard problem' for the discipline, one that has always been eager to distance itself from the charge of anecdote and anthropomorphism (Mitchell and Thompson, 1997). Rushen (1991), in a tough critique, confesses to a wide-ranging scepticism for claims about animal welfare based upon poorly derived and poorly interpreted physiological and behavioural data, particularly when research results appear to counter-intuitively support certain forms of intensive husbandry practice. Lawrence, in his 2008 review, reports on the widespread impression that applied behaviour science is 'soft' relative to other disciplines, the cause, he suggests, being that it is often 'overly descriptive or because it tends not to be focused on mechanisms or because it openly investigates issues such as animal feelings' (2008: 12). The varied disciplinary components of welfare science have undoubtedly got better at this but the continued concerns over 'evidence' and 'measurement' are demonstrated in the current drive to enrich and legitimate 'evidence-based veterinary medicine' (EBVM). More anecdotally, these concerns are reflected in the title of the 2017 Universities Federation for Animal Welfare (UFAW) annual conference, *Measuring animal welfare and applying scientific advances – Why is it still so difficult?*. One problem, emphasized today in the collaborative discourse of 'One Health', is that animal welfare science is not always perceived (largely unfairly we would claim) to have yet established similar degrees of evidential power as human medicine with which it is often compared. While EBVM is certainly expanding within clinical veterinary medicine (see Cockcroft and Holmes 2008: 2, who specifically target their 'Handbook' of EBVM at 'veterinary surgeons in non-academic, non-referral practices), the 'real-world' research and reporting methods (Muhlhausler 2013) associated with animal welfare science do not always fit so well with the established procedures of 'evidence-based' science (Holmes and Cockcroft, 2004; Keene, 2000), for which randomised control trials and systematic reviews have become the new 'gold standard'. As the Royal College of Veterinary Surgeons (2012: 2) point out:

Veterinary science still has relatively small numbers of published systematic reviews (255 published up to August 2012). It has been argued that the existing systematic review methods may not be directly applicable to certain areas of veterinary science (such as food and feed safety) but guidelines for the application of systematic review methodology in veterinary related issues will undoubtedly be more common in the future.

Evidence, evidential power and scientific 'uncertainty' remain a challenge for animal welfare science both normatively (Sandoe et al., 2004; FAWC, 2014) and ethically (Campbell, 2014), made arguably all the more important by the fact that animal welfare sits uniquely but not always comfortably between two sets of understandings, that of science and its empirical referentials and that of society and its cultural and ethical practices. Yet, paradoxically, as much social science moves further and further away from the structures and strictures of positivism, arguing for the importance of practice and context over objective knowledge and the unique legitimacy of 'evidence', veterinary medicine (and by association, animal welfare science) seems to be undergoing something of a reverse evidence revolution – in theory at least. Whether it actually alters what clinicians and researchers do is a moot point. The drive towards EBVM (and evidence-based animal welfare science is implicitly included in this) has been described not as an increase in objectivity but an obscuring of the inevitable subjectivity of knowledge making and an eschewal of intuition (Goldenberg, 2006). It is also, one might argue, a negation of the context and relational specificity of evidence. For Rollin (1995) the issue is less the lack of answers than 'the failure to ask the right questions', a phrase that is echoed in Despret (2016), in the Preface to which, Latour (2016: viii) asks, 'why is it that scientific knowledge about animals should be created under such artificial conditions to get rid of all the equally artificial situations in which humans encounter animals.'

Sentience, subjectivity and anthropomorphism

It has taken a long time for sentience – the ability to feel, perceive, be conscious, exhibit preferences and experience subjectivity – to be recognized as a capacity that matters among farm animals (Rollin, 1990), though many farmers would readily admit to it (Woods, 2010). While it fundamentally underscores the concept of farm animal welfare (Dawkins, 1980, 1990, 2012; Duncan, 1993, 2006; Proctor, 2012), it still remains, for some, both conceptually and empirically elusive. Dawkins (2012) argues that sentience in farmed animals has become an unnecessary and insoluble conundrum that detracts from more achievable and normative objectives. Demonstrating and assessing subjective experiences, positive (or negative) emotions and affective states and their impact upon behaviour among pet and food animals also raises particular descriptive (Yeates and Main, 2008) and methodological difficulties (Désire et al., 2002; Boissy et al., 2007), not the least being the capacity to distinguish apparent cognitive emotional response from whether an animal feels positive or negative (Paul et al., 2005). As Duncan (2005: 485) puts it: 'The problem with a feeling is that it is a subjective state, and therefore is only available to the animal experiencing it' (cf. Nagel, 1974 though see also Wemelsfelder, 2007). Welfare science's response to these difficulties has been inventive, innovative and interdisciplinary. The degree to which an animal is willing to 'work' to attain something it needs or likes (or undertake some behaviour it needs, ethologically, or wants to perform), or indeed avoid something it doesn't, was initially developed as an indicator of poor welfare (if that need or want is denied; Dawkins, 1983, though see Duncan, 2005). Borrowing essentially from microeconomics and notions of cost, demand and elasticity, techniques such as 'preference' or 'motivational testing' have become adapted to the detection of positive needs or wants (Jensen and Pedersen, 2008; Edgar et al., 2016). From human psychology, learning and decision-making theory, the notion of 'cognitive bias' has been employed as a mechanism to demonstrate the impact of emotional states on behaviour, thereby permitting their assessment (Mendl et al., 2009). Finally, concern for facilitating some degree of natural or normal behaviour in kept animals has led to an interrogation on the very nature of 'natural' and 'normal' within intensely domesticated species and, from that, how current behaviours, including social activity, might be adapting (positively or negatively) to the animal's physical and social environments as a consequence of post-domestication genetic change resulting from intense selection. In response, another particular branch of applied ethology/welfare science draws on molecular biology, neuroscience and epigenetics for the study of such welfare-relevant parameters as stress, reproductive capacities and behaviour through analysis of animal genotypes. In doing so, offers a particular approach to understanding, and potentially addressing, many of the detrimental effects of domestication (Jensen and Anderson, 2005; Jenson et al., 2008; Jensen, 2014).

More problematic has been the notion of anthropomorphism. The tendency to ascribe 'human' feelings and motivations to animals has been the bête noir of animal behavioural science for most of its existence and avoiding it has been a driving force in experimental empiricist methodology, particular when the 'feelings', 'choices' and 'preferences' of farm animals are being investigated. As Dawkins (2012: 35) writes:

The critical, doubting, skeptical methods of science are thus the friend, not the enemy, of the idea that animals may have thoughts and feelings a bit like ours. Anthropomorphism, by discouraging and ridiculing such skepticism, does a disservice not only to ethology but to a wider acceptance of consciousness in other species.

Nevertheless, anthropomorphism has been used creatively and effectively to test the reliability of scientific welfare assessments (Wemelsfelder and Lawrence, 2001; Wemelsfelder, 2007), and, indeed, to derive initial hypotheses about animal behaviour and 'whole animal' expressivity of emotions and feelings. Beyond empiricism, anthropomorphism is, in Webster's terms (2011), a 'fruitful fallacy' and, for some, remains considered as a prerequisite for empathy with non-humans in general (Bekoff, 2007; Butterfield et al., 2012). As we shall see below, although welfare science has tried hard to avoid anthropomorphic assumptions from influencing empiricism, anthropomorphism plays a very significant role in the representation of farm animal welfare to generate food product value: happy chickens sell better than sad ones.

Naturalness and a 'good life'

The final empirical challenge for farm animal welfare science that we want to identify is that of 'naturalness'. As we shall see below, citizens and consumers frequently associate 'good' farm animal welfare with notions of 'natural' environments, natural behaviour and, to a certain degree, natural bodies. Higher welfare is linked, in many people's minds, with greater degrees of 'naturalness', leading to the common association of organic production methods with higher levels of farm animal welfare (Harper and Makatouni, 2002; Hovi et al., 2003). Although animal science may respond, with a degree of legitimacy, that following generations of selective breeding, manipulation and artificialization, there is little that is 'natural' about either farm environments or farm animals (Duncan and Fraser et al., 1997), the emphasis that the public, and the retailers who supply them, place on the 'natural' means that welfare science has had to respond in providing empirical measures and indicators of what Rollin calls an animal's *telos* (the essence and purpose of an animal) and, critically, developing on-farm strategies for enhancing it, whether it be introducing dust-bath facilities and perches into chicken broiler sheds or hidden refuges for young pigs.

In 2009, the FAWC introduced a slightly different approach to the concept of animal welfare. Forever associated with the 'five freedoms', FAWC argued that 'an animal's quality of life can be classified as a life not worth living, a life worth living and a good life' (2009: 17). Taking the first as simply unacceptable within livestock farming, FAWC defines a 'life worth living' as one in which the balance of an animal's experiences must be positive over its lifetime. All livestock raised within the UK should, as a legal requirement, have a life worth living, though FAWC fully recognizes that this is not always the case.

> Achievement of a life worth living requires provision of an animal's needs and certain wants, and care by all involved. Wants are those resources that an animal may not need to survive or to avoid developing abnormal behaviour, but nevertheless improve its quality of life. They may well stem from learned behaviours so that once an animal has become accustomed to their provision then withdrawal may lead to an adverse mental experience. They may also be innate such as space to play, to groom or engage in other normal behaviours. Giving an animal a life worth living therefore requires skilled and conscientious stockmanship above all else, together with good husbandry, considerate handling and transport, and humane slaughter. (FAWC, 2009: 15)

The concept of a 'good life' goes further than this.

> Not only must there be full compliance with the law but also with examples of good practice described in the Welfare Code. In addition, good welfare should be a main aim of husbandry with disease controlled by the strictest measures and with minimal prevalence, normal behaviour, availability of environmental choices and harmless wants, a ban on most, if not all, mutilations, certain husbandry practices (including the manner of death) prescribed or forbidden, opportunities provided for an animal's comfort, pleasure, interest and confidence, and the highest standards of veterinary care. Above all else, the highest standard of stockmanship has to be provided. (FAWC, 2009: 16)

Though grounded in the 'five freedoms', a 'good life' for a farmed animal is nevertheless a largely aspirational status and one that is far from being achieved in all contemporary intensive husbandry systems.

> It is hard to conceive how certain systems of husbandry could ever satisfy the requirements of a good life because of their inherent limitations. Examples include the barren battery cage for laying hens, and the long-term housing of beef cattle on slats, denied access to pasture. (FAWC, 2009: 16)

We cite FAWC's approach at length here for two reasons: first, because the concepts of a 'life worth living' and a 'good life' are increasingly entering the lexicon of farm animal welfare; and, second, because both enshrine the complexity of welfare as an empirically problematic combination of science and ethics. Both terms imply societally determined value judgements (in the words 'good' and 'worth') which are increasingly at odds with the current emphasis on an empirically rich, evidence-driven animal welfare science. Ironically perhaps, and following a trend observable in the rise of evidence-based medicine, there is the risk of a growing polarity between an increasingly evidence-driven approach to health on the one hand (whether human or animal) and less empirically rich, but nonetheless equally vital, approach to welfare (again, whether human or animal).

Nevertheless, in its relatively short forty-year history, animal welfare science and applied ethology have provided empirical evidence to the notion that farm animals can not only suffer from the conditions and practices of intensive (and other) husbandry systems but, perhaps more importantly, have distinct and identifiable needs and wants (Dawkins, 2012; FAWC, 2012a). Through its engagement with farming practice, welfare science has shown how these needs and wants can be identified and why, in many cases, they should be met even if some of them have no specific production value. As a result, production practices have changed either as a result of legislative interdiction or as a result of consumer/retailer pressure. Hence in many countries, practices such as pig castration without anaesthetic, sow gestation crates and battery housing systems have been banned while regulatory standards have been imposed across an entire range of welfare parameters from stocking densities and housing dimensions to medicine use and slaughter methods. Welfare science has shown how welfare matters to the animals concerned. How that mattering is taken into account, and the value that societies, consumers and those individuals charged with the care of animals place on that mattering in the face of economic necessities and the need for profitable farming systems are what we turn to next.

With the broader food chain, the critical intersection of animal welfare science and food supply arguably comes in the mechanisms and procedures for assessment: the assessment of conformity to mandatory welfare standards as well as assessment for meeting voluntary higher welfare objectives. As food chain actors, consumers, non-governmental organizations (NGOs) and government increasingly require producers to be able to demonstrate that they are meeting both mandatory and additional standards, welfare science has turned more and more to the development of assessment protocols. We shall therefore return to welfare science, and the development and operation of these assessment protocols in Chapter 4.

Ethical engagement

Our argument thus far has been that for animal welfare to be given value, it has first to be rendered identifiable and calculable. It has to be 'detached'

(Callon and Muniesa, 2003). Animal welfare science has, to a large degree, begun to achieve this through an experimental and empirical engagement with what matters to animals, though a word of warning is offered by Yeates et al. (2011), who argue that the current disciplinary configuration of animal welfare science cannot and should not be seen as necessarily embracing all that is or might be considered as animal welfare. Or to put it in the words of Karel et al. (2007): 'science should refrain from the ambition to monopolize knowledge (and therefore *judgement*) about animal welfare' (2007: 293, emphasis in the original). Of course, that science did not emerge from nothing. It was born both out of recognition of public ethical concerns over intensive husbandry (Fraser, 1999), such as those identified by Harrison (1964) and acknowledged by the Brambell Committee, and out of a committed practical scientific concern for, in Webster's words, 'what we can do for them' (1994: 127). Welfare science has been called a 'bridging concept' (Fraser et al., 1997) for this reason, linking an empirical scientific approach to a normative societal ethical concern. Yet implicit here in both is not only a sense of (relative) ethical representation (who speaks for animals, albeit within the broader acceptance of the legitimacy of animal husbandry) but also recognition of prior ethical value.

> Any conception of animal welfare inherently involves values because it pertains to what is *better* or *worse* for animals. The different research approaches and interpretations that scientists use in assessing animal welfare reflect value-laden presuppositions about what *is* better or worse for animals [...]. Moreover, these differences cannot be turned into purely empirical issues by any known type of scientific research. (Fraser et al., 1997: 188, emphasis in original)

Some welfare scientists have argued strongly that the process of scientific welfare assessment be distinct from the process of ethical judgement and moral positioning (Broom, 1991: 4168). Opinions vary. For those who reject the husbandry, killing and consumption of farm animals, the very notion of on-farm 'welfare' starts from an unacceptable ethical premise (Cole, 2011). Others within welfare science clearly recognize that different scientific conceptions of animal welfare, many of which emerge from varying ethical as well as scientific starting points, can lead to conflicting conclusions about how animals can be treated (Fraser et al., 1997: 202). The end result is that the welfare of farm animals across different production systems – and critically, the assessment of that welfare – is often complex, potentially contradictory, confusing to consumers and, in being so, potentially useful to those interests who might seek to intentionally differentiate and segment the market value of animal products. For farm animal welfare, both as an empirical science and as a citizen concern has to operate within the framework of an economically viable food and farming sector. In this, meeting socially and scientifically acceptable welfare standards works both ways: as a potential constraint to low price production chains and as a potential source of added value to quality production chains. The result has been an unfortunate polarization, to produce cheap food for humans by means often seen as unethical or to produce more ethical foods that only some will be able to afford. Such differences, we shall argue below, become the currency of economization.

If, in simple terms, science provides the means to identify and measure the welfare, both good and poor, of farm animals, then societal norms, expressed either through evidentially based legislative requirements, or through good practices – or at least socially and/or professionally acceptable practices – or via consumer choices, set the parameters of acceptability. But what is acceptable and to whom?

Building on Evans and Miele (2012), we might assert that the lives and the welfare of farm animals, as sources of human food, matter in a societal sense in a number of ways: first, from a Hobbesian or Kantian perspective, because our treatment and care of them (whether indirectly or directly) reflect (and reinforces) our sense of our own moral status and values, either collectively or individually. Second, they matter because farm animals and their products form part of a broader representational and semiotic universe of language, concepts, symbols and meanings within which we cooperate and co-empathize. Third, we care for farm animal lives because we touch and ultimately ingest those animal bodies and animal body products into our own selves, thereby involving embodied material and sensory interactions that concern us most directly, whether it be through nutritional needs, gastronomic excess or bodily health. Clearly, both individual and societal responses to these concerns can vary enormously.

For some individuals or communities, the raising, killing and consuming of farm animals and their products remain simply and unequivocally morally and/ or physically abhorrent. For others it is acceptable as long as various safeguards and procedures are put into place and respected to minimize avoidable suffering. For others still, specific concern for the well-being of animals destined to be killed and consumed by humans is largely misplaced and unnecessary. Numerous surveys undertaken over the last ten years (e.g. Phillips et al., 2012; Eurobarometer, 2005, 2007; Kjaernes et al., 2008; IGD, 2009) confirm that the second of these categorizations reflects the increasingly predominant view among European citizens, though others also point to the widespread rise of vegetarianism and veganism (Vegetarian Society, 2014).

Although one can trace the formation of the first animal welfare organizations to the mid-nineteenth century, the development and generalization of 'factory' or intensive livestock farming by the middle of the twentieth century is, as we have seen above, a key pre-curser for the emergence of popular (as well as scientific) engagement with the ethics of livestock farming and the welfare of farm animals. In the preface of Ruth Harrison's landmark book, the American biologist Rachel Carson wrote: 'I hope it will spark a consumers' revolt of such proportions that this vast new agricultural industry will be forced to mend its ways' (Carson, 1964: viii).

Harrison's claim was that intensive production methods were, at least in part, unethical in ways that those of pre-industrialized agriculture were not. The existing moral limits of animal agriculture were, it was claimed, exceeded or were deemed no longer appropriate or relevant to the new technologies and infrastructures of 'factory' farming. Harrison's own critique of factory farming was one of popular ethics and morality. She wrote:

> The arguments against factory farming are essentially based on humanitarianism and quality [of life]; the arguments for factory farming, such as they are, are economic arguments. (Harrison, 1964: 194)

In this polarization (economic utilitarianism on one side, humanitarianism and consequentialism on the other), she pitched a popular and traditional public view of livestock farming – one that was bucolic, rather romanticized and somewhat idealized – against the apparent brutality of modern intensive animal confinement and mutilation. Here was born an almost ideological distinction between 'traditional/extensive' and 'modern/intensive' that is still very much with us today (QA Research, 2013).

Individual acts of animal cruelty, outlawed in pre-existing legislation, are replaced it is often claimed by the systematic inhumanity of industrialized production practices that deprived living animals of light, space, company and natural environments while subjecting them to almost permanent states of pain, suffering and discomfort. In a second Preface to Harrison's book, Sydney Jennings (a former president of the British Veterinary Association) writes: 'How far will man claim the right to inflict bodily discomfort and cause mental anguish to birds and animals if factory farming methods appear to require it?' (Harrison, 1964: ix).

Carson's hope, however, did not materialize, though, as Rollin (2013) points out, a generation was energized over issues of farm animal welfare. In the end, there was no 'consumers' revolt' but there has been consumer pressure, though often indistinguishable from retailer and food industry–led practices of market segmentation and differentiation. If anything, consumers and citizens have, on the whole, become inured to many of the methods and the metrics of industrial, intensive animal production. We might argue that, at one level, certain mutilations (such as the beak trimming of laying hens or the removal of pigs' tails) and the culling of unwanted or uneconomic animals are an integral component of modern farming systems (and accepted as such or at least unchallenged as such by the majority of citizens and consumers). At another level, permanent confinement within indoor and artificialized environments is becoming so commonplace for a growing number of farmed species that traditional refrains such as 'all cows eat grass' seem positively anachronistic. Lives are becoming shorter, weight gain faster, outputs – whether they be litres of milk or the number of eggs laid – greater.

This is taking place, however, behind the growing raft of what are felt as increasingly effective animal welfare legislation, codes of practice and assurance schemes that have come into being over the last thirty or so years (see Chapter 4). Citizens and consumers feel, according to studies in different EU states, not only that levels of farmed animal welfare have improved but that they are being taken care of through public legislation (Eurobarometer, 2007). While there may still be many further improvements to be made, responsibility for these is increasingly held to lie with the farmers and the retailers rather than with any profound changes to food production systems, or indeed with consumers themselves. The paradox is summed up by the IGD (2009): by believing that animals have been treated well, in conformity to robust legislative standards, consumers are alleviated of the guilt they may feel about consuming the flesh or products of farmed animals.

So, for the most part citizen concern for farm animal welfare has rarely led to large-scale acts of militancy or even explicit political engagement. The principal exception to this within the UK was the widely supported and sometimes violent movement against the live shipment of young calves and sheep to Europe in the mid-1990s. Live shipments of sheep and young male calves born to dairy cows had increased steadily in the 1980 and early 1990s following the establishment of the Single European Market and the relaxation of rules governing animal transport times. The banning in the UK, on welfare grounds, of veal crates in 1990 was also a factor as producers sought other means of obtaining value from unproductive animals. The subsequent large-scale opposition to live transport, coordinated by the UK's leading animal welfare NGOs – the RSPCA and Compassion in World Farming (CIWF) – was unique in its dramatic mobilization of an otherwise un-politicized middle class (Benton and Redfearn, 1996). Yet, in a perceptive paper, Howkins and Merricks (2000) situate mobilization within a context of British countryside politics and an enduring pro-livestock farming welfarism, rather than any genuine political radicalization or opposition to animal production.

With the possible exception of the live exports issue (and, though for different reasons, the support for the hunting ban in 2004), numerous surveys have shown that widespread and general concern for the welfare of farmed animals in the UK is strong but rarely backed up by specific intentional actions (Evans and Miele, 2008). Rather, it is exercised, first, through broad general support for the growing volume of legislative and regulative actions on the part of governments and the food sector, second, through popular expressions of disquiet over singular and often highly mediatized acts of intentional cruelty, third, through membership of and support for pro-welfare organizations and, finally, where possible and desirable, at least among the more engaged and critical consumers, through food purchasing choices. Though hardly revolutionary, such support and such actions have nevertheless provided a broad level of consistent societal backing for socially and politically defined notions of what is ethically 'acceptable' and what is not. For the most part, led and mobilized by the principal animal welfare NGOs (the RSPCA and CIWF in the UK), examples include popular support for the banning of long-distance animal transport, the replacement of battery cages for egg-laying hens by enriched cage, colony or free-range systems, the interdiction of castration of piglets without pain relief and, most recently, concern over the growth of non-stun slaughter. While some observers express alarm that this mobilization results from and reinforces a misleadingly simplistic polarization between what are perceived of as being inherently high welfare and inherently poor welfare production systems or styles that continue to this today (Fraser, 2014), excessive levels of confinement, intrusive body manipulations, inhumane treatments, excessive stocking densities, behavioural deprivation, high levels of persistent lameness, slaughter without stunning and so on are now generically considered unacceptable within a broad section of society. We have arguably reached a point at which welfare concern might now be considered an almost 'mainstream phenomenon' (Rollin et al., 2011). Nevertheless, more radical lobbies and organizations continue to manifest their strong opposition to intensive livestock systems and the treatment of animals within them. Bodies like 'Animal Aid' in the UK, while they may lack strong or numerically important support within society in general, nonetheless play an increasingly significant role, on the one hand, in defining and challenging the limits of acceptability in animal treatment (by drawing attention to individual and systematic acts producing animal suffering, sometimes obtained through illegal means) and, on the other hand, in generating unwanted publicity for producers and food chain actors, including retailers.

Accounts of the social definition of ethical standards in farming and of the moral limits to the treatment of animals often hold livestock farmers and stockpersons apart. Animal farmers seem caught 'in the middle', between the economic imperatives of an increasingly verticalized food system and the moral approbation of an increasingly distant consumer society. And yet, as the FAWC states (2007: 2), 'stockmanship is the single most important influence on the welfare of farm animals'. If citizens and consumers define what are the socially acceptable ethical standards for the treatment of farm animals through a combination of utilitarian consequentialism, anthropomorphism, fashion politics and biological self-interest, farmers and those charged with the care of animals tend to display a more deontological ethical engagement with their stock and its welfare. Where individual animal productivity is closely associated with health and welfare, professional identity, farming culture and notions of 'good practice' create a context for both a 'duty of' and a 'responsibility for' care (Gatward, 2001; Wilkie, 2005, 2010; Dockes and Kling Eveillard, 2006; Van Huik and Bock, 2007). Although both of these vary considerably across the different production sectors, with beef and dairy farmers typically demonstrating closer relations to individual animals than say broiler producers (Kjaernes et al., 2009), this sense of 'duty' towards a professional moral code is, we would argue, substantively different as a form of ethical engagement to that of consumers and citizens. There are other differences too. Farmers and stock-keepers share space, dwelling, daily rhythms and, to a certain extent, work, labour and suffering with their animals (Porcher, 2006, 2009, 2011; Despret and Porcher, 2007). This can create a context not only of material dependency but also of an affective codependency. As a number of researchers have pointed out, the welfare of livestock can be strongly influenced by the nature of the relationship or bond that exists between stockperson and farm animal (Hemsworth and Coleman, 1998; Boivin et al., 2001; Waiblinger et al., 2006). We shall develop this more specifically in the following chapter.

Increasingly though, this deontological moral engagement is being brought into question both from within and without the livestock sector. Of the former, Porcher (2011) writes:

> The industrial organization of work, the denial of the intersubjective bond between farmers and animals and the repression of work rationales that are not economically based have triggered a deterioration, if not a perversion, of the relationship between workers and animals. (2011: 6)

A growing regulatory regime, the increasing use of standards, certification and assurance among food chain actors and particularly retailers (which we consider in some detail in Chapter 4), the narrowing of economic margins and the inevitable economies of scale are all, it is argued by Porcher and others (Anthony, 2003), weakening the strength of this deontological engagement. Moreover, the time-deepened moral framework upon which it rests is increasing being challenged by the alternative ethical priorities being promoted by consumers, ever distanced from what some argue are the inevitable realities of contemporary (cheap) food production and susceptible to often highly anthropomorphized accounts of animal well-being (Miele, 2011).

Economic engagement

Our third referential for understanding contemporary engagement with farm animal welfare is economic. At one level, it is evident that a healthy animal will be more profitable than a sick or suffering one and that increases in the welfare of an animal will, up to a point, lead to increases in productivity. McInerny (2004: 3) put it in acknowledgedly 'clinical' terms:

> In the same way as a machine or other physical capital is maintained, repaired and otherwise managed to sustain its flow of productive services, so animals will be fed, housed, and maintained in an appropriately healthy state to the extent it is economically worthwhile to do so. Because capital inevitably wears out (depreciates), at some point it has to be scrapped (culled) and replaced to maintain productive capacity. For animals representing goods-in-progress, they need to receive inputs of care and feeding only to the extent that the cost of this is covered by the value of final saleable product.

Concern for basic welfare is therefore good economic sense and, in a rather circular fashion, productivity is used as an indicator of good welfare. However, as McInerney (2004) shows, the relationship between productivity and welfare is not a simple linear one.

McInerney's conceptual model of this relationship (Chart 2.2) shows how the 'natural' welfare of an animal can be improved through husbandry, through protection from predators and disease, regular food and water and so on, and such improvements may yield increases in animal productivity up to the point where 'maximum' welfare is reached (point B in the chart). From this point on, although further gains in productivity can be made, welfare declines, ultimately to the point where the animal becomes unfit and no longer productive. Critically, the optimum position (point C in the chart) is variable, depending upon consumer choice (higher welfare, less productive, higher cost or lower welfare, more productive, lower cost) and production system (intensive, extensive, etc.).

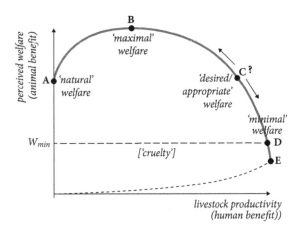

Chart 2.2 Conflicts between animal welfare and productivity. Source: McInerney (2004).

For farmers, poor welfare has a cost. At one level, it leads to reduced productivity. At another, resolving the welfare needs of suffering animals has a cost (or loss in the case of culled animals) as does compliance with regulatory standards. Where poor welfare and animal suffering become an issue or concern for individuals or society in broader terms, then human welfare may be reduced because of empathy and concern for the animals concerned (FAWC, 2011):

> Thus, farm animal suffering can be seen as a 'negative externality' of livestock production in much the same way as environmental pollution is considered by economists as a negative externality of industrial production. Externalities can be a major source of market failure in economies (i.e. they result in an allocation of resources such that the quantities of different goods and services produced are non-optimal from society's point of view, meaning that human welfare is lower than it might have been). (FAWC, 2011: 6)

For those engaged and committed consumers concerned by farm animal welfare, there is a cost in purchasing products from identifiably high welfare production systems. Yet, over the last fifteen or so years, we have seen considerable growth in a highly competitive choice-driven market for higher welfare animal products. As we have argued elsewhere (Buller, 2013a), ethics is the new marketplace and farm animal welfare has become increasingly exposed to different forms of demand-led governance where market segmentation, consumer choice and brand fidelity become critical drivers. Although the expansion of farm animal welfare legislation has created a rising base-level standard across the board, food chain actors are now mobilizing animal welfare as an additional and differential component of product quality and brand identity (Buller and Roe,

2012). This facilitates both product and brand segmentation (e.g. between 'basic' and 'quality' ranges or between individual retailers) and acts to regulate producer or manufacturer access to retailer shelves (where access is increasingly dependent upon compliance to an assurance or certification regime). In short, farm animal welfare has shifted, over the last fifteen or so years, from being an issue of largely ethical concern (the meeting of socially acceptable universal standards) to an issue of market creation (the market-driven differentiation of standards).

Farm animal welfare has not always been a focus of market consideration. Healthy, productive animals are always likely to be more valuable than unhealthy, unproductive ones as long as product value (either as material substance or as reproductive potential) is the primary economic concern. Throughout the history of animal farming, successive developments in technology, pharmaceuticals and husbandry technique have sought to increase the health and growth of livestock, within the desired parameters of production cycles, thereby contributing to the profitability of both the sector and individual farms. Contemporary animal welfare science grew up very much within this broad optic, its mission being to ascertain and improve the ability of farm animals to cope with the demands made on the stability of their physiological and psychological states by contemporary farming techniques (Broom, 2011): failure to cope results in failure to grow, failure to reproduce or death (Broom, 2001).

Whether animals could cope or not has not been, until relatively recently, a factor in the differentiation of animal products. Although battery chickens and calves in veal crates were the focus of early campaigns and boycotts, the issue for the emerging numbers of concerned citizens and consumers was that comparative welfare states were neither measured nor identified within food supply chains. Moreover, in the absence of specific evidence to the contrary, the pursuit of choice and cheap food encouraged a broad disengagement accompanied with a general confidence in the food industry and its ability to produce food according to the largely assumed moral and ethical standards of the time.

Two factors contributed to the eventual entry of farm animal welfare into the commercial marketplace. The first was the emergence of growing scientific evidence of the manifest failures among dairy and meat producers to meet these moral and ethical standards. Intensive 'factory farming' techniques not only introduced greater demands on animals' ability to 'cope' but also included levels of built-in wastage that inherently challenged ideas of individual animal care and welfare. As evidence of failing standards became available, and as mechanisms for assessing on-farm welfare became more robust, the potential for differentiating between individual farm, supply chains and entire production systems grew. The second factor was the commercial need among food chain actors and, most notably, retailers to both create additional value through the segmentation of otherwise fairly homogenous product sectors, such as pork or chicken, and strengthen customer fidelity to specific product brands, in-house labels or indeed to entire retail companies (Hughes, 1996; Morelli, 1997; Codron et al., 2005; Busch, 2010).

The UK food scares of the last thirty years (salmonella in eggs, BSE in cattle, Foot and Mouth, bovine TB, horsemeat contamination or substitution, etc.) raised consumer concern for the provenance of food and the transparency of food chains. It also put pressure on retailers and food chain actors to be able to demonstrate that they had met legally required due diligence in ensuring the quality of the food on their shelves. Although many recorded falls in animal product sales during or immediately following each of these food scares, marketing strategies, quality assurance mechanisms and greater segmentation – all of which we explore in Chapter 5 – quickly re-established former purchase levels (Lloyd et al., 2004), with one or two notable exceptions (Pugh, 1990; Howkins and Merricks, 2000). Today, animal welfare is a significant element in retail product and brand segmentation (Vanhonacker et al., 2007; IGD, 2009; Kjaernes et al., 2009).

Elsewhere (Buller and Roe, 2012, 2013), we have sought to use Michel Callon's radical approach to the understanding of markets (1998) and, more specifically, the concept of 'economization' (Calsikan and Callon, 2009) to help us understand the process by which farm animal welfare has become 'performed' within the market for animal products. It is useful to recall those arguments here. Economization, they define in the following way:

> the processes that constitute the behaviours, organizations, institutions and, more generally, the objects in a particular society which are tentatively and often controversially qualified, by scholars and/or lay people, as 'economic'.
> (2009: 370)

Animal welfare is a biological and physiological state as experienced by the animal. However, as we have seen, it has rewardable 'value' in addition to any ethical or moral value: to the farmer in terms of added productivity and, possibly, sale price and to the food chain actor and retailer as a source of potential 'value added' where consumers are willing to pay for extra welfare standards over and above legal minima. As the Farm Animal Welfare Committee has pointed out (FAWC, 2011), these added values are constructed from what are often very different bases. For the producer, value lies in health and fitness of the animal.

For the retailer, it lies in the assured conformity of the production system to agreed standards. For the consumer, that value derives from the perceived 'naturalness' of the animal's living conditions. For each of these actors, the welfare of the animal is constituted in different ways.

> So it doesn't matter whether we know what animal welfare actually is; we need only to know how to capture the responses to it within the framework of economic behaviour. (McInerney, 2004: 11)

For us, as social scientists, that 'economic behaviour' is our entry point into 'economization'. For markets to exist, argues Callon (1998: 51), *homo economicus* must be 'formatted, framed and equipped with prostheses which help him in his calculations and which are, for the most part, produced by economics'. Here, retailers and the supermarket play a key role in the configuration of economic agency (Alworth, 2010). Traditionally, argues Latour (2005), explanations of consumer choice behaviour were based either on belief in a sort of preordained or inherent trope of optima-maximization (*homo economicus*) or on subservience to some powerful economic infrastructure. Now, however, 'prostheses' (or what Latour terms, 'plug-ins') abound.

> If you look at a supermarket in this way, a bewildering array of devices is underlined, each having the capacity to provide you with the possibility of carrying out calculations somewhat more competently. Even when one has to make the mundane decision about which kind of sliced ham to choose, you benefit from dozens of measurement instruments that capacitate the subject as a consumer – from labels, trademarks, barcodes, weight and measurement chains, indexes, prices, consumer journals, conversations with fellow shoppers, advertisements, and so on. (Latour, 2005: 210)

In their useful summary of the key points of Callon's 'practical approach' to markets, Araujo and Kjellberg (2009) draw out three key features: its empirical focus on 'the practical interactions between different types of entities, incorporating both social and material elements' (199); its highlighting of markets 'as outcomes of co-configuration' and its emphasis on situated and ever-changing performances involving more than just human actors. As a result, they argue (2009: 201): 'attention is directed toward the multiplicity of agential configurations that are being enacted as part of unfolding market practices'.

The emergence of the free-range egg sector in the late 1980s and 1990s illustrates how the welfare 'market' is effectively assembled, as developments in the economization of farm animals, mobilizing new and different interpretations of 'good welfare', coupled with advances in veterinary science, and through a series of market-based technologies, labelling devices and innovative assessment protocols, led to a reshaping and a reconfiguration of the 'object' of farm animal welfare as epitomized in the novel concept of 'free range' (Buller and Roe, 2013). Miele (2013a) similarly employs Caliskan and Callon's concept of economization to show how the growing market for halal meat, and the qualification of halal products, raises particular questions for the manner in which 'welfare' becomes defined and mobilized as value, confronting scientific with religious interpretations of animal suffering.

We shall return, in a later chapter, to a more detailed analysis of specific plug-ins, prostheses or 'market devices' (Cochoy, 2007: 7) employed in the marketization of farm animal welfare. For now, we wish to retain, in particular, the focus in the work of Callon and his collaborators on the 'performance' of market practice and the heterogeneity of what we might consider to be market actors. In the field of food animal welfare, it is the animal material body and the perceived quality of the animal's life that impacts upon consumer (and retailer) choice through an assemblage of market devices, such as labels and assurance certificates, that intervene actively in the construction of markets. FAWC (2011) observes that the form in which animal products are sold can greatly influence the extent to which welfare provenance is given value. Moreover, different parts of the animal's body not only command very different prices but differentially reflect welfare concerns to the consumer. We have argued elsewhere (Buller and Roe, 2013) that this influence can go further still in that it can directly impact upon how welfare itself is measured and assessed. Along with FAWC, we acknowledge that a significant proportion of animal products go into processed food production, where provenance is rarely identifiable to consumers. Yet focusing on the mechanisms by which actors, such as retail buyers and shelf managers, construct both the market for and the consumers of farm animal welfare illustrates clearly the pertinence of this 'practical' and 'performative' approach which underpins the following chapters of this volume.

Chapter 3

Food Animal Care

In this chapter, we turn to the practical activity of working with farm animals in the commercial farming environment. In recent years, the food retail sector has significantly increased its attention to on-farm practices to ensure that product claims for better welfare map onto, as much as possible, demonstrably better experiences for the animals (see Chapter 4). A key element of this is the day-to-day practical relationship stockpersons have with the animals they work with. While some of the welfare improvements behind new production systems can be achieved through changes to the physical infrastructure of the farm, greater attention is now being paid to the management practices that support a positive daily relationship between stockperson and animals. This chapter contributes to the debate around the nature and qualities of the stockperson–animal interaction (Burton et al., 2012), an interaction that underpins many of the claims for higher animal welfare in the food market. We achieve this through an analysis of descriptive accounts of humans and animals interacting in the commercial farming environment. In doing so, we draw specifically from reflections and observations from farmers and stockpersons about this kind of work.

We develop here an argument for animal stockpersons to be reconsidered as animal carepersons in recognition of the changing understanding of farm animals as sentient creatures. We provide empirical details about how cultural and economic processes around the production of higher welfare food are, in turn, having an effect on the experience of carrying out farm animal care work on the farm. As our study shows, adequate and good care for individual farm animals is still being negotiated within both existing and novel production systems with a higher welfare remit. Mol et al.'s (2010: 14) concept of care as 'ongoing tinkerings with shifting tensions between different demands to care' is useful in the farm context. Their approach embraces the complexity of delivering care. It is suited to thinking about care for an other as an achievement alongside other demands which may be in tension with care delivery – minimizing costs, personal challenges, competitive advantage – each being well-recognized characteristics of the commercial industrialized, food animal production environment.

The fieldwork that features in this chapter is drawn from a two-week ethnography in July 2009 when Roe shadowed the work of stockpersons on an Oxfordshire farm in the UK. Since it was a mixed-use farm, it was possible to gain experience of the varied styles of relationship that different farm animal species establish with stockpersons, and at different life stages (including a newly hatched chick, established herd cow, ewe and young pig). Additionally, in-depth interviews were carried out with farm managers and all levels of stockpersons working on the mixed-use, organic certified farm. The interviews were carried out to understand more about how to improve animal welfare through the dynamics of the daily stockperson–animal interaction. In this example, the farm management had identified an interest in addressing the farm's stockperson culture as a route to continue to make farm animal welfare improvements. Before developing this however, we wish to elaborate briefly on our conceptual approach to the understanding of care as a means of redefining the stockperson as a farm animal careperson.

Mol et al. (2010) identify good care and modern technology as sharing an uneasy relationship, commonly felt throughout the twentieth century. This uneasy relationship can be seen both in the broad context in which Harrrison's *Animal Machines* was written and, as we have seen above, in the influence it went on to have. Take, for example, the chick-vaccinating machine that will be described later in this chapter. It is a technology that delivers a precise measure of vaccine as part of the health care package for only hours-old chicks. It is part of the care package but could also be identified as a brute piece of heavy machinery being used in proximity to the fragile young life of an hours-old fluffy chick. Part of the achievement, in using this piece of technology to deliver care, is the result of concern for both the working hours and conditions of the human operator to ensure he/she can carry out the job effectively and carefully, and in the regular maintenance of the machine. As Mol et al. (2010) stress, technologies (human–machine in partnership) themselves need caring for in order to work effectively. This is a theme we develop further below.

Five assumptions underpin the following empirically driven analysis of the stockperson–animal interaction. First, contrary to much of the literature on human–animal relations on farm, this chapter examines this interaction as enacting care between two sentient beings – human and animal. Second, the locus of influence or power is displaced from the stockperson into the relationship actively formed as a consequence of an individual animal or an animal collective's agency. Third, animal careperson–animal relations are characterized as forged through habitual practices of animal care. Fourth, our interpretation is attentive to the environmental contingencies and dynamics that enact different behavioural responses in animal, human and technologies.

Finally, we give particular attention to the significance of embodied memories about how to 'work' with a flock/herd of animals, or an individual animal, that are often difficult to articulate in words.

The chapter is organized as follows. Two opening sections – 'Previous encounters' and 'Contexts of care' – introduce the existing literature and policy relevant to the study of the stockperson–animal relationship. This is followed by 'Observing care' which contains a number of closely analysed empirical observations about how care is performed including the daily checks on the animals, trust, skills in handling animals, questions around speed, care and food. We end this particular section with a discussion on judging negligence. This is then followed by close ethnographic observations in a section entitled 'Making animals killable'. The chapter ends with 'Animal care economized' that makes a number of overall points about the stockperson–animal relationship.

Previous encounters

Qualitative studies are quite novel within the farm animal welfare literature, despite a growing interest in on-farm practice from food supply chain actors and animal welfare NGOs. Often fictional accounts stand in place of actual documented encounters between humans and animals in making public the circumstances in which animals are raised and the human experiences and feelings associated with that raising. Rather than encouraging debate based on animal welfare science and an understanding of whether animals are, or are not, having a life that meets their needs and is 'worth living', this has indulged a culture that largely opts to keep potentially upsetting animal-related events out of public view. The result of this lack of debate is often a general confusion over whether acceptable welfare standards can be met within industrialized commercial settings. The primary focus of modern food animal production after all has not been the welfare and quality of life of the sentient being at the centre of the system, but rather its general productivity; and this despite growing evidence of the potentially higher value of products from improved welfare systems. Nevertheless, the concept of, on the one hand, the sentient being and, on the other, the commodity sit uneasily together and yet it is precisely the coalition of these two different modes of orderings that the stockperson is challenged to negotiate in everyday practice – at one turn evoking the meaning of the animal as sentient and having feelings, and at another turn evoking the meaning of the animal as an edible commodity. Moreover, the stockperson is required to do this alongside negotiating care for their own emotional well-being as they adapt to the daily challenges of their role.

Psychologists have been the predominant voice in studies of the practical care relations between farm animal and stockperson, though this work has failed to situate this care within a wider context. Breuer et al. (2003) concluded that negative handling of heifers increased their fear of humans, while Coleman et al. (2003) considered how personality may affect treatment of animals, arguing that 'a person [...] sensitive to the behaviour of an animal may affect that person's behaviour towards an animal making him or her more sensitive to the animal's responses to handling' (Coleman et al., 2003: 198). These studies though interesting do not seek to engage with the complexity of daily pressures and demands that are typical within the dynamic farming environment and which places stress upon, and thereby shape, the human–animal relations on a farm. The beliefs, attitudes and views elicited from farmers in these various studies draw predominantly from the farmer's expert knowledges of operating a farming business. They largely fail to engage with a farmer's lay, practical knowledges of farming, the daily iterations of practices in a changing, dynamic community of fellow farm workers, farm animals, machinery and the seasonal meteorological challenges of the environment. Burton et al. (2012) offer an exception to these predominantly psychological approaches by developing a sociological framework to address how a farm's 'culture' influences the behaviour of stockpersons and by recognizing the practical challenges of behaviour change within the stockperson community may act as a driver for animal welfare improvement. Through taking a practical, ethnographic, analytical approach to studying stockperson–animal interaction on the farm, some of the more-than-human challenges of making change happen are identified.

To study care practices of sentient beings in the animal farming context, a methodology is used which enables the *observation, participation and close study of human/food animal encounters*. Although social science literature has made an important contribution to the study of contemporary food and agriculture policies and market regulation, there is a scarcity of contemporary ethnographic studies in both geography and sociology that give attention 'to those who implement the associated [welfare] measures and practices on farm' (Hubbard et al., 2007, though see Roe et al., 2011 as a possible exception to this general observation). Fewer still seek to engage in the emotional experiences of working with farm animals – though notable exceptions here include Chapman and Crowden (2005), Law (2008, 2010) and the aforementioned Burton et al. (2012). In comparison there are many notable literary depictions of the life, killing and death of farm animals where we quickly learn how these events affect humans emotionally, and can affect animals emotionally too. There are scenes of farm animals giving birth, tackling animal illness or awkward behaviours in Sterchi's

The Cow (1988) and Berger's *Pig Earth* (1979); scenes of slaughter of animals in peasant culture in Hardy's *Jude the Obscure (1895)* and scenes of industrial scale slaughter-houses in Sinclair's *The Jungle* (1914) and the killing/euthanasia of animals in Coetzee's *Disgrace* (1999). In these rich, detailed literary narrations that span over 100 years, the affective, emotional, physicality of encounters is strongly conveyed, interestingly more often in relation to a singular animal rather than a number of animals. These contrast strongly with undercover exposes of animal cruelty to livestock publicized on the internet, for example turkeys kicked around as footballs, which created headlines back in 2007 (The Daily Mail, 2007). Along similar lines, more recent studies of farmers and/or stockpersons tend to interpret their views and attitudes as predominantly responding to the need to conform to quality assurance schemes, to find a place within the infrastructure of the agro-food industry (Fearne and Walters, 2004; FAWC, 2005) or to be participants in the market for higher welfare products (Hubbard et al., 2007), rather than in terms of their relationship with their animals. Exceptionally, in their cross-disciplinary, qualitative study, Horseman et al. (2014) used in-depth interviews to address the barriers and limitations farmers experience when trying to treat lameness in dairy cattle. This study demonstrates the significance of giving attention to the perception of an animal's or group of animals' health situation and how that relates to human action to tackle it.

> It is not simply a question of farmers' ability to detect lameness but rather their ability to call what they are seeing as lameness and to understand the value of promptly treating all lame cows, especially early onset lameness. (Horseman et al., 2014: 164)

Contexts of care

Farm animals are kept in environments where they rely on humans for their basic needs. Humans must ensure they are fed to avoid hunger or thirst; are given shelter so they are free from discomfort; can live without pain, injury or disease, or fear and distress; and are able to express normal behaviour. These expectations (the 'five freedoms', see Chapter 2) can be met through a complex arrangement of farm animal care practices that stretch through the life of the animal, or even before. Some may be related to selective breeding techniques that manifest, or allow to persist, known welfare problems within intensive farming systems. Yet, despite the nature of these responsibilities, the daily activities of farming animals are rarely referred to as care. For example, in the work of Rhoda Wilkie (2005, 2010), the language of care is not used when describing the social, emotional and material infrastructure that shapes stockperson activities. Nor is the term 'care' used to describe the attitudes displayed towards the animal at different points in the animal's lifetime.

Our study critically engages with Wilkie's work which identifies four attitudinal categories a stockperson holds for different animals (in the case of her study, cattle) in the herd. These are 'concerned detachment', 'concerned attachment', 'detached detachment' and 'attached attachment'. She recognizes that a farmer may shift their position with regard to an animal over the course of the animal's lifetime depending upon the quality of interaction between a farmer and an individual or group of animals. Wilkie uses these categories, first, to identify how the animal is commoditized, de-commoditized and re-commoditized during the different interactions between stockperson and animal and, second, to respond to the question of how willing a farmer might be to 'reconnect with their animals' (Curry Report, 2002). Wilkie's work is relevant here for it identifies a socio-affective component to the job that is often overlooked, and critically which itself becomes a disincentive to greater connection (Wilkie, 2005). In other words, she sees the potential for emotional connection with the farm animal as itself a barrier towards developing empathic relations with an animal. In looking in detail at animal care practices, we ask what does this barrier for developing empathic relations consist of in practice?

Within the broader context of a rise in public anxieties about the welfare of farm animals, over the last decade there has been a recent surge of interest in the governance of the stockperson–farm animal relations (FAWC, 2007). There are two connected reasons for this. First, as we see above, there is a growing movement within animal welfare science to approach the definition and assessment of welfare directly from the animal's point of view rather than relying on the evaluation of the resources, management and environmental factors that might contribute to an individual animal's welfare. At a European level this approach is linked to the 1997 Amsterdam Treaty that recognizes animals as 'sentient beings' and to the scientific development of animal-based welfare assessment measures (e.g. Welfare Quality®, 2004–2009) that respond directly to this recognition of sentience. Scientific measures such as fear-avoidance tests, lameness and gait scoring, normal behaviour and body condition, directly and indirectly, are correlated as indication of good or poor stock management. Second, UK food market retailers such as Waitrose, Tesco's and Marks and Spencer, who compete in the premium food market of higher welfare meat and dairy products, have started to reward farmers that meet additional stockmanship criteria (e.g. Tesco's project 2008–2009; Sainsbury's Dairy Development 2017). In response to this changing farm animal welfare context, the UK Farm Animal Welfare Council stated in 2007 that the relation between stockperson and farm animal is the 'single most important influence on the welfare of farm animals' (FAWC, 2007: 5) and proposed some essentials of stockmanship:

Knowledge of animal husbandry. Sound knowledge of the biology and husbandry of farm animals, including how their needs may be best provided for in all circumstances.

Skills in animal husbandry. Demonstrable skills in observation, handling, care and treatment of animals, and problem detection and resolution.

Personal qualities. Affinity and empathy with animals, dedication and patience. (FAWC, 2007: 7)

The UK FAWC report of 2007 additionally gave a comprehensive overview of how the training and education of stockmanship could be improved. The FAWC report was however more circumspect with respect to the daily nature of stockperson activity and the circumstances and events that might regularly challenge stockperson knowledge, stretch their skills and test their endurance in actual care practice.

Improving understanding of the detail and circumstance of stockperson work can only contribute to efforts to comprehend and formally assess evolving stockperson practices within the changing governance structures for farm animal welfare. Becoming more enlightened about the realities of how the work of stockpersons can improve farm animal welfare, but also how pressures on stockpersons can lead to failings in farm animal welfare, marks an important cultural shift. It is a shift that is increasingly influencing the governance structures around farm animal welfare work. Stockperson labour is enrolled into the economization that is driving welfare improvements. For farms who wish to be part of the market for higher welfare foodstuffs, developing a culture of improved care for the animals is one of many steps towards receiving a successful audit from a farm assurance company that can facilitate entry into the market (see Chapters 4 and 5 for more details). It is within this commercial context of the benefits of a good farm animal welfare audit that the notion of commercializing 'good care' for animals is placed.

It is worth noting at this point that there are particular well-used agricultural terms with which we might take issue in our drive to breathe fresh air and a new vision about what working with farm animals actually entails. 'Stock husbandry' is the traditional term for expressing the work of a stockperson. This term is laden with rather dated gender assumptions that cast the man, the husband, looking after their animals in much the same way as they would their wife. 'Husbandry is the masculine caring for the land' (Burden, 2006: 22), and we can extend this to the animals living on the land. Historically, the label 'care' is associated more with feminine roles. However, care work is increasingly normalized as a gender-neutral role throughout the human caring professions. Yet this change is not widely applied and discussed in relation to the role of the stockperson, despite the feminization of certain stockperson roles, for example, poultry work. The benefits of thinking about the stockperson as a careperson immediately opens access to a wealth of literature, policies, shared experiences and ideology about the demands of being a carer as relevant and recognizable with respect to the animal farming context. To rename stockpersons as food animal carepersons encourages changes in expectations and ideology surrounding farm animal production, retailing and consumption of the sentient farm animal being. Additionally, to support this move we must recognize that the farm animal is no longer an object but has its own agency to affect the emotional lives of those working with them. The animal is no longer conceived as mute, inanimate, inert stock, but sentient and affecting. The implications of interpreting animal agency in farm animal studies have already significant momentum (Miele, 2012; Buller, 2013b, 2014). We have a similar aversion to the term 'stock' which reduces the status of the animal to a chattel and a 'unit of production', suggesting nothing of its vitality and sentience. In this volume, we prefer to use the term 'food' or 'farmed animals' that more properly describes the purpose given to these animals' lives.

Observing care

Methodologically, this chapter uses ethnographic participant observations and in-depth structured interviews to develop a narrative about encounters between animals and humans on the farm. It draws on the fieldwork described in the introduction to this chapter. This narrative engages directly with the challenge to interpret specific events when animals, materialities and technologies are brought together. As opposed to solely interpreting these events in terms of the human's experience, space is given to outline how such events impact upon and reconfigure a range of non-human materiality (including that of the living animal but also others) and technologies both tangible like farm machinery and veterinary medicine, and intangible like farm assurance scheme protocols and farm management ideology. To do this, we draw upon the work of science and technology studies scholars (Law, 2004; Mol, 2003; Barad, 2007; Haraway, 2008) to inform the interpretation of events on farm. This conceptual bricolage takes forward growing interest in social science, in phenomenology and in science and technology studies to renew attention to embodied human and non-human practices. This body of work, associated in part with non-representational theory (Thrift, 2008; Anderson and Harrison, 2011), emphasizes the study of bodily movement and practices and importantly argues that these are shaping and are shaped by the material environment that the body is situated within. Most significantly, it argues that bodily practices in turn shape thought processes and thus challenges the classic Enlightenment position that the mind controls the body. These interpretative concerns frame the approach taken here to investigate how the environment/the animal/technology affords human care-full and care-less activities. These concerns also support interpretations of daily and routine events, responses to which cannot be wholly attributed to rational thought but instead relate to how the multispecies environment is configured. Our emotional selves become sensorially engaged with the world that enables us to walk or eat without thinking very much about how to do it. In the same way, farm animal careperson practices are carried out in ways that do not always involve reflective consideration of what is done and why, as they have become habituated by experience. Moreover, we might push this a little further by suggesting that what people do may not always be aligned with the broader emotional conscience of the individual. Instead, actual events configure their action to be played out in a particular way. The language of choice is not used within this interpretative framework as the analysis moves to an understanding of how thought and action are framed by the broader environment.

Ethical principles, advocated, for example, by animal rights writers like Singer (1995 [1974]) and Regan (2004) and the work of animal welfare scientists seeking to articulate the capacities of the sentient being (e.g. Webster, 2006; Dawkins, 2012), are of little use to the animal careperson carrying out their daily tasks. For their writings are of little immediate and practical value when standing in a field of cattle or a shed full of poultry, caught up in the daily processes and practices of working with an animal to meet its needs and those of the animal caretaker. As Brandth (2006: 20) writes: 'Farm work accommodates bodies in various ways: The products of farming, food, accommodate consumer bodies. But more important, perhaps, working with animals is corporeal work and contains aspects of care work and emotional work. Animals need to be fed, kept clean, warm and content. They may get sick or die.' Taking Brandth's interest in the corporeal nature of farm animal work, we examine on-farm practices as illustrations of embodied knowledges, practices and skills that carry with them emotional competencies.

Animal caretakers have shared and learnt through embodied, sensual knowledges how to communicate not only with different species, but with different breeds and different individual farm animals. Our concern is to comprehend how animal caretakers communicate with animals in their care, through a discussion of events that take place between human and animal(s). It becomes clear, through these examples, the paramount need to establish some degree of shared understanding between human and animal.

Checking the animals

Every day each group of animals is checked on the farm; the furthest field is visited first, driven to in an all-terrain vehicle (ATV); each house of chickens is gently walked through. Each animal whether sheep, cattle, pig or poultry is encouraged to its feet, a signal that it is responsive, physically able and thus displaying signs of good, rather than poor, health and welfare. This is called 'doing the checks' on the animals; however it also builds up a regular co-presencing of humans and animals. It activity constructs subtle forms of communication through the regularity of the practice over consecutive days, weeks, months or years, often carried out by the same person each time. From this repeated practice grows a relationship with a herd of cattle, a group of pigs, a flock of sheep or poultry from which one can identify communicative elements from human to animal(s) and from animal(s) to human. Animals showing signs of poor health can be easily spotted through this practice, through their walking gait: the slow, awkward rise to their feet or their failure to get up at all. The pitch of the background noise in a henhouse can reveal to the trained ear that the occupants are more stressed than on another day. The subtlety to this intercommunication between a food animal careperson and the animals in their care is highly nuanced and one which an untrained eye, ear, body strains to pick up from a few visits (see Table 3.1). This daily activity also establishes starting points for more complex interactions between food animal careperson and food animals that hopefully will result in there being less stress for all sentient beings involved. More complex interactions could include the activities of moving animals from one field to another, tending to an animal that is ill or injured, moving the cattle longer distances across the farm once routes and routines are established with leaders of the group. Yet such complex daily activities can also regularize poor care practices.

In the four extracts detailed below (Table 3.1), the vulnerability of both human and animal is present in the sensibility that motivates the move towards intra-communications – observing the eyes, shuffling slowly – to gesture a meaning, or a comprehension of each-other's co-presencing in order to avoid what Harrison has described as a 'withdrawal of meaning and the break-up of comprehension [...] when there is little or nothing to be said – when, as we say, the world falls apart' (2008: 425). Elsewhere (Roe and Greenhough, 2014) the challenges

Table 3.1 Examples of food animal caretakers talking about communicating with farm animals (from fieldwork undertaken in 2009)

Example 1:

Farm animal careperson A: I think it's the same voice and it's important to keep a fairly level voice and not an excitable one, and not to shout and yell and bawl. You've got to be quiet, you can't go in and walk as a normal person would walk. You've got to go in and walk quietly and shuffle round the birds but equally you've got to make sure every bird stands up. So it's a case of getting that balance right.

Example 2:

Farm animal careperson B: Well we was always taught that if you went in a field with a herd of cows you always had a stick in your hand. And a cow that had got a calf she'd bowl you over. But then you look at a cow and you know what she's going to do before she does it, it's body language. Like our old man used to say watch his eyes, watch his eyes, he'll tell you which way he's going. That's how we was brought up.

Roe: So that's what you do now to read the animals, what the animal wants to do …

Farm animal careperson B: You can read it, you can read what they're going to do before they do it.

Roe: That's a real skill that is.

Farm animal careperson B: See I think like vets, and this is just my opinion, they'll look at a herd of cows and they won't see nothing. It's the farmer that picks the cow out that's wrong.

Example 3:

Farm animal careperson C: You know, they're all right, so, when we've calved indoors, if the cows not happy when you're tagging the calf, you can almost see a different colour in the eyes but they're, sort of, like a, I don't know, like a blue colour to me.

Example 4:

Farm animal careperson B: Cattle are very big animals and if you try and rush them, try and rush them through gates and that, you will find that they'll pull a lot of your fences down. So you've got to just, you know, take it easy with them.

Roe: So is it about the pace at which you move …

Farm animal careperson B: Yes.

Roe: Go at their pace?

Farm animal careperson B: Yeah. Every, sort of, group of cattle has a ring leader as I like to call them and it's, so long as you keep that ring leader moving where you want them to the rest will generally follow. But then you've got them all in a confined space in a yard somewhere, you've just got to be, you know, give them that bit of time. Give them a bit of respect and then they'll work through the way you want them to. You can start hollering and shouting at cattle and it doesn't make the slightest bit of difference, it just stirs them up.

---

of rounding up cattle have demonstrated the improvisatory angle to habitual practices of working with farm animals.

Trust

Animal carepersons are frequently on their own with animals. Should personal communication fail between them and the animals, a feeling of being physically vulnerable can be there. Here a food animal caretaker describes it as 'trust' in describing how he plans his escape route from cattle should his communication skills' fail (Table 3.2).

Trust is secondary to the primary establishment of communication. This second stage of trust is what is developed from repeated positive embodied communication practices. The context that facilitates trust cannot be ignored, as the establishment of trust between animal and humans goes on to enable easier animal handling when an animal is sick and in pain or in a strange place such as the abattoir. Ultimately, the trust relations between animal/food animal and careperson out on the farm, forged during everyday encounters, teach us the value of communication between sentient bodies. The communication can amount to no more than 'a quick word', or a slow-paced reassuringly repeated set of calming practices; each is valuable in context for developing trust and hence better care for humans and animals on the farm. In the case of the food animal careperson, good care is nearly always negotiated as a balance towards the best interests of the food animal as a collective rather than the individual animal.

Despite changes in food animal farming towards improving the infrastructure to ensure animals are well cared for, there is still an expectation that people either have or don't have some innate, natural empathy towards livestock that shapes how they carry out their work with animals.

> I do think people either have a natural empathy with livestock or not. And I think that empathy is sort of transferable between the species. If you haven't got it, then you really haven't got it. But I think there's a level of sort of basic connection. And then I think when you ... work with an experience – if you like the different types of animals, you start to learn about how they behave and why they do things and what's likely to upset them or spook them or whether they are behaving in a natural way. (Farm Manager, interviewed in 2009)

Too much emphasis on the position outlined by this manager might suggest that there is little further to add to guarantee animals are well cared for than the innate empathy of the carer. Through further empirical examples, we explore whether getting the right person to perform a task is all you need, or whether creating an environment where they can work to the best of their ability with

Table 3.2 Examples of food animal caretakers talking about trust (from fieldwork undertaken in 2009)

Food animal careperson B: They do trust me. You know, I do trust them as well but I'm always wary that one just might turn a bit funny. I've always got my escape route planned and …

Roe: Really, what in your head?

Food animal careperson B: Yes, yeah, well if the mother's this side I know that I can get away the other way.

---

animals might also be a factor. As Conradson (2003) has commented, care-taking tasks involve both physical and emotional labour. Caring for farm animals is no exception. Yet we argue understanding the role of a food animal careperson means looking beyond the human individual to the institutional context, the specific animal breeds and histories, the physical infrastructure and indoor–outdoor environment within which they work. It is from studying the broader context that the capacity to care well unfolds. To illustrate this point, in the following subsection three further examples are analysed as broad context within which care tasks are being carried out.

Practices

Figure 3.1 shows a chick vaccinator at work vaccinating one of approximately 6,000, barely a few hours-old, chicks. Holding each one very briefly he will vaccinate the whole batch in a 3-hour time period to protect them from disease. One cannot avoid recognizing the place of technology in the ongoing care of these chicks' lives. Still within their eggshells they were kept alive and nurtured to grow in an incubator. For three weeks the eggs were turned mechanically, imitating the behaviour of a mother hen if she had had the chance to sit on her own eggs. In effect the incubator took on the role of primary carer for the eggs and the chicks growing inside. The vaccinator uses a similar piece of precision technology to give a dose of vaccine to chicks, to support their health within the crowded, high-density environment of chicks growing into chickens that characterizes their life experience.

In a second example, a hatchery careperson is carrying out the 'chick take-off'. This involves sifting through freshly hatched eggs. Over the previous three weeks, the hatchery careperson has tended to the incubating eggs. The chick take-off involves filtering out those chicks which are deformed or that have not hatched properly often because they remain stuck to their shells.

Figure 3.1 Chick vaccinator example of Wilkie's (2005) 'detached detachment'. Photograph: Roe.

> Against a constant background of cheeps, intermixed with the sharp alarmed shrill cry of singular chicks, with the words 'There, there. Its okay, I'm here' she deftly breaks the blood capillaries and neck of a deformed chick with the back of her thumb on the corner of the crate. (Extract from author's ethnographic research notes, 2009)

This act of killing is the delivery of what is accepted as best care for deformed chicks. Notable is the tenderness in her voice and the gentleness in her handling of these tiny, fluffy yellow bodies during this killing act.

On farm the spaces where care is practised and performed are the fields, yards, pens, cattle crush, the race, barns and sheds. Like Parr and Philo's (2003) study of how care for humans is constituted by subjectivities and care practices played out within and through space, the same is the case for farm animal care. More generally the care follows the animals across the varied farm spaces, but there are some more medicalized care tasks that do require specialized spaces to restrain the animals to ensure effective 'care' delivery. Most notable among these is the cattle crush, which this third example discusses. Cattle crush technology has eased the process of caring for industrially farmed animals, as very large, strong animals can be safely restrained while giving them individual attention. A calf is held in the crush in order to receive a nutritional mineral tablet to help its growth that replaces minerals absent in the farm habitat. While this maintains the digestive health of the cow, it also supports the healthy growth of an animal that is commercially valuable. We witness machine, human, animal and mineral assembling to deliver intimate care practices that characterize the relationship between farm animal and careperson, eased through well-maintained and suitable technology.

> The clang and roar of the cattle crush, the anxious bellows of the cow, the smaller size of the calf, the strength of the farmer's fingers to pry open the jaw of this calf, the rehearsed veterinary skills to direct the tablet down the throat rather then the oesophagus, the caress of the throat to encourage the calf to swallow, assemble in these moments of care. (Extract from author's ethnographic research notes, 2009, and see Figure 3.2)

What links these three examples together is that the health and welfare needs of different farm animals – the vaccination of chicks, the culling of deformed chicks and the delivery of a mineral tablet – are all instances of care delivery, yet they each draw on different animal-handling skills and emotional involvement. Animal health issues are being dealt with through vaccinations and mineral

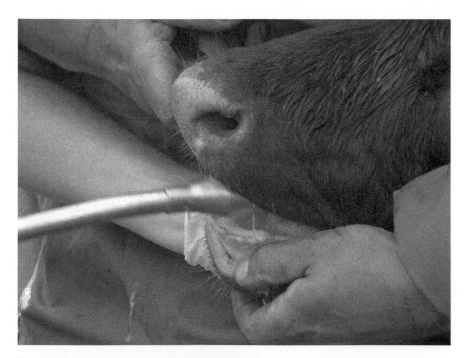

Figure 3.2 Delivering the bolus. Photograph: Roe.

tablets in the first and third examples, while suitability for life as a broiler chick growing to be a chicken for the table is assessed in the second example. We begin to examine the practices of being a farm animal careperson through these three examples, particularly in relation to how the human–animal relationship is managed in these different examples. We return to discuss the thinking of Wilkie (2005) and her analysis of farm animals as 'sentient commodities' (2010). Wilkie would describe the vaccinator as holding an attitude of 'detached detachment' (see Figure 3.1) to the chicks he handles. The hatchery worker, in contrast, might be said to hold an attitude of 'concerned detachment'. Yet in the third example the farmer and vet are very focused on the individual animal, adapting themselves to its size and shape and to the emotional, embodied response it makes to being put in and then held in the crush. They approach their task with 'concerned detachment'; a mixture of technological proficiencies, human skills and embodied sensitivities for the vulnerability of the body being cared for, whether a fearful body or a fragile body.

As Chapter 2 has outlined, farm animal care practices need to be studied within the context of food regulatory, scientific and market-led governance activities. Throughout the empirical examples given within this chapter the background context is that these animals' lives are a consequence of specific 'economic' material practices that are affecting how they live and the selection of these actual animal bodies to live to grow into food. This context shapes the experience of animal carepersons working with food animals. In a previously published paper (Buller and Roe, 2013), we introduced the term 'co-modifying' as a way of grasping the profundity of the implications of this entanglement between scientific knowledge-making practices, civil anxieties and the integration of farm animal welfare values into market performativity. This term 'co-modifying' refers to how the practice and process of turning the concept of animal welfare as a set of abstract values into material practices are not homogenous or static but are context-dependent, species-specific and market-suitable. Through the examples above one can begin to get a sense of the complexities of what food animal careperson work entails in practice as a consequence of the mass industrialization of food animal production (even though, in the example above, these are organic broiler chicks). Our analysis offers a critical analytical perspective on what has happened, is happening and may happen with a view to remaining alert to how stockperson care practices are being shaped, modified, co-modified by technical, social, material and institutional arrangements in the economization process and are, as a result, delivering what are deemed as acceptable welfare standards for food animals. In what follows, we ask how are the processes and practices of species-specific farm animal care being modified and co-modified in the evolving context of what is market suitable? To borrow from Haraway (2008): what happens when the market and farm animal welfare meet in the nexus of practices of care delivery between stockperson and animal?

Speed, care and food

One of the central characteristics of the modern food animal industry is the drive to speed everything up, largely in order to reduce farm staff and feed costs. An animal that needs less time spent caring for it, that eats less food and perhaps requires less indoor heating because of its shorter life is cheaper to produce, leading to stable or improved profit margins. Mechanized and biological processes are tinkered with to speed up animal production, carcass processing and distribution to the shop shelf. Held against these economic objectives, the notion of speeding up a life hardly seems synonymous with good animal care. Yet two of the care practices discussed above – the killing of a deformed chick and vaccination – were both carried out at high speed. Speed, we argue, can be an important component in delivering good care in certain contexts because it can help manage the socio-affective bond between human careperson and the animal, particularly when carrying out emotionally demanding work. Yet inversely, speed can also result in too little time for a socio-affective bond to establish and flourish and thus can impede care. In the following analysis, we consider these points within the economization of food animal care.

The vaccinator above took pride in the speed with which he handled chicks. He presented an attitude akin to a production-line worker, privileging speed and accuracy over giving attentive care (which would involve pausing and reflecting while handling each and every individual chick). But even the hatchery worker, who has started work at 6 am, is equally keen to get through the task of preparing the newly hatched chicks to be sold and moved to another organic chicken farm. Both hatchery worker and vaccinator are handling the lives of thousands of chicks that morning (overall some 17 million chickens are slaughtered each week in the UK). For the lay observer, it is often the speed with which individual animals are handled in intensive farming production that appears abhorrent, unnatural and of inherently poor welfare. Speed of handling and the sheer volumes of animals involved are not factors that are commonly associated with notions of care and respect for the living animal. Yet, both of the practices discussed here reveal a more nuanced interpretation of speedy practices within the practice of caring for animals that become food.

Turning our attention briefly to the slow food movement and its opposite, the fast-food movement, both of these are primarily focused on the duration of time within the consumption experience; the first to decelerate the consumption experience and to create a multiplicity of food formats, the latter to accelerate the eating experience and to create a homogeneity of food formats across spaces (Murdoch, 2006). Both use time to represent the food supply chain to the consumer. In the farm practices we have described above, time unfolds as a component of the actual quality of the care practices and the context in which they occur within the supply network. For the most part, this is unseen yet it may underpin claims that appear in brand commitments, quality assurance schemes and ultimately on food packaging. Examining time as a factor in the experience of caring of an other within industrialized farming is to accept that while capital values speed over slowness in order to manage the demands of mass production, there may be other additional reasons for speed that relate to the experiences of being an embodied, emotional human being and that equip one to care effectively.

A different way of considering the role of speed in care is to explore how it might be valued as enabling detachment from adverse emotional connections that can develop by dwelling too long in the moment. Speed may be valued personally by the vaccinator because it enables a detachment, to dampen the socio-affective connection to the fragile, warm, vulnerable, living and breathing body that passes between his fingertips; each individual bird barely lingers long enough to become a conscious living presence; there is little desire to dwell in the moment to allow thoughts or feelings to rise in response to what is held in his fingertips. The vaccinator is a subject who not only thinks and feels, but also performs their work through bodily gestures of limbs, digits, muscles, organs and bones working together; and this body enables him to know how to care but also places him vulnerable to the potentially difficult feelings should he linger too long in the moment. By lessening the time holding the body of each chick and barely sensing its livingness, the affects that convey the social realities and affective emotional sensations about the practices he is carrying out are denied purchase and so in effect he demonstrates a tactic for caring for his emotional self. It is worth pointing out that there is no suggestion that the vaccinator does his job badly because of his speed.

In contrast, in the second example, where the stockperson selects and identifies those chicks whose deformities render them unviable under the standards of the broiler industry, the rhythm of work is punctuated by an occasional slowing down. Scanning for normality is a practice of relative brevity; fingers, palms and hands cradling, then a swift turn of the chick in the hand, the human eye focusing on visually checking for 'normality' and the chick is placed in a freshly prepared out tray. However, once an abnormal chick is identified, to be removed and killed, time slows as the gestures and sounds of additional care are practised and uttered. The chick is held shielded in one hand or cupped in two; soothing sounds for the chick and herself are made: 'There, there', she says. The thumb is readied as a button to push life out of the chick by the breaking of its neck on the hard edge of the table. It is done with 'concerned detachment' (Wilkie, 2005). Wilkie's aforementioned study dwells upon the emotional paradox associated with livestock production summed up in the line: 'Workers enjoy working with animals but are instrumental in preparing them for slaughter' (2005: 226). In this second example, it is a very premature slaughter that we are witnessing, not at the point of life when it is big enough to furnish a Sunday dinner table, but rather a size only suited for feeding pet or zoo snakes. The slowing down that this careful extinguishing of life demands brings attention to these moments when contradictory feelings and challenging thoughts can be experienced. We suggest that in these practices there are moments when some disposition of detachment becomes necessary for the careperson's own sense of self-care.

Self-care for the food animal careperson becomes part and parcel of delivering care to the food animal whether as part of an animal–human–machine care-delivery assemblage, such as the process of vaccinating chicks, or when in the act of 'thumbing-out' life to those chicks deemed physically unsuitable for further growth and development. Here then are complex, multiple and sometimes seemingly contradictory care practices. 'Good care' is, for Mol and her colleagues (Mol et al., 2010: 14), a 'persistent tinkering in a world full of complex ambivalence and shifting tensions'. In these two examples, we witness the shifting tensions of caring for the self and caring for the animal along with ambivalence for the individual that speedy activity can offer, both of which form part of the economization of care.

How can these 'tinkerings' associated with meeting an animal's welfare needs be characterized, interpreted, within the process of economization of care? How and where does the economization of food animal welfare create ambivalences? In the two examples that this section began with, we can already start to witness the shifting balance between care for the animal, care for the human, between the different material qualities associated with care. The inanimate vaccinating machine has a legitimate place within the health and care of poultry within intensive production systems despite the material contrast it presents to the lives that pass before it. If the deformed chicks were not killed, they would likely endure a life of pain and suffering and unable to carry out normal behaviours. The act of killing these chicks is part of the economization of care in a system that depends upon huge numbers. If individual chicks are not vaccinated, the risk of endemic disease threatens entire flocks. Again and again, it is the size and scale of the poultry population, the housing and the method of production that create the context for what is done to ensure good care within the economization of food animal welfare.

Returning finally to the third example, delivering the bolus to the cattle: this is a task not carried with any great speed, rather there is a steadiness as animal after animal is brought through the crush. This is a task carried out maybe once a year; it is not as routinized as the first two examples which may be a near-daily occurrence for the humans involved. In this third example, it is important to not overlook the experienced practical skills for handling the mouth of the cow by the farmer, and the accuracy of the vet inserting the tablet down the throat of the calf. These gestures subtly indicate how the bodily sensibilities of farmer and vet are present in how they tackle this delicate and intrusive procedure. If this is not done 'carefully' the calf could be hurt. The success of this procedure is found in the collective understandings between the food animal carepersons and members of the cattle herd. The daily visit when the animals are checked has developed an understanding between human and cattle. This has also fostered animal knowledge of the field environment where it is not unusual to see humans standing in and among them. Thus when the cows are encouraged to move, through gestures by now familiar human carers, they are calm as they are readied to enter the crush. The animals do not respond with fear or trepidation, but trust. Of course, this is background context, but it is very much a part of the continual making, and remaking, of care within the economization of farm animal welfare. The development of trust and confidence between this herd of animals and the carepersons has been a long-term, and time-intensive, investment. Yet in the act of delivering the bolus, the formation of a positive relationship between cattle, between herd and humans is valued when all goes smoothly during a time of close proximity to large, potentially dangerous animals.

Judging negligence

However, there are incidents where there can be disagreement on the farm as to whether the best care is taking place. These indicate the complex set of negotiations and contingencies that shape actual practices of caring and questions about how much is sufficient. Table 3.3 presents detail on three incidents that occurred, or were recounted, during fieldwork, where it was felt animals were not receiving sufficient, or good-enough care. Someone passed judgement that the best interests of the animal were not being met. The place and value of good care in the economy of farm animal welfare were evident as it

Table 3.3 Three reports of insufficient care (from fieldwork undertaken in 2009)

Incident 1:
'You've just got to get the basics right and it's amazing how much time we spend chasing people up to make sure that the animals have food, and water, and are there where they are supposed to be; which is pretty fundamental really.' (Farm Manager)

Incident 2:
The vet whilst checking the sheep, grabs a ewe wearing a prolapse strap. Loosening it they turn pale and angry as deep sores are revealed where the strap was cutting into the ewe's body. As the ewe is held, the vet calls across for me to bring the fly-strike spray-gun to preventatively treat the exposed flesh. I can see the vet's anger towards the humans' responsible and empathy for this ewe is bringing her close to tears. Afterwards, as we are leaving the field the vet mutters: 'We should get prosecuted for that. It's unacceptable.' (Extract from Roe's ethnography)

Incident 3:
A food animal careperson looks critically at the height of the entrance to the arcs in the sow-pens: 'It's too high. It's above their knee level. I am the only person who perceives that as a problem. I can walk past those pigs and I can cry, because to me that is so, so, so wrong. But everybody else just thinks I am making a fuss. Nobody else perceives it as being a problem. But it really eats away at me.'

---

was suggested that the animal's economic value could be undermined if a case of negligence was found.

These incidents draw on the observations of those not directly responsible either for the day-to-day management of the animals or for negotiating the challenges of providing continuous good-enough care. They raise issues associated with whether there can be sufficient agreement about what is good-enough care among a collective of food animal carepersons at a level of detail beyond the formal assessment and auditing processes of the food industry. We might ask what role should the opinion of the onlooker, not directly involved in the care of farmed animals (whether a farm worker or member of the public observing farm practices from afar), have in challenging standards or care? And more to the point, how do changes to cultures of care practices happen within the complexity of practical negotiations that an animal caretaker performs daily in relation to the sentient farm animal or flock or herd?

We began this chapter by identifying five assumptions underlying our approach to the understanding of stockperson care practices. In some ways, those assumptions might be relevant for all forms of care. Yet there are specific characteristics we identify in both the ideological and practical expectations of being a food animal caregiver. A food animal careperson must work with a food animal that is a food resource while also being a sentient being capable of passivity, withdrawal and vulnerability. A food animal careperson must have the personal sensibility to be capable of taking part in a food animal economy that breeds and keeps animals either to be killed and eaten as meat, or to produce products like milk or eggs for food consumption, or to be killed because they are an unavoidable by-product of the food animal industry.

A food animal careperson must actively build a positive relationship with animals that facilitates non-verbal intra-communication between human and animal(s) to successfully achieve cooperation with regular tasks of feeding, cleaning, checking they are healthy and mobile, and moving them from field or pen to elsewhere without causing stress, anxiety or injury to either human or animal. They need to engage with an animal body's tendency towards passivity and withdrawal from a relationship with a human.

Finally, a food animal careperson needs to be responsive to an animal's suffering and to do what is possible to relieve it; in other words to directly engage with the vulnerability of an animal's body – which may lead to killing it. In the next section, we specifically address how food animals are made killable on the farm.

Making an animal killable

What is markedly different about the care expressed for animals as opposed to that for humans is that society operates to a different legal code of ethical practice for food animal care than that for humans, or indeed for pet and companion animals. We have given ourselves the right to kill a healthy animal for consumption within the food industry, to kill a food animal if it is suffering even if this prevents it becoming human food and to kill an animal that, for various reasons, has no economic value. The killing of farmed animals for human consumption is a topic that has attracted debate throughout human history and today continues to dominate ethical philosophy (Singer, 1974), populist books on meat eating (Foer, 2010), animal slaughter within religious doctrines (www. diarel.eu) and accounts from inside abattoirs written as both fiction (Sinclair, 2002 [1914]) and non-fiction (Eisnitz, 1997; Roe, 2010; Pachirat, 2013). What is notable is that the spaces that have attracted this attention are predominantly the official sites of mass slaughter of animals – the abattoir. What is left out of most of these narratives[1] is the killing on the farm of individual or batches of animals as part of routinized farming practice and herd/flock management

---

[1]Exception Hugh Fernley Whittingstall Chicken Out Campaign TV programme from instead a broiler shed where daily culls were filmed and discussed.

(and as distinct from the killing of animals on farm as a result of any one-off or exceptional biosecurity event, for example, foot and mouth disease; see Law, 2010). Consequently, the general public are far less aware of the killing practices often initiated by food animal carepersons. The thought, feeling and practices that surround the killing of animals as a form of care on the farm have very different motivations to the automated slaughter lines in large-scale facilities that turn animal into meat, as the following examples illustrate.

When caring is killing

There is an expectation that a food animal careperson knows when to kill an animal as part of his or her practice of relating to and recognizing species-specific suffering and how to act on the decision that to care could well mean one should kill the animal. Care for the vulnerable and sick body inevitably raises the question of whether the animal in effect becomes killable. In reality, as our previous example in the hatchery house illustrates, this question is often also raised for otherwise healthy farm animals that cannot, for various productive reasons, enter the food chain. Many otherwise healthy farm animals do lose their way on the journey to becoming a commodity; most often it is shortly after birth;[2] for example, perhaps they are of a gender that is not used in commercial production (e.g. male calves in a dairy herd), or because they are simply too numerous to be efficiently raised (e.g. an excessive number of piglets born to a sow). Where there is no market for what might be termed 'excess' animals, they must be culled to limit the ongoing costs to the farm business. Other animals may be killed on farms because they are ill, injured or suffering, or because they are simply considered poor 'do-ers', unlikely to reach appropriate slaughter weight in the required time or to be productive in other ways. The killing of animals on farm is the outcome of complex and conflicting norms that are established differently around healthy and sick animals. This is dependent upon their status as a potential commodity or a failed commodity. The thoughtful and practical task of relating these different habits of killing to different animals is a task the food animal careperson is often required to do. While at times it may be relatively easy to justify killing as a form of caring (e.g. to end suffering), the responsibility and judgement call required can be demanding. We can witness the emotional or socio-affective response to performing different ways to make an animal or animals killable in the examples that follow.

---

[2]Most notably, the routine killing of male chicks in egg production and male calves in milk production are two established and routine animals that on birth are made killable.

The following five examples illustrate these complex sentiments and motivations for killing practices. The first three outline practices and sentiments expressed by a single food animal careperson. The following two examples refer to the opinions and the sentiments expressed by two individuals on the farm who have had veterinary training. A comparison is made between the food animal careperson and the veterinarian who are involved with different types of killing events on the farm. These differences, as will be discussed, relate to socio-affective or emotional response to killing an individual animal in contrast to killing a large number of animals, despite both being perceived as acts of care. We note, at the outset, that the positive experience of killing an individual sick animal, in contrast to killing healthy animals, is referred to by the farm animal careperson as an event where 'killing is wonderful'.

Killing as shameful

Farm animals are killed purposefully for meat but are also euthanized. While there is a high-level awareness of pet animal euthanasia – to put an animal to sleep that is no longer wanted by its owners, and for whom no alternative home can be found, or because of poor health often near the end of its natural lifespan – the place of euthanasia within farming is perhaps less well understood. Food animals are given life so they can be killed and eaten. However, as the following examples demonstrate, animals may need to be killed on the farm. In such cases, it is the farm animal careperson who can be responsible for the act of killing, a very different task from their major role – to keep a healthy, well-cared-for animal growing steadily towards the weight when it will be slaughtered for meat.

> The other hard thing I've had to do since I've been here and I had to do it very early on after I came here and it really, really upset me. I have had to go in and kill whole flocks of birds that were healthy, because we didn't have a market for them. No I can do it. I am actually very good at killing chickens. But by God it is not nice. And you are doing it and tears are running down your face. But you know what you've got to do. And its one of those jobs where sort of go out after dark, when everybody else has finished and you just sit in the shed and plough your way through them. And that is really horrible, you know. You've got tears running down your face while you are doing it but you've got to do it. (Interview with Food animal careperson A, 2009)
>
> I spend a morning in the hatchery. The final act is ending the life/killing the organic chicks successfully hatched that morning for whom no market can be found. I know that the macerator will be used to bring a swift death to three or four trays of fluffy chicks. I've seen the dead chicks go through the

machine and a black dustbin bag of pale brown meaty mush is the output. The person I have spent the morning with handling the chicks does not want me to witness her putting the live chicks through the macerator. (Extract from author's ethnographic research notes, 2009)

The farm animal careperson cited above experiences shame about what she has to do, conveying an uneasy relationship with the responsibility for animal death. Shame here lies in her description of not wanting to be watched hand-wringing the necks of adult chickens, or indicating that she didn't want the interviewer present during the process of killing the chicks. Wolfe (2008) might refer to what the food animal careperson is experiencing here as the 'pressure' of reality overtaking her. This is a task she has to do as part of her work: something she feels she is very good at, but it is not pleasant. Her tears make the event real to her as one of sorrow. She is experiencing 'the weight and gravity of our moral responsibilities' towards the poultry being killed with her own hands and her tears articulate its 'unspeakability', the failure of words to confront this reality (Wolfe, 2008: 14). J.M. Coetzee describes the character of David in his novel *Disgrace* going through a similar moment of grief when responding with private tears to his role in the killing or euthanizing of unwanted pet animals (1999).

This food animal careperson cited above also expresses dismay at the killing individually by hand of a large number of chickens. The size of the group was not lost on her, felt directly over a lengthy period of time as one by one she individually handled every bird to wring its neck. We might return here to our theme of speed and slowness – macerating is fast and mechanical and thus preferred, neck-wringing individual birds is slow and manual and the weight of the task is felt more keenly. The care quotient for the food animal careperson drops as the task is slowed.

> Well it's not bad killing an injured or sick bird. Is easy. You know you are doing it for the benefit of the bird. Killing a healthy bird because you've failed is very, very hard. And that's something I have enormous difficulty coming to grips with. I mean you've got to do it from a welfare purpose if you've got nowhere to put the bird, you've got nowhere to move the bird to because you haven't got enough room or whatever reason. (Interview with food animal careperson A, 2009)
>
> Killing is hard. But I'd actually say if you've got a sick or injured animal. It's a wonderful sensation. This is going to sound really awful. I firmly believe that the ability to euthanize is a gift. And that's the last gift we can give any animal. If it's in pain or its suffering, or it doesn't have any quality of life. And I feel very,

very strongly here … err … particular with the pigs and the sheep, we don't cull soon enough. (Interview with food animal careperson, A, 2009)

At a different stage during the interview, the same food animal careperson explains how killing is a gift when one is exposed to the suffering of an individual farm animal. For the majority of farm animals, this may be the only time when they are related to as an individual sentient animal rather than as a number in a group, herd or flock (Buller, 2013c).

There is a surprising power and energy to how the 'gift' of euthanasia is expressed by this and other food animal carepersons and vets when discussing sick animals. The act of killing as euthanasia can indeed be a moment of singularity, a rarer one-on-one relationship with an animal to be almost cherished, as distinct from more routine killings. Here when a sick, suffering animal is in a state of vulnerability, it is treated as an individual during the act of euthanasia with communication between the careperson and the cared-for reassuring the latter that they are being looked after. There is, however, more to sentience than simply the capacity to suffer.

> The vet is rung to be told the news that the cow has died before the slaughterperson has arrived. She feels frustrated and in someway she has failed. This cow was very thin but had one calf. A few days earlier both cow and calf were brought in off the pasture into a shed on the farm-yard to receive close veterinary attention which included doses of antibiotics. The hope was that the cow could recover but after two days of antibiotics and no sign of recovery the decision was made to have the cow shot on the farm. This reduces the stress on the animal from being taken off farm for slaughter and also ultimately ends the suffering of the sick animal. However it appears that decision was taken too late, the cow dies before the slaughterperson arrives. This burst of frustration and an immediate sense of failure is because of the strength in veterinary ideology that it is their duty to put an animal out of its suffering, to decide when it needs to die. (Extract from author's ethnographic research notes, 2009)

> So, it's an acceptance that in domestication, you do the best thing you can, but sometimes you do end up taking lives … and I think that's part of it. So, I'm really big on this and we've had loads of people here, in the past, who … and I've said to XXXX 'I don't want to employ anybody else who wont kill things' … because it's a responsibility that you have to kill things and do it well. And, it's a big one. So many animals on farms just get left to die because they can't bear to put them down … and for me, that's like saying 'I can't do the job'. So, that would be like a nurse and a client who won't use a bed pan … well, sorry, this jobs not for you then. (Interview with farm manger, 2009)

Killing is part of the food animal care collective. It has an intrinsic role in how farms are run and yet here is perhaps an area where if we respond to the animal as a fellow embodied creature, rather than as an animal with capacities or contractual utilitarian rights, then a rush of sensibilities, sympathies, shared vulnerabilities, finitude and suffering enter.

> What is 'indeterminate' is not our compassion for the suffering of non-human animals, but rather the very idea that 'rights' and 'entitlement' bear anything other than a completely contingent relationship (derived from the historically and ideologically specific character of our juridical and political institutions and the picture of the subject of rights that they provide) to the question of justice for non-human animals. (Wolfe, 2008: 22)

Questions then must be asked back on human society about how it deals with suffering, sentient human bodies. Is euthanasia as the approach for killing the suffering body interchangeable with killing the sentient?

Animal care economized

This chapter has developed an understanding of the work of food animal carepersons as primarily a practical engagement with farm animals, work that involves feeling and responding to the needs of the animal through and with the body. But this is also work that is subject to the effect of events beyond the immediate on-farm environment. As the discussions of different events/ encounters with farm animals make plain, what is witnessed shapes the ability for the stockperson to take different actions, along with previous experience and the broader context in which they are working. An encounter/event may offer juxtapositions between cultural ideas afforded to the stockperson and observant ethnographer, through the materialities and sensualities as they affectively resonate in various ways. To capture this has required close study of the movement/gesture/expression of bodies during encounters. Within these encounters animal and human work together to produce food for humans, achieved through numerous practical tasks where both human and animal show care for each other's well-being, each other's needs and potential fragilities. The focus on what happens in practice, rather than attitudes and opinions about farm animal care, has fostered here the opportunity to investigate elements to the farm animal careperson–farm animal relation. This helps to understand how the market for farm animal welfare is being actualized on farm, where and how it matches market expectations, and how, and why, it may fail to meet those expectations. If one can tackle vulnerabilities to particular constituent matters, for example that can lead to a lack of motivation to fully carry out the potential positive care to animals in one's job, one might also understand what needs to be done to improve animal welfare. How does 'good enough' care take place? Such a process-based study to animal welfare doesn't assess the achievement of standards, but looks at the process by which welfare is attained in practice with openness to how events, and responses to them, make the question of what is the right thing to do more contentious.

If we compare, for a moment, animal welfare to human health care (Mol, 2008), we might understand the food animal careperson as an exemplar of a care professional whose practices of care are not hindered by the logic of choice circulating around an autonomous patient (the animal cannot verbalize choice). Neither are they hindered by the assumed in-animacy of the animal they care for. Instead the care relationship is between two sentient beings that have emotional lives each affecting the care they give and receive. This care flows not only from human to animal but also from animal to human. The animal is expected to be careful not to harm the humans they work with and to develop a care for establishing good relations with the humans that work with them. Animals that don't express this care for humans are often killed because their awkwardness is costly to maintain good care for the other animals and good care of the humans tasked to work with them.

Second, we have seen in these examples how the task of caring is part of the economization of animal welfare. In the food animal care collective one cannot escape events, where a logic of care is shaped by the logic of capital, but equally how the logic of capital supports the logic of care. Although less immediately apparent, the logic of capital is, of course, present in human health care. The food animal care collective is an illustration of the interplay between the logic of care and the logic of capital around key moral and practical concerns of how to kill, how to communicate and how to empathize with, and respond to, the suffering of another human or animal. Good care is more than what one farm animal careperson on their own can achieve: it is achieved by a collective. This chapter has described who and what comprise the collective on the farm; for example, technology, human-friendly animals, understanding management for the emotional demands of the role of farm animal careperson, animal-friendly humans. However we must not forget the influence of other sites, other geographies that are significant agents in making it possible to offer good care for food animals: the practices of consumers in supermarkets, the corporate commitments of food retailers to include good food animal welfare within their brand, good practice in the food processing sector. Improving understanding of what happens on farm can only work to develop and inspire better care practices for both the humans and animals who live and work alongside each other. Consumers, for example, what do they imagine/know about stockmanship? Miele and Evans (2010) find that consumers of welfare-friendly foodstuffs imagine a production system, rather than levels of individual care that animals might expect to receive, the result, possibly, of the relative invisibility of farm animals in the everyday landscapes; out of sight of the majority of human habitations. Broiler chickens and pigs are predominantly kept indoors in the UK and of over 10 million pigs slaughtered in the UK in 2013, only 3 per cent lived their whole life outdoors in free-range units (Agriculture and Horticulture Development Board, 2014). Only those people living in the countryside, or who regularly walk through livestock farmed land, have arguably most potential to encounter animals and question the observed practices of care the animals are experiencing.

Finally, within wider society, stockpersons or farm animal carepersons are valued not as thinkers, writers or spokespersons to the wider world but because we need human beings that can cope and perform the demands of caring for vulnerable, mortal non-human animals in the context of modern, intensive livestock farming. An important skill they require to carry out this role affectively and effectively is communication and empathy with another species. Interestingly Wolfe (2008) writes that the 'wound' between humans and animals can never be healed but only deepened if thought, writing and speech continue to be the ways we try to suture it. It will not be through utilitarian animal rights theory that the curing will be done. Like Wolfe, we feel this literature is abstracted from the actual practices that are the real ongoing iterations of human–animal relationships, and it is for those reasons this chapter has focused on the practices that bring food animals and their carers into relationship with each, a relationship that, in terms of numbers, in terms of ubiquity and universality, is arguably the most significant of all the human–animal relationships in our society.

Chapter 4

Selling Welfare

Once killed and the carcass subdivided into cuts, the welfare of the animal or bird might appear to be no longer an immediate concern. Although the animal's liveliness can impact the quality of the meat product right up to and even during the process of slaughter (Ferguson and Warner, 2008; Roe, 2010), attention shifts during processing to more prosaic issues of product condition, presentation and consumer health and safety. Yet, animal welfare is increasingly being used to sell animal products; meat is described or advertised as 'welfare friendly', eggs are 'free range'. Although the term 'welfare-friendly pork' is common in advertising across Europe, establishing a sense of direct material and aesthetic connectivity between the perceived quality of the product and the quality of the life, 'pork' is also both semantically (and intentionally so) and materially distinct from the living pig from whence it came. Food chains and food products capture, assemble and mobilize the welfare of animals in a manner that, as we have argued throughout this volume, seeks to re-engage a vital and 'more-than-material' connection between the consumer and the consumed as co-possessors of a sentient life for which being treated well matters. Food chain actors construct and qualify the welfare of farmed animals through mechanisms and devices that are both visible and invisible. Such instruments can be employed to redefine the very sense of welfare or certainly the manner in which welfare is understood and perceived by consumers (Labatut et al., 2009). The meaning of welfare is thus manufactured and re-manufactured (Jackson et al., 2011). Certain parameters of animal welfare may be emphasized, such as an animal or bird's access to outdoors or natural pasture, while others may be hidden, such as the experience at killing or what are considered necessary mutilations. Consider, for example, this quotation from a French veal processing company, interviewed in 2007 as part of our Welfare Quality© research:

> It was a gamble to put images of living calves on the same 2-page display as an escalope of veal. My idea was that city-dwellers, increasingly disconnected from the realities of agriculture and what took place in the countryside, was no longer susceptible to such images ... What we wanted to say in these brochures was that here was the farmer, attentive, almost 'maternal' towards

their calves; this was what it meant to be a farmer – to be maternal, with a knowledge and understanding of the young animal. We sincerely thought that this was the message to get across. But, journalists, especially those working for women's' magazines, in which our products were advertised, did not want to suggest what happened in an abattoir, maintaining that the juxtaposition of the live animal and the piece of meat was wholly incompatible. We get into 'Oh that's a pretty calf, I don't want to eat that'. So now, we show only recipes and cooking. (Representative of veal processing firm, interviewed 2007)

Welfare is, in this way, reassembled through multidirectional semiotic and material flows that transgress the distinctiveness of production and consumption concerns. Citing Probyn (1999), Stassart and Whatmore (2003: 450), for whom, as we have seen above, food becomes 'a ready messenger of connectedness and affectivity', have put this rather well:

The stuff of food constantly shifts register between matter and meaning; animal and meat; calories and flavours, stretching and folding the time/spaces of here and now, 'us' and 'them', producing and consuming in complex and contested ways.

Two key assertions underlie this book. The first, which we specifically addressed in the previous chapter, is that farm animal welfare is, above all, a form of practice. The welfare science that we considered in Chapter 2 seeks either to identify scientifically defined levels at which animals can no longer cope satisfactorily with environmental, material and social conditions of their confinement and begin to suffer unacceptably or to promote positive stimuli which enhance animal experience. The achievement of acceptable or good welfare depends, first and foremost, upon practices of human–animal interaction. The second key assertion, which we develop in this chapter, is that the welfare of farm animals has become increasingly commodified within the food chain either as a component of added product or brand value or as a form of food chain legitimation and assurance or as a form of alternative ethical consumption practice. This has given rise to a more competitive approach to welfare criteria, their measurement and their deployment at different points within the food chain. The resulting tension between these two approaches, the scientific and the economic, has not only characterized the rapid development of farm animal welfare as a 'consumer' or food industry concern but also led to a significant re-framing of the meaning of welfare itself.

If Chapter 3 looked at on-farm welfare as a practice of care, Chapter 2 concluded that the growing visibility of farm animal health and welfare in the food chain results from two principal drivers: the need for food chain actors, from producers to retailers, to demonstrate to consumers and citizens verifiable conformity to both public and private regulation governing the treatment of farm animals; and the desire among food chain actors to segment food markets thus establishing differential pricing structures.

In this chapter, we consider the mechanisms of that commodification and marketing by examining the manner in which farm animal welfare is assembled through the food supply chain (as opposed to how it is *practised* on the farm). We present this in the form of four frames: frame one, diligence and responsibility; frame two, segmentation; frame three, assurance and frame four, labelling. Drawing upon our own empirical research conducted through a number of funded research projects over the last ten years, we chart the development of welfare standards and criteria within the food sector, identifying the key but very different roles that legislation, retailing and NGOs have played in that development. We consider the processes and practices of assurance and labelling, drawing upon recent research, and explore the manner in which assurance schemes operate 'on the ground'.

An important point here is that welfare is *assembled* within the agro-food network. Different actors assemble it and give it normative meaning in different ways. It is assembled scientifically, ethically, aesthetically, commercially, through practices of care, through anthropomorphic sensibility, through broader notions of food quality, through a sense of responsibility and so on. For these assemblages to be accepted by all relevant parties, a degree of convergence over objectives is required, certain conventions need to be established and certain material forms, objects and devices have to be agreed upon. A number of writers have turned to 'convention theory' (Boltanski and Thévenot, 1991) to understand how quality is assembled or constructed in the food chain (e.g. Sylvander, 1995; Thevenot, 1995; Stassart, 2003; Bonne and Verbeke, 2008). For Sylvander et al. (2006), the establishing of a quality convention can be seen as a four-stage process involving motivation (arising often from some sort of social crisis creating uncertainty), relevance (developing a response to the crisis that is relevant for the actors concerned and to the market), coherence (allowing for the coordination of different actors in the project) and legitimation (the resulting convention will need to fit within institutional and legal frameworks). As we shall show in what follows, this is a valuable framework for considering the emergence of farm animal welfare – a socially co-constructed quality within food products – as the subject of conventions established between producers, retailers, consumers and others.

A second point is that such conventions are often operationalized through what is often a heterogeneous assemblage of distinct objects, procedures and techniques; what Callon et al. (2007) refer to as 'market devices': the 'material and discursive assemblages that intervene in the construction of markets' (Muniesa et al., 2007: 2). As we shall show below, specific market devices – in this case, certificates, brochures, labels, audit forms, inspections, brands – play an important role in establishing and formalizing the conventions that enable the welfare of farmed animals to become marketable. One example of how markets can be 'civilized' in this way is provided by Miele and Lever (2013) who investigate the development of the Welfare Quality© assessment protocol as just such a 'techno-ethical device' for enabling the marketization of animal welfare. Another comes from Stassart and Jamar's (2005) study of quality beef production in Belgium (and the particular 'device' of the carving table). These authors demonstrate how quality conventions assemble through commonly agreed rules and practices of engagement, the materiality of the animals, their corporeality and behaviour with socially constructed notions of product quality and collective social performance. Together, these constitute a set of standards, which renders this particular 'quality' economic and thereby marketable.

Frame one: Responsibilization and the shifting governance of food supply chains

Our starting point is that farm animal welfare has become a key marketing term in a number of countries including those of North America and Northern Europe, but particularly in the UK, for product quality in food supply chains. The shift from welfare as a statutory condition of animal production to welfare as a marketable quality of product commercialization has everything to do with the critical function that retailers now play in regulating food supply chains under what Burch and Lawrence (2009) term the 'third food regime'. The growing role and presence of key NGOs, who have perceived the benefits of securing a more consumer-oriented approach to addressing issues of farm animal welfare, is also critical.

The transformation by which UK retailers have gradually taken control from manufacturers and processors of the organization and management of the food supply chains has been widely documented (Marsden and Wrigley, 1995; Marsden et al., 2000; Wilkinson, 2002; Burch and Lawrence, 2007), although this model is not always applicable across the whole of Europe where manufacturers and producer groups still dominate (see Roe and Higgin, 2008). Staying with the UK model, this takeover has been achieved, as Burch and Lawrence (2005) explain, first, by the enormous purchasing power of a relatively small number of increasingly globally focused retailer groups and, second, by the growth of retailers own brands which have gradually replaced manufacturers brands on supermarket shelves. More recently, as Burch and Lawrence (2005) argue, supermarket brands have gone further than merely replacing or imitating manufacturers' brands, they now 'are at the leading edge in terms of meeting consumer demands for a range of new food products' (2005: 2). This, they maintain, represents the emergence of a new 'third' food regime: 'characterised by flexible manufacturing and high levels of innovation, as supermarkets restructure the agri-food supply chain in order to satisfy highly segmented niche markets for a range of new agri-food commodities' (Lawrence, 2005). The setting of standards, the deployment of new private governance and regulatory arrangements and the development of exclusive supply contracts are some of the many devices employed by retailers in this restructuring process (Marsden et al., 2000). More and more, as Marsden et al. (2000) note, regulatory activities that, in the past, would have been associated with governments are bestowed upon corporate private-sector retailer interests.

Shifts in consumer culture and in the proximity of retailers to consumer interests have made this food chain transformation and this transference of regulatory power possible. As consumption and consumer interests become ever more important in policy-making, retailers thus come to see themselves as representing certain of those interests within the food chain (Marsden et al., 1998; Dixon, 2002) through explicit or implicit corporate social responsibility. For Marsden et al. (2000), this has three implications, each of which is relevant here. First, it leads to competition between retailers based upon the construction and maintenance of quality, rather than just price. Second, the development of private/retailer food regulation is directed towards procedures of production rather than simply products (see also Renard, 2005). Third, in the pursuit of quality-based competition, the private regulations imposed upon their suppliers by retailers frequently tend to go beyond legal minimal standards. Vroom (1985) suggests that this is the consequence of a deficient state regulatory strategy or falling citizen confidence in governmental regulatory capacity (Freidberg, 2003a) though Marsden et al. (2000) disagree, an important point to which we shall return below. Certainly, within the field of farm animal welfare, competitive private standards have raised the bar on a number of welfare variables, such as for example stocking densities in broiler sheds, well under current statutory maxima. Whether this is driven in response to scientific evidence of the welfare benefit of such change or for reasons of segmentation and brand identity, or simply to avoid negative attention, is a moot point (Hatanaka et al., 2005).

The growing power of certain food sector interests and their proximity to consumers, coupled with a diminished role for the State in both regulation and enforcement, place a burden of responsibility upon the former to show, or be able to show, by demonstrating 'due diligence', that they have done everything in their power to ensure full compliance with legal requirements throughout the product's 'life'. Introduced in the UK by the 1990 Food Safety Act, the notion of due diligence is an interesting reversal of the traditional obligation that only engaged the responsibility of food chain actors for the compliance of a product while under their own direct control (Henson, 2008). As a form of 'experimentalist governance' (Sabel and Zeitlin, 2008), due diligence has been a necessary accompaniment to the process by which retailers have extended both their economic reach further and further down their supply chains (Busch, 2010) and their ethico-political reach as 'representatives' of consumer demand. Consequently, meeting the requirements of due diligence has had a major impact upon how the 'quality' of foods is defined, assessed and verified.

Also indicative of broader shifts in the governance of food, it is increasingly non-governmental organizations, or NGOs, rather than government 'watchdogs', parliamentarians or concerned citizens and consumers that are holding retailers and corporate food outlets to task for their commitment to issues like welfare. Bodies such as Compassion in World Farming, the Royal Society for the Protection of Animals (RSPCA) and World Animal Protection, to name but three operating out of the UK, play a critical role both in identifying and highlighting issues of poor welfare inherent in production systems through campaigning but also in actively promoting good practice, through award schemes or, in the case of the RSPCA, by running their own accreditation schemes for high welfare production systems. Recent campaigns by such bodies on issues of lameness, mutilations, animal housing, sow stalls, humane slaughter and animal transport combine credible scientific evidence and targeted political action with popular mandate. That these campaigns are aimed increasingly at food chain actors rather than at governments and regulatory authorities again reveals the changing nature of food and welfare governance. Going back some thirty years, Hollands, in his 1985 review of the politicization of animal rights in the UK, emphasized the critical importance of formal political action for NGOs, through parliamentary lobbying and the prescribed processes of law making (Hollands, 1985). Today NGOs and other actors have learnt that as much, if not more, can be achieved by seeking to directly influence food chain actors into adopting change. Freidberg (2004) calls this the 'ethical complex' whereby NGOs have come to participate in the governance of supermarket supply chains, creating 'a condition compelling supermarkets to respond, in various ways, to NGO demands for ethical sourcing' (514). Although her examples are drawn principally from what might be called 'fair trade', others (Hughes, 2001; Wilkins et al., 2005) have similarly identified the growing role of NGOs in pushing normative concerns such as farm animal welfare (Elzen et al., 2011) across different communities of interests within the market sector. To a degree, each 'side' legitimates the other. Freidberg (2004: 521) again:

> In all cases, the supermarkets' efforts to appear socially responsible have depended on certain NGOs for information, advice, and public displays of approval, whether in the form of press releases, labels, or participation in the supermarkets' own reform initiatives.

The annual *Business Benchmark on Farm Animal Welfare* (Amus and Sullivan, 2014), produced jointly by Compassion in World Farming and World Animal Protection, offers a review of how global food companies perform with respect to achieving animal welfare goals. Its aim is:

> To improve corporate reporting on farm animal welfare management, policies, practices, processes and performance and, over time, to contribute to improvements in the farm animal welfare practices and performance of food companies. (Amos and Sullivan, 2014: 2)

The 2014 Benchmark covers some eighty global food companies including producers, restaurants, retailers and food manufacturers. All are ranked by performance against a number of key criteria such as stated commitment to welfare, the setting of welfare targets and a series of more traditional welfare assessments involving method of slaughter, transport time and so on. In a similar vein, the 'Good Egg Award', also established by Compassion in World Farming, has been given to food companies that have committed to use cage-free egg products since 2007.

What is clear from all of this is that for retailers, farm animal welfare standards are more than simply economics (or indeed, science). Achieving higher welfare standards has cost implications both for producers (e.g. having to reduce stocking densities or slow down growth rates) and for retailers, who are unlikely to be able to translate all higher production costs directly to all consumers. Drawing on a neo-institutionalist perspective, Ransom (2007) sees the growing involvement of retailers and food sector actors in private welfare regulation as being closely linked to institutional and organizational dynamics, reflecting mimetic responses to an uncertain and anxious regulatory and scientific environment. Dixon (2002) emphasizes rather the importance of the cultural circuits in adding value to products, such as, in her case, chicken. 'The product design process', she argues (2002: 150), 'retailing practices, food knowledges and discourse production highlight how even the most economically powerful actors must negotiate daily with the cultural landscape'.

Occasionally, that 'cultural landscape' may come to oppose or even vilify the corporate massivity, profits and broader impacts of some of the larger retailers and food outlets (Vorley, 2007). Issues such as their contribution to the emergence of 'food deserts' (Guy et al., 2004), upon commodity prices such as milk (Bonanno and Lopez, 2005) or upon distant producers in emerging economies (Dolan and Humphrey, 2000; Wilkinson 2002), have all been well documented. Indeed the growth of alternative food markets and outlets over the last thirty or so years has been partly explained through consumer dissatisfaction with these ubiquitous retail structures (Smith et al., 2014). Yet, in their capacity to generate and profit from quality standards on entire production chains, retailers and corporate food outlets may serve a critical function; they absolve consumers from the need to act ethically themselves. In the field of farm animal welfare, this is an important attribute. Countless surveys demonstrate that while consumers or citizens describe themselves as concerned about the welfare of farmed animals, few wish to act upon this concern in their own purchasing behaviour. Rather, they prefer, in their majority, to feel that welfare is taken care of within food supply chains so that the food available on retailer shelves is healthy, safe and complies with societally approved standards. Whether one accepts the current standards to be sufficient to maintain welfare or not, retailers and corporate food outlets have proved remarkably effective in aligning their production chains to legal standards as an obligation of due diligence and, as we have seen above, have on occasion gone beyond them. This is no claim for the ethical superiority of food retailers. As Freidberg (2003b: 29) points out, their recent 'ethical turn' may well be 'a benign by-product of an intensively competitive retail market'.

Nevertheless, because of their size and the scale of their operations, corporate retailers and large food service operations can have a significant impact upon how their suppliers, or their own 'in-house' producers, address the welfare of farmed animals. They may, argue Matheny and Leahy (2007: 355), be more effective than statutory regulators.

> Retailers are becoming the most potent force in setting animal welfare standards and will be the major engine for influencing animal welfare change. They can move faster than Governments, can cut off a supplier's livelihoods by stopping contracts and can ignore international trade agreements. While Europe as a whole has to adhere to the World Trade Organization and cannot bar imports on animal welfare grounds, retailers are free to do so. (Bayvel, 2005: 794 – after Spedding, 2000)

In 2007, the food chain McDonald's announced that it would move its entire UK and European supply chain to non-caged eggs over the subsequent fifteen years.

Given that, in any one year, McDonald's were using around 120 million eggs in their 'breakfast menu' alone, this single move would likely have a significant effect on the number of caged bird production systems in at least some of the countries concerned. In 2015, McDonald's in North America made a similar announcement, affecting, they estimate, around 8 million egg-laying hens.

Frame two: Segmentation, profit and branding

We might distinguish strategies for introducing animal welfare as a component of food product quality that are inclusive from those that are exclusive. The former will address concerns of brand integrity, due diligence, food safety, legal compliance and baseline consumer expectations; the latter will respond to a more segmented market where welfare is associated with differential product or brand quality and often price. A retailer, food service outlet or manufacturer may decide, as McDonald's above, that their entire production chain for a given product or raw material or even brand should meet specific welfare (or indeed other normative) criteria. These might be imposed upon their producers through contractual obligation or through mandatory compliance with an assurance or certification scheme. For most retailers, outlets and manufacturers, such inclusive strategies would be based upon one of three approaches: a comprehensive form of quality assurance/auditing, whether it be a baseline scheme demonstrating conformity to mandatory standards such as EurepGAP (Campbell, 2005), now known as GLOBALGAP and formed originally by a group of thirteen European retailers keen to streamline good agricultural practice standards emerging across different quality certification and auditing procedures for their supply chains (Ransom, 2007); a national-level assurance scheme such as the UK's Assured Food Standards (also known as the 'Red Tractor' scheme) or the French *Label Rouge*, delivering mandatory and occasionally higher standards; or one of many private standards established independently by many retailers and often, for some welfare criteria, going higher than mandatory standards (Buller and Roe, 2010), as the following extract from the website of UK retailer 'Waitrose' testifies (Table 4.1).

Establishing a supply chain conforming to inclusive generic quality standards may also be a sound commercial decision in which animal welfare plays only a minor role, as the following two quotations from our interviews with food chain actors undertaken as part of the Welfare Quality© research demonstrate:

> It would be wrong to say that our strategy is driven by animal welfare but I think that it's certainly our strategy that we want to drive and nurture growth in the free range sector. And we deliberately select particularly the retail customers that we

work with to be those that want to see some growth in that sector [...] because we want to be reliant less on the cage egg sector because that will become increasingly a trading function and as with anything where you are trading commodities you have good years and bad years but you can't manage that or predict for that to any great degree. But free range is much more consistent in terms of where we can deliver reasonably consistent revenues and incomes and profit. (Interview with representative of UK egg supplier, selling to major retailers, 2007)

Table 4.1 Waitrose description of their egg supply

What's special about Waitrose eggs?
- All of the fresh hens' eggs we sell are free range – we were the first supermarket to do this and we've been doing it for years.
- All of our hen's eggs are collected and inspected by hand.
- All of our hen's eggs are laid on the British mainland, mostly in England and some in Scotland and Wales.
- Our eggs are laid on farms we know and trust.
- All our hens are housed in much smaller flock sizes than the UK standard.

Source: Waitrose website (2015) at: http://www.waitrose.com/home/inspiration/about_ waitrose/about_our_food/eggs.html

Here there is economic potential but also a pragmatic approach to both customer demand and producer sustainability:

> At any one moment, the various procedures and assurance conditions that the farmers respect are there for a reason, for an objective: to produce a product under conditions which are going to be judged as largely satisfactory. These conditions are not idealistic, a hen sitting on top of a pile of hay laying an egg a day for the family. People want eggs that are available at a cost that is affordable by a family but are also capable of sustaining the income of the produce. (Interview with representative of French egg manufacturer, 2007)

Although retailers and food outlets generally adopt inclusive quality strategies as a baseline, many will segment product lines on the basis of differential quality characteristics including animal welfare. The capacity for different animal products to sustain segmentation, however, varies considerably. Eggs, for example, have become archetypical of the possibilities of segmentation with retailers variously stocking cage eggs, barn eggs, free-range eggs, organic free-range eggs, traditional free-range eggs, total freedom eggs, omega-enriched free-range eggs and so on. Pork, on the other hand, as relatively cheap meat offering a relatively narrow range of tastes and coming from a shrinking number of different commercial breeds has been traditionally far less segmented. For the pork sector, varying welfare standards offer the prospect of price differentiation. How a single product such as a whole chicken might be segmented through the supply chain is demonstrated in Chart 4.1.

Broiler chicken production has become highly industrialized and vertically integrated within the UK with four key processors (2 Sisters, Moy Park, Faccenda and Cargill) accounting for 86 per cent (Dickinson, 2014) of all birds (some covering all stages from breeding to processing) and four key retailers (Tesco, Asda, Sainsbury's and Morrisons) accounting for 84 per cent of sales to consumers. Key actors such as these seek to develop a range of products covering different potential markets and consumer demands. At one end of the scale are the value range products that generally conform to standards based upon statutory minimal requirements for animal welfare or reflected in a generic assurance scheme such as the UK's 'Red Tractor/Assured Food Standards' (see below). At the time of writing, a whole chicken of this kind is being sold in a major UK retailer at £2.48 per kilogram. At the other end of the scale, a whole organic chicken, produced under full organic free-range certification with higher welfare standards, currently sells at £6.50 per kilogram at the same retailer.

Jackson et al. (2006) provide an illuminating account of how the UK retailer Marks and Spencer's developed an entirely new quality chicken product, the Oakham chicken brand in 2003, in an attempt to meet the perceived needs of

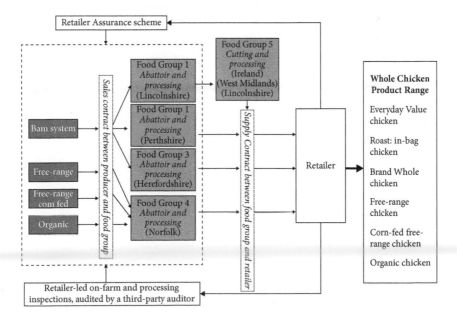

Chart 4.1 Whole chicken supply chain for major UK retailer.

the retailer's consumer base for a slower-growing, higher welfare bird. At the same time the product allowed the store to differentiate itself and its products from its competitors by appropriating an alternative discourse of sourcing. The authors quote Marks and Spencer's agricultural technologist at the time:

> This intensively produced chicken is a commodity, or was a commodity, and what we needed to do was to differentiate our chicken off compared to the rest of the high street. So, it was about looking at what our customers [wanted] ... starting off at the other end, whereas normally we go at the farm end and work upwards towards the consumer. (Jackson et al., 2011: 63)

Two factors are nonetheless critical to the use of direct or indirect welfare criteria for the market segmentation of animal products. The first of these is a certain permissive flexibility in the manner in which welfare claims are both made and justified. The second is an effective *bundling* of welfare claims with other criteria of product quality.

As Chapter 2 has demonstrated, assessing the welfare of farm animals is highly complex, combining animal needs and wants, physiological and psychological responses as well as embodied, animal-based and external environmental components. Although welfare is a measurable state (Broom, 2010), levels of good or bad welfare are, in many ways, socioculturally determined. Governments, informed by welfare science, might establish legal minima or maxima for such variables as stocking densities and stun-to-bleed times, along with broad principles such as the 'five freedoms' (see Chapter 2) and a general 'duty of care' (see Chapter 3). Yet, these may vary significantly from country to country (see Chapter 5). Beyond these legal thresholds, different non-governmental actors, whether they are retailers or animal welfare NGOs, construct the meaning and the value of 'welfare' as they see fit – through standards, through packaging design and labels and through advertising.

Compassion in World Farming recently compared (2012) welfare standards across a range of non-statutory assurance schemes. While there was broad agreement on the overall principles (and all surveyed schemes complied with statutory standards), variations were revealed across a number of criteria (see Table 4.2). Schmid and Kilchsperger's (2010) comparative assessment of private NGO and retailer-led welfare standards across Europe similarly identifies significant variation across a range of production systems and species types and little overall consistency. Thresholds differ: certain aspects of welfare are addressed by some schemes and not by others, some offer very specific maxima or minima, others more vague aspirational guidance, others still making vague allusions to animal well-being.

Table 4.2 Different standards under comparative welfare assurance schemes for dairy calves and broiler chickens

Scheme	Assured Dairy Farms	RSPCA Freedom Food	Soil Association (Organic)
Appropriate weaning age for dairy calves	Minimum 5 weeks	Minimum 5 weeks and must be eating at least 1 kg calf starter per day	Minimum 12 weeks

Scheme	Assured Chicken Production (Standard)	Assured Chicken Production (Free Range)	RSPCA Freedom Food (Minimum)	RSPCA Freedom Food (Free Range)	Soil Association
	All figures are in kg/m²				
Broiler chickens low indoor stocking density (maximum)	38	27.5	30	27	21

Source: Compassion in World Farming (2012).
Note: Figures for 2012. Some have subsequently been revised.

As welfare becomes enrolled as a component of competitive claims for brand or product quality, the field is ripe for different actors to not only set different standards but also represent welfare in different ways.

> Free-range birds are reared for longer and enjoy an outdoor life, which results in improved flavour and texture. We encourage them to explore outdoors by providing a combination of trees and man-made shelters. We also give them perches and pecking objects – such as shiny discs and wooden blocks – to encourage natural behaviours, and provide straw bales so that they can jump, play and exercise. It's fantastic to watch them – they're very happy chickens! (https://realfood.tesco.com/our-food/home-on-the-range.html, accessed 9 July 2017)

The notion of a 'happy chicken' has an anthropomorphic and empathetic appeal with which consumers can immediately associate, though it has little scientific meaning or empirical validity. Elsewhere, we have documented the use of images and discourses of benevolent animal-friendly husbandry in the commercialization of animal products (Buller and Cesar, 2007; Roe and Higgin, 2008) from cartoon cows in lush green fields to smiling roving pigs. Miele (2012) observes the increasing use of marketing messages that refer specifically to the emotional states of farm animals such as curiosity and happiness and argues for their potency.

> By bringing to the foreground the life of the animals and leaving in the background the quality of the food, these marketing messages might act as subjectifiers (Latour, 2005) for promoting a stronger involvement of consumers into the life of farm animals, and for expressing a form of care for farm animals (Miele and Evans, 2010). However, many of these marketing messages are ambivalent since the happiness of the animals is presented as instrumental in the better taste of the food. Therefore, they may also attract more materially concerned consumers. In both cases, however, the caring and materially concerned consumers are collected or associated together (Latour, 2005: 78) by the invention of the happy chicken, which allows different modes of relating to, and enacting of, issues of animal welfare. (Miele, 2012: 2087)

Of course, the consumer does not know – cannot know – whether the individual animal that yielded the meat, eggs or milk being bought actually experienced any of these emotional states. Despite the implied subjectivities of such marketing mechanisms, the individual animal remains undefined.

The quote from Miele above serves also to introduce the second factor that facilitates the use of welfare in segmentation; 'happiness is presented as instrumental in the better taste of food', she writes (2012: 2087). Welfare is rarely if ever a stand-alone quality in the segmentation, marketing and consumption of food products. It is more frequently bundled together with broader and more multifaceted notions of quality that include taste, type of animal feed, authenticity, provenance, traceability, environmental impact, human health, bucolic aesthetics, nostalgia, naturality, even colour. The advocate and primary driver of the higher welfare Oakham brand, as recounted in Jackson et al. (2006: 64), is quick to acknowledge that: 'Our customers told us they wanted chicken to "taste like it used to taste"'. Here, higher welfare becomes associated with tradition and nostalgic references to what are perceived as pre-intensive production systems. Certainly the major retailers are fully aware of the supporting rather than headlining, role of welfare in product marketing as revealed in the following quotations from our interviews with food chain actors undertaken as part of the Welfare Quality© research:

Yes, and that is all about eating quality because the other thing to say is you can have all this fancy animal welfare but if it doesn't taste good, there is no point in having it so it has to be the whole package, animal welfare is a contributory factor. (Interview, representative of major UK supermarket)

The first concern is not welfare, no, it really isn't. It is far more in terms of quality and food security – perhaps welfare is part of this but it is not a priority part. What is the priority is product quality; the tenderness of the meat is one of the first things. We are constantly thinking about this, what is the priority. (Interview, category manager major French supermarket)

Recent decades have seen well-documented and substantive changes in the nature and definition of food quality (Bernués et al., 2003; Grunert, 2005) as a demand-driven food supply sector moves increasingly towards accounting for perceived quality and extrinsic quality cues (including both risk avoidance and ethical elements) as much as for the more traditional intrinsic qualities (taste, composition, etc.). In line with the observation by Marsden et al. (2000, see above) that private food regulation places greater emphasis on process than product, Caswell et al. (1998) distinguish a range of quality attributes in food supply chains stretching from animal welfare to the presence or absence of foodborne pathogens commenting that 'they are rarely implemented in isolation' (1998: 549). Northen (2000) similarly identifies an array of quality attributes found within British beef and lamb assurance schemes noting that many of these are not communicated to the consumer but are selectively employed in strategies of product communication.

Bundling quality attributes is an effective mechanism for establishing a recognizable brand (Richardson et al., 1996) which Jackson et al. (2011: 59) define as: 'a narrative process where brands are developed and "storied" in ways that are consistent with the commercial positioning of the firm and the personal investments of the brand developers'. Brands, argue Leitch and Davenport (2007: 47), are best understood as systems of meaning rather than as objects, 'controlled representation of an organization's identity' as brand theory becomes more focused on brand consumption than brand production. In UK food retailing, brands play an important role in defining the relative positions of the major supermarkets as retailer brands, with their coherent assurance processes, come to replace individual manufacturers' brands. Burt (2000) sees in this a crucial repositioning of retail branding from lower-quality/lower-price attributes to higher-quality brand alternatives; as he puts it: 'from "me too" copies of existing products to the development of new innovative products in high value markets' (2000: 885). Particular retailers thus become associated in consumers'/citizens' minds with specific quality attributes, including those related to the welfare of farm animals, while NGOs, like Compassion in World Farming, reinforce such associations through their supermarket awards and comparative surveys of retailer performance in promoting higher welfare production. Concern for brand identity is not restricted to retailers and food companies. The RSPCA have recently changed the name of their internationally recognized assurance and certification scheme from 'Freedom Food' to 'RSPCA Assured', arguing that the former nomenclature failed to make the connection in consumers' minds with the organization behind it. 'People know and trust the RSPCA name', said the scheme's CEO recently, 'so we hope by using it, will simplify our message on animal welfare' (Cooper, 2015).

Animal welfare then has become an almost ubiquitous (albeit varied) and necessary component of product segmentation and quality branding. It is not necessarily visible on food packaging or consumer information, but it is there in corporate social responsibility statements, in private assurance scheme criteria and in selective instances of product and brand advertising. Ironically perhaps, where higher welfare was initially an element in the segmentation and differentiation of distinct niche products, competitive standard setting and the generalization of standard use have, if anything, reduced the power of welfare as a dynamic of segmentation as more generic products assume higher standard levels. Though production system labelling for shell eggs, introduced in 2004, is widely held to have stimulated the growth in sales of free-range eggs and the decline of caged eggs (Buller and Roe, 2013), recent figures show that the volume of sales of eggs from caged systems has started to rise again as caged-system welfare, under new EU legislation, starts to translate into welfare improvements. Similarly, for broiler production in the UK, birds from production systems that go beyond statutory requirements (including organic and free range) still represent under one fifth of total UK broiler production (Table 4.3).

Table 4.3 Market split, broiler production in the UK

Production type	% of birds grown in the UK
Standard quality chickens (meeting statutory requirements)	82
Higher welfare chickens (private/retail assurance)	14
Free range	3
Organic	1

Source: Dickinson (2014).

Frame three: Assurance

Our third framing in what we interpret as the progressive presence of the animal, as living subject, within a food chain that stretches from farm to shelf, and possibly beyond, engaging producer and consumer in a reinforcing ethic of care, is that of assurance. Assurance is the framing mechanism by which segmentation and branding, addressed above, are legitimated and bounded. It is defined by Baines and Ryan (2002) as comprising three aims: to demonstrate regulatory compliance, to ensure product quality and to communicate information to consumers (see also Manning et al., 2006). It is, thereby, a key element in linking production and consumption. Assurance has become in recent years arguably the predominant form of welfare governance in animal-origin food chains. While assurance schemes have not replaced statutory minimal standards (and many retain those standards), they have, through their component assessment procedures, audits, certifications and inspections, emerged as a de facto regulatory regime. Moreover, they have become primary drivers in the development and refinement of welfare assessment. The largest of them in Britain, the Red Tractor Assurance scheme, initially established by the UK National Farmers' Union in 2000 and run by Assured Food Standards, currently extends to 95 per cent of all the litres of fresh milk produced in Britain, 82 per cent of finished cattle, 65 per cent of finished sheep, 85 per cent of UK pigs at slaughter and 90 per cent of UK broiler production (Assured Food Standards, 2015). In this section, we want to argue three points. First, we want to demonstrate how the practices of on-farm assurance assessment impact upon the relationship of farmers and their work to food supply chains and the actors that constitute them. Second, we maintain that fundamental shifts in the means of assessing the welfare of farm animals within assurance schemes are having a potentially far-reaching effect upon how animal lives are presented within the food supply chain and, ultimately, to consumers. Finally, we want to explore the contention that the growth of private assurance as a means of governing welfare practices on the farm and in the slaughterhouse is becoming so widely used that it is impacting upon the form and intent of statutory regulation. Before considering the first of these, we briefly trace the development of assurance schemes as a mechanism for introducing welfare criteria into quality standards.

In May 2000, the UK Farm Animal Welfare Council (as it was then) announced that it would hitherto take what it called a 'food chain' approach to farm animal welfare, recognizing that the standards under which animals are produced are effectively a quality characteristic of the products consumed. FAWC stated its belief that:

it is not logical to act as though the concerns in our society about animal welfare relate only to British livestock production. Nor do we believe that consumers should be prevented from making informed choices with regard to the welfare provenance of the livestock products, which they choose to consume. In this context, however, if properly implemented farm assurance schemes offer a means whereby the link between animal production conditions and the final food product can be made clear. If this is to be achieved, it is essential that the assurances provided not only by retailers, but also by the catering and food processing industries, should be equally informative and trustworthy to command consumer confidence. (FAWC, 2000: v)

The first decade of the current century saw a new emphasis placed upon the role of non-statutory assurance as a means of addressing animal welfare. Several factors contributed to this emphasis. The UK Policy Commission Report on Farming and Food, published in 2002, considered such schemes as addressing what was seen at the time as being the country's 'poor animal health record' though the Commission equally regarded assurance as a viable way of adding value to agricultural outputs and thereby increasing farm incomes. Retailers had begun to operationalize private or proprietary assurance schemes for their own suppliers in response to the 1990 Food Safety Act's requirement that they show due diligence in achieving legal compliance and as a means of reassuring consumers that standards had been met. During the 1990s, a number of professional sector bodies set up specific assurance schemes for their members, largely as a means of promoting their products and restoring public confidence in production standards following a number of food and animal health scares. These various schemes were constructed around legal requirements and non-mandatory codes of practice. They include, in the UK, Assured British Meat, the National Dairy Farm Assured Scheme, Assured Chicken Production, Assured British Pigs, Agriculture and Horticulture Development Board's Beef and Lamb Quality Standard Mark schemes, most of which have been subsequently regrouped, as independent subsidiaries, under the Red Tractor or Assured Food Standard scheme (though not the Lion Egg Quality scheme, started in 1998, nor the entirely independent Genesis Quality Assurance scheme which is nonetheless recognized under Red Tractor). Finally, coming at the issue from a slightly different angle, the RSPCA established its welfare assurance scheme, Freedom Food, in 1992 to specifically address farm animal welfare, while the Soil Association has, since 1973, acted as the principal certification body for organic agriculture in the UK. All of these share a broadly similar form: a list of required practices and standards; an assessment carried out by third-party assessors that are accredited with the United Kingdom

Accreditation Service (UKAS) and some form of accreditation statement, label or certification to demonstrate that the facility and/or supply chain is compliant.

The recent interest in short supply chains among food scholars has drawn attention to the mechanism by which quality is constructed at the local, producer level. Marsden et al. (2000), for example, present the case of Llyn Beef in Wales where a cooperative of local producers got together to develop and market locally produced beef under their own assured quality standards. Similarly, Stassart (2003) documents the mobilization of a beef producer group in Belgium around a particular set of values and instruments of quality and its determination. In both studies, producers seek to establish a new set of relationships with consumers based upon the values and meanings of quality. In Stassart's (2003) study, this has led him to focus specifically on the various modes of ordering (after Law, 1994) that accompany the translation of quality within the food chain while Marsden et al. (2000) emphasize the re-socializing and re-spatializing of food that subsequently occurs. Both studies however encompass the 'alterity' that to some extent defines much of the 'alternative' food network phenomenon (Maye et al., 2007). While the 'narrative convenience' of distinguishing 'alternative' and 'mainstream' food chains is often overly simplistic (Goodman et al., 2012: 104), conventional, vertically integrated food systems do tend to adopt a somewhat different approach to defining the parameters of quality (Henson and Reardon, 2005) often reflecting the agendas of supply chain captains, even though these parameters may ultimately depend upon the practices of husbandry and animal care at the micro-level.

The performance of farm inspection

At their centre, assurance schemes are, first, a set of proscribed parameters or criteria and, second, a procedure and a performance of assessment. Although assurance schemes cover many fields, our interest here is primarily in their application to farm animal welfare. Taking the example of the Assured Food Standards (Red Tractor) for pigs, we find thirteen broad categories of standards (Table 4.4).

Within these categories, specific standards relating to the welfare of the animals include:

- sufficient access to food and drinking water
- the existence and implementation of a veterinary health plan
- the recording of health and welfare indicators (such as litter sizes, mortality rates, weaning rates, facial scarring, tail biting)

Table 4.4 Categories of inspected standards: assured food standards for pigs, 2014

Standard	Defined aim
Documents and procedures	Plans and procedures in place to ensure safe and legal food production
Staff and labour providers	All staff are trained and competent to carry out the activities they do
Traceability and assurance status	Clear identification of livestock to deliver food chain traceability
Vermin control	Effective and responsible control of birds, rodents, insects and other animals to prevent contamination and food safety risk
Housing, shelter and handling facilities	Safe, comfortable and hygienic housing for all livestock, including youngstock and those close to giving birth
Feed and water	• All livestock receive a daily diet sufficient to maintain full health • Animal feed is suitable and traceable • On-farm mixing produces safe animal feed • Feed remains clean, palatable and free from contamination
Animal health and welfare	• Proactive management of the health and welfare of all livestock through planning and reviewing • The health and welfare of all livestock is being checked and managed by appropriate people • Effective and appropriate management of sick or injured livestock
Biosecurity and disease control	Effective biosecurity measures to prevent the spread of disease and protect food safety and animal health
Animal medicines and husbandry procedures	• Responsible and competent use of medicines and veterinary treatments • Safe, secure and responsible management of medicines • Prevention of contamination in food
Fallen stock	Fallen stock promptly removed, stored and disposed of to prevent environmental contamination and spread of disease
Livestock transport	• The health and welfare of livestock is managed during transportation • Well-managed transportation • Controls to prevent the spread of disease
Environmental protection and contamination control	• A well-maintained farm • No contamination, pollution or spread of disease from any potential contaminants or wastes

Standard	Defined aim
Outdoor pigs	The welfare requirements of outdoor pigs are met at all times.

Source: Derived from Assured Food Standards for Pigs (2014) available at: https://assurance. redtractor.org.uk/contentfiles/Farmers-5615.pdf

- access to enrichment
- daily inspection of animals for signs of ill health, poor welfare or injury
- minimum weaning duration
- handling without injury and stress
- regularity of veterinary visits
- isolation facilities for sick animals
- presence of staff trained in euthanasia techniques
- limited conditions under which tail docking and teeth reduction are permitted

Farmers would generally expect to be assessed on the full set of criteria every twelve or eighteen months depending upon the type of scheme. A certified third-party assessment company or, in some cases, the scheme's own certified assessors would undertake the assessment. If standards are not met, farmers are generally given a set time period to conform or, in the case of certain standards, are suspended from the scheme until rectification. Suspension or removal from the scheme may have a considerable impact upon a producer's ability to sell his or her product.

Elsewhere (Roe et al., 2011), as part of an empirical investigation in animal welfare assurance schemes, we have argued that the process of assurance scheme on-farm inspection or assessment, despite the levels of proscription involved, is an important moment in the mobilization of farm animal welfare, yet it remains relatively understudied. Citing Lowe et al.'s (1997: 11) reminder that 'actors construct their worlds from what is around them, that is by designating and associating entities which they select, define and link together', we have been concerned to understand how farm animals and their welfare, as subjects of both care and assessment, are perceived and accounted for by assessors during assessment procedures. In practice, assurance assessments are a combination of the proscriptive and the impressionistic. A good part of any assessment refers to required documents being available and accessible. Yet, for assessors:

> it's just using your eyes and ears, your nose and talking to people really to get to know and I don't follow the tick boxes. The paperwork documentation side of it yes, I would follow that … but a lot of it you look and you can see. (Assessor, Interview: Roe et al., 2011: 75)

Although UKAS rules limit the ability of assessors or inspectors to give advice during an assessment, it is clear from our research that there are often considerable layers of practical sympathy (particularly with regard to farmer stress during the assessment visit), collective responsibility (the sense that inspectors are, in many cases, there to help make farmer more successful) and professional detachment (Roe et al., 2011). Nevertheless, the driving impetus is never far away:

> It might sound a bit strange but to say to people that the first impression of a farm is important because that is where the food is coming from. So you shouldn't be ashamed of consumers seeing these farms and if someone takes care and interest in the way their farm looks the chances are they will take more care and interest in the animals as well. (Assurance Scheme Manager, Interview: Roe et al., 2011: 75)

Collectively, these assessed standards of husbandry practice, animal care, record keeping and risk avoidance emerge as a de facto model of 'best practice', or at least the scheme architects' interpretation of best practice. Increasingly, they are becoming the 'only practice' as few retailers, if any, will sell products that do not come from quality-assured lines. Farm assessments are an assemblage of different knowledges, practices, rules and relations combining welfare science, husbandry and retailer/consumer expectations with the farmer somewhat precariously positioned within them (Hubbard et al., 2007). Yet, these multiple methodological components are not necessarily dissolvable into a single whole. 'You can't walk around a pig building with a lap-top and muddy boots', said one assessor (quoted in Roe et al., 2011: 77). How the welfare of farm animals is assessed becomes critical.

Assessing welfare

The second argument we wish to develop here is that key changes in the means of assessing the welfare of farm animals within assurance schemes are altering the way animal lives are presented within the food supply chain.

The welfare of farm animals is a multidimensional concept difficult to define and even more difficult to measure. As we saw in Chapter 2, welfare science has progressively adopted diverse approaches to the classification and assessment of animal welfare states. Yet no single measure can cover all the dimensions of welfare. The growth of assurance schemes has nevertheless necessitated the development of practical on-farm welfare assessments in a way that legislative compliance never did (Sorensen and Fraser, 2010). Protocols have had to be put into place and sets of measurable welfare parameters established and agreed. Individual measurements may be aggregated to form composite indicators (Botreau et al., 2007) and these themselves may be combined to form 'iceberg indicators', key elements that reveal a range of different processes at work (Heath et al., 2014).

Traditionally, welfare assessment has relied heavily on input, management, resource or environmental measures of farm animal welfare, those that indicate levels of provision and/or protection. For example, a common response to the first of the 'five freedoms' (see Chapter 2), 'freedom from hunger and thirst', might well be the establishment of a minimum number of water points or feeders per given number of animals. Similarly, the second 'freedom' (freedom from discomfort) may well engender a measure of resting space or floor type per animal. Following the physiological thrust of welfare science, assurance schemes were initially developed around such input-based metrics for these represented, at the time, the most efficient means of determining the appropriate conditions of husbandry. What they can't tell however is how the animal is responding to these conditions or indeed to any other factors that might impact on their welfare. They say little, if anything, about the animal and its physical or its mental state, whether that is positive or negative.

Now, a growing emphasis is placed on 'outcome'- or 'animal'-based measures of welfare (Main et al., 2012). These seek to assess actual welfare by establishing indicators or measures of physical and/or mental states ranging, for example, from mortality, body condition (including scarring or the presence of lesions or wounds) and lameness to human avoidance, use of enrichments and antagonistic behaviour (Main et al., 2007). Animal-based measures give the most direct insight into how animals are coping within their own environment (Whay et al., 2003; Whay, 2007). They are especially valuable for those bodies or organizations that seek to make claims about the particular welfare advantages of their systems of products. Measuring animal-based outcomes is not though without difficulty: there is, writes Whay (2007: 18), a potentially 'high level of subjectivity within this type of assessment and interpretation of the significance of the results to the animals themselves presents an ongoing challenge'. Furthermore, farms or even systems that might score poorly on resource- or input-based measures, sometimes, paradoxically score highly when animal-based measures are employed (Bracke, 2007). So considerable attention has been given to achieving workable, consistent and effective assessments of welfare outcomes that are able to operate within the context of farm assurance schemes alongside more conventional resource measures (Whay et al., 2003; Blokhuis et al., 2010; Main et al. 2012).

Our interest in these outcome- or animal-based measures is twofold. On the one hand, there is their potential to alter the farmer–animal relationship. On the other, they have the possibility to alter the consumer–animal relationship. The impact of these outcome measures is felt right through the food chain (Buller and Roe, 2010). Outcome measures are often held to be inherently more subjective than input or resource measures. How does one gauge the degree of apparent anxiety displayed by a dairy cow in the presence of humans and how does one ensure inter-observer reliability; how much play might be used to indicate positive welfare state? How does one aggregate individual expressions of behaviour into a composite and valid assessment of on-farm practice (Botreau et al., 2007)? Yet the observation of on-farm inspections shows that impressions and subjective accounting are common informal accompaniments to even conventional input-based farm assessment procedures (Miele, 2012; Roe et al., 2011), though the conclusions drawn from them can be problematic and inconsistent (Palczynski et al., 2016). For farmers, outcome-based measures implicitly or explicitly engage their own physical and affective relationship with their animals (Kielland et al., 2010); they might reveal or imply inattention or failures in care practices, suggesting changes in management style, though they are just as likely to reveal the effects of systemic issues in production systems (e.g. overcrowding leading to fighting and poor body conditions or poor flooring leading to lameness). While the exposure of such issues is important, their resolution might lie beyond the immediate action frame, or indeed responsibility, of a farmer seeking compliance within a regulatory framework for an assurance scheme (Roe et al., 2011; Rushen et al., 2014). More challenging for welfare assessment has been the quantification of positive emotional states in farm animals (Boissy et al., 2007). One approach, known as qualitative behaviour assessment (Wemelsfelder et al., 2000; Wemelsfelder, 2007; Wemelsfelder and Mullan, 2014), unambiguously engages with assessor subjectivity and creative anthropomorphism (reinterpreted as shared physicality) in an effort to identify positive welfare states. Although outcome-based and qualitative assessments generally take longer to undertake than input measures, they do bring it all back to the animal and to animal lives, thereby ultimately allowing assurance procedures to make more legitimate claims about how husbandry practices and systems impact upon individual and group welfare.

Although not widely adopted by all assurance schemes at the present time, a number of experimental protocols for animal-based assessments have or are being developed, for example, the Welfare Quality protocols (Welfare Quality, 2009a, b, c) or the AssureWel project (AssureWel, 2015). This latter is a system of welfare outcome assessment for the principal farmed species that is being developed by collaboration between the RSPCA, the Soil Association and the University of Bristol. As an example, Table 4.5 identifies the AssureWel outcome measures currently designed for pigs while Table 4.6 provides a more detailed example of the assessment of enrichment.

For consumers, further up the chain, outcome-based assessments present a challenge. One the one hand, they may be used to claim a greater validity in accounting for animal lives. 'For herd health', claim one major UK retailer on their published welfare information sheet, 'we use an "outcome based" system to ensure we focus on the cow's health' (Sainsbury.co.uk, 2014). They create a link between product and individual animal; reference to an index of lameness, for example, evokes a sensibility to the notion of a lame animal; an indicator of positive welfare state based upon enrichment behaviour may evoke notions of animal 'happiness'. Information and claims about farm animals, their individual material presence and behaviour within production systems can therefore be conveyed to consumers in a way that input-based measures avoid, creating, in Miele's (2012: 2087) words, 'more complex moral relationship between human and nonhuman animals, a search for different intimacies between humans and [in her case] chickens'.

However, on the other hand, and by the same token, such indicators may also lose their potency when they appear to call into question entire systems of production particularly when staples, like milk, are concerned (Webster, 2010).

Table 4.5 Core outcome-based measures as developed by AssureWel scheme

Measure		Measure	
1	Enrichment use	9	Tail lesions
2	Lameness	10	Shoulder lesions
3	Tail docking	11	Vulva lesions
4	Nose ringing	12	Manure on the body
5	Ear and flank biting	13	Leg swellings
6	Pigs needing further care	14	Skin conditions
7	Hospital Pen	15	Body condition
8	Body marks	16	Mortality

Source: http://www.assurewel.org/pigs

Table 4.6 Extract from assessment protocol for pigs, 2014

Enrichment use Pen measure

Observation: Observe and record the oral behaviour of standing and sitting pigs in the pen (ignore lying pigs). Assess quickly to avoid double counting pigs already assessed.

Record the number of standing and sitting pigs:

1. *Using enrichment* = Investigating a suitable manipulable substrate or object provided for enrichment
   - Include if snout/mouth is manipulating straw, hay, wood(chip), sawdust, mushroom compost, peat, (or other material that enables proper investigation and manipulation)
   - OR in contact with an object/toy such as a hanging object or ball.
   - Only include if these objects/substrates have been provided by the producer as enrichment.
   - In outdoor systems, include manipulation of turf or clean areas of ground (i.e. not contaminated with manure).
2. *Manipulating other* = No. pigs manipulating other pigs, pen equipment/floor/ muck
   - Include if the snout/mouth is in contact with any part of another pig.
   - Include if the snout/mouth is in contact with muck or the floor, fixtures or fittings of the pen. Pay attention at feeders or drinkers to discriminate between manipulation of pen furniture and eating/drinking.
   - In outdoor systems, include rooting in dunging area or manipulation of areas of ground contaminated with manure.
3. *Stone chewing* = Manipulating a stone or stones with the snout or mouth – often audible.

Source: http://www.assurewel.org/Portals/2/Documents/Pigs/Generic%20Finishing%20 Pig%20protocol%20-%20v.1.pdf

Relatively high levels of recorded lameness in dairy herds and sheep flocks (Barker et al., 2010; Main et al. 2010; Main et al., 2012) have had little immediate impact on consumer purchasing. As Webster (2009: 145) argues:

> The best-designed and most scientifically-robust monitoring protocol cannot be expected to succeed unless it leads to effective action to promote and improve welfare on-farm.

Assurance and the governance of welfare

The final point we want to make here sees assurance as a dynamic and original mode of welfare governance (Henson and Reardon, 2005). We have already identified above the growing role of retailer power within the restructured world of food regulation. Assurance schemes and their use in farm animal health and welfare provide an example of what Power (1994) refers to as the 'audit explosion'; the extension of the practice of auditing into new areas of social and economic life through mechanisms of inspection and accountability, with a concomitant multiplication of consumption-facing regulatory agencies and actors both public and private (in this case, public bodies like UKAS and the Food Standards Agency alongside the private regulatory powers of retailers). In this manner, the audit-as-assurance is, in large part, replacing or at least superceding state regulation as the driving mechanism for the delivery of welfare goals. At the same time, it is partially rewriting or re-framing those goals to meet the market-driven cultures of the new regulators, the assurance scheme 'captains'. Not that this necessarily implies a defunct system of state regulation. Rather it suggests an imbrication of private and public actions, driven by different goals yet achieving, temporarily at least and with some cost to certain actors, potentially improved welfare standards. In this way, through shifts that Scott (2003) suggests represent a move from the 'regulatory' to the 'post-regulatory' state:

> The broader shifts in the political economy of the nation-state, and the increasing 'consumer'-led transfer of power down the food chain to retailers [...] have combined to empower retailers as harbingers of public policy through private and corporatist means. (Marsden et al., 1998: 488)

Assurance schemes serve the food chain 'captains' well, allowing them to demonstrate conformity to minimum legal requirements, and in places go well beyond them to avoid any risk of legal liability through producer failure (Humphrey and Schmitz, 2008). At the same time, they are able to transfer the burden (and the cost) of food chain responsibility down the line to individual producers (Busch, 2007). Competition between retailers over their quality and ethical credentials has certainly led to an upward pressure on certain standards and for some observers can help drive subsequent legislative change (Fulponi, 2007). As we have shown elsewhere (Buller and Roe, 2013), retailers began pushing free-range eggs in their supply chains some time before the ban on battery systems came into force.

Yet, as a form of regulation, assurance schemes do present problems at both 'ends' of the chain. With assurance schemes becoming the norm, rather than a component of specialist or alternative niche products commanding higher prices from ethically driven consumers, conformity and accreditation represent an additional and yet unavoidable cost for producers as without these, access to markets can become restricted (Fearne and Walters, 2004). A common criticism is that some of the requirements of assurance schemes are perceived by farmers as merely 'tick box' actions, driven by consumer, rather than production considerations and having little or no relevance to farm practice or the welfare of animals. There is evidence too of wider structural changes occurring as a consequence of assurance scheme expansion. Livestock markets, the traditional site of animal purchase and exchange prior to slaughter and processing within food supply chains, have been gradually replaced by individual contracts between producers and either abattoirs or manufacturers and retailers. Abattoirs themselves, increasingly owned by large food groups, have responded to this new role by increasing capacity, becoming more centralized with faster and faster throughputs (Northen, 2000). Finally, for consumers, the multiplication of assurance schemes, with their different parameters and standards (few of which are actually displayed) rather than being a source of transparency, has become a source of confusion and misinterpretation, leading increasingly to calls for more coherent and straightforward comparative information at point of sale (FAWC, 2006). It is to this that we now turn in the final section of this chapter.

Frame four: Labelling

Many assurance schemes specifying the respect of distinct welfare standards are, to all intents and purposes, 'invisible' to conventional shoppers and consumers. A retailer might stipulate on its web pages and corporate social responsibility statement that, for example, no caged eggs are used in its own brand processed food, but there may be little if anything to indicate this on the product itself. Fresh meat may be produced to RSPCA-assured standards but there may be no clue to this at the butcher's counter. Other schemes and levels of compliance however may be specifically identifiable through on-product labels, statements or packaging styles. If the former are all about selling – or creating confidence in – a brand or retailer identity and its reputational capital, the latter are largely about creating a distinct niche market aimed at specifically concerned consumers. Farm animal welfare is thereby differentially 'framed' by food actors through labels and product information. Coming back to Çalışkan and Callon (2010: 12), labels might be understood as 'so many pre-calculated operations' constituting the calculative capacities of different agencies. This though endows them with a normativity and intentionality that is not always born out in practice; consumers don't necessarily read them and are frequently confused by them, particularly when it comes to animal welfare (Schroder and McEachern, 2004; Evans and Miele, 2008). Animal welfare is a peculiar product, in many ways suggestive of what Karpik (2010) refers to as a 'singularity', a product defined by a multidimensional, uncertain and incommensurable quality (Hutter, 2011). Such products, he argues, are selected by informed consumers on the basis of these, sometimes elusive, qualities rather than price. To assist them in the making of that selection, various 'judgement devices' (which echo Callon and Muniesa's 'market devices') are employed, foremost among which, for our purposes here, are brands and labels. Labels occupy a somewhat dualistic terrain between standardization and distinction (Beregson et al., 2014), between the need to demonstrate conformity and adherence to a set of (often hidden) standards and the need, for the consumers and the retailers, to distinguish themselves and the strength of their engagement. They are shaped by material, regulatory, semiotic, scientific and aesthetic considerations, a coming together of exchange, normalizing and representational practices (Kjellberg and Helgesson, 2007).

As assurance schemes have multiplied, so the debate on labelling has intensified (e.g. www.labellingmatters.org; Farm Animal Welfare Forum, 2011). Food labelling performs different functions for different interests though four principal rationales stand out:

- Labelling enables markets to be segmented and thereby create and justify additional market value for producers/industry/retailers.

- Labelling informs differentiated consumers and enables them to make a choice according to the different selection criteria they have.

- Labelling demonstrates conformity to required rules, shows transparency and establishes due diligence thereby facilitating public surveillance and confidence.

- Labelling/branding encourages customer fidelity.

There is a *fifth* rationale which we might term the bio-political rationale. Labelling is also a way for governments (and not always just governments) to influence markets and the way consumers make selections about food for what are often multiple sociopolitical and economic reasons. By referring to specific attributes of products, labels offer 'cues' to aid buyers (whether consumers themselves or retailers buying from their suppliers) to choose to purchase certain things and not buy other things, leading ultimately to shifts within the supply (Bernues et al., 2003). Generally, there is a distinction between extrinsic and intrinsic attributes within labelling. Intrinsic attributes are qualities that are part of the product itself (such as its fat content and nutritional value but also its fitness for use – say for a stew or for a roast). They are sometimes referred to as 'sensory cues' (Veale et al., 2006). They are often subjective, though they may also be informed by experience ('this cut of meat was delicious last time'). Extrinsic attributes refer to the price, the process or origin of the product, production system and so on. These rely on more objective criteria for determination. For consumers, extrinsic factors are often interpreted as affecting intrinsic attributes – for example, assuming that a free-range chicken might taste better (Bernués et al., 2003). From a marketing perspective, extrinsic attributes or cues are interesting because they can be altered and manipulated without any material change to the product (Oude-Ophuis and Van Trijp, 1995).

One goal of labelling is to create specific purchasing behaviour or to change purchasing behaviour. Some labelling schemes are designed to produce behaviour change among existing consumers (the introduction of a retailer's low-salt ready-meals range allows consumers to shift to the purchase of low-salt products). Others generate new consumers and are targeted to a market that is out there but has not been specifically addressed (so these might be people who always wanted low-salt meals and are now purchasing them from that particular retailer). Of course, it might work the other way. By identifying some products as being 'less good' with respect to whatever parameter is being selected, and therefore cheaper, it might become equally sought after. One thinks of the infamous and well-reported impact of Jamie Oliver's 'Fowl Dinners' TV programme broadcast in the UK in 2008 which led to a dramatic increase not only in the sale of organic and free-range chickens but also in the sale of basic-level poultry which became relatively cheaper. To what extent does welfare labelling become an inclusive or an exclusive practice? To what extent is it catering for a fairly restricted demand from a fairly restricted set of consumers, rather than being inclusive, allowing the maximum number of people access to higher welfare conditions? Time and time again, research has identified the persistent gap between what people say influences them in their purchasing choices and what they actually buy (Eurobarometer, 2005, 2014). This is particularly the case for animal welfare where repeated consumer surveys identify this as something all consumers say they are concerned about but few act upon that concern in a consistent way in their purchasing decisions.

There are many reasons for distinctively labelling a product with specific properties. Leaving aside nutritional and 'environmental labelling' or 'eco-labelling', the standard ways in which animal welfare becomes specifically integrated into product labels or advertising is either by proxy, through origin or provenance labelling, through the identification of compliance with explicit higher welfare assurance schemes (such as the distinctive blue icon of the RSPCA's former 'Freedom Food' label) or by reference to distinctive production systems (such as 'free range'). Of these, country of origin labelling is, in many ways, the most straightforward. Although agricultural produce is traded all over the world, many people feel more secure in the knowledge of where their food comes from (Eurobarometer, 2014). National governments and citizens frequently trust in, and defend, the idea of a national agricultural identity and country of origin or provenance labelling is often regarded as a proxy for other considerations; that a particular country will be 'better' across a range of parameters including such things as taste, welfare, environmental considerations and the institutional and legal regulation of, and adherence to, such parameters (Skarstad et al., 2007). The intensity of this sentiment does vary from country to country and from product to product (Kjaernes et al., 2009). Rationales other than product quality also underpin country of origin and provenance labelling. Following the BSE crisis of the late 1980s and early 1990s, the EU introduced mandatory origin labelling for beef under Regulation 1760/2000 (and other later regulations – see Table 4.7) though it failed to prevent the infamous 'horsemeat scandal' of 2013 in Europe (Barnett et al., 2016). Since 1 April 2015, there is now across the EU country of origin or place of provenance (rearing and slaughter) indication for fresh, chilled and frozen meat of pigs, sheep, goats and poultry following

Table 4.7 Compulsory country of origin beef labelling system (EU)

Compulsory Country of Origin Beef labelling system (EU) Operators or organizations marketing European or imported beef are obliged to label the beef at all stages of the marketing process. When the product is not pre-wrapped, they must supply relevant information in written and visible form to the consumer at the point of sale. Labelling must include the following information: • the reference number or code establishing the link between the meat and the animal (or group of animals) from which the meat was derived; • slaughtered in (country where slaughter took place and licence number of the slaughterhouse); and • cutting/cut in (country where cutting was performed and licence number of the cutting plant). Moreover, since 1 January 2002, operators must also indicate: • the country where the animals were born; • the country where the animals were fattened/bred; and • the country where the animals were slaughtered. Where the beef is derived from an animal born, bred and slaughtered in a single country, this information may be grouped together under one heading, Origin, followed by the name of the country in question. By way of derogation, imported meat for which not all compulsory information is available is labelled Origin: non-EU, followed by the name of the non-EU country in which it was slaughtered. Complementary items may be included as voluntary labelling additions.

Source: Derived from Regulation (EC) No 1760/2000

Regulation 1337/2013. Milk is the notable exception here. We might also include the EU protected designation of origin (PDO) and protected geographical indicator (PGI) rules as a more localized form of 'Voluntary Place of Origin' labelling. Under their internal production rules, specific forms and practices (including higher welfare procedures) can be specified.

There are relatively few specific on-product animal welfare labels demonstrating approved conformity to particular welfare assurance or certification schemes within the EU, though their number is increasing (FAWC, 2006; Compassion in World Farming, 2012). The most well known is the RSPCA's Freedom Food (now renamed RSPCA Assured) which covers, at the last estimate, some 257 million farmed fish and animals (see Chart 4.2), though the distinctive label is by no means always used on individual products. Others include the *Neuland* scheme in Germany, the French *Thierry Schweitzer* label in Alsace and the US 'Animal Welfare Approved' label. Far more common are the more generic assurance scheme labels that, while they might include animal welfare, are generally based upon producers meeting legal minimum standards across a wide range of production criteria (though some of the required standards may be higher than legal minima). Examples of these labels would include the UK's Red Tractor label and Lion Mark and the French *Label* Rouge, all of which are generally displayed on product packaging. Also increasingly common are food products specifically labelled as 'Organic', signifying conformity to a set of more specific criteria, including those of animal welfare. Many of these schemes, like the welfare-specific schemes mentioned above, go significantly beyond legal requirements with respect to, for example, the animal's environment (stocking densities, bedding, outdoor access), its treatment (restricted use of medicines) and its observation (animal-based assessment measures).

Research on the impact of these specific food labels on consumer choice and behaviour reveals a number of sometimes rather contradictory tendencies. Olesen et al. (2010), employing a non-hypothetical choice experiment to determine Norwegian consumers' willingness to pay a price premium for organic and animal welfare-labelled salmon, and found that while higher welfare can, among concerned consumers, elicit a willingness to pay a higher price, aesthetic criteria, which mitigate against paler organic salmon, are also significant. More importantly however, Norwegian consumers' belief that their country's welfare standards are generally high limits the market for foreign products with additional welfare requirements. There is little doubt that welfare labels respond to a growing demand among concerned consumers willing to pay higher prices (McEachern and Warnaby, 2008), though this needs to be set against the relatively lower prioritization of animal welfare as an actual driver for individual purchasing

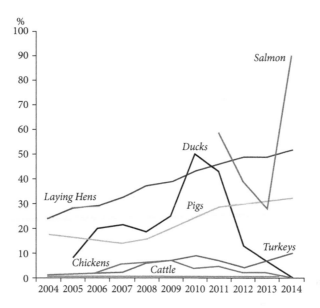

Chart 4.2 Number of animals farmed under RSPCA standards. Source: From RSPCA Trustees Report and Accounts (2014).

decisions among more general populations less willing to pay premium prices (Eurobarometer, 2005; Grunert, 2011). The most recent survey, undertaken for the European Commission by the Food Chain Evaluation Consortium in 2015, confirms this.

> Our survey asked respondents to spontaneously state the three main purchase criteria they use when buying meat. The main purchase criteria used are aspects of quality, mainly presentation and durability (66%) and price, mainly in unit terms (16%). Only 2% of meat purchases cited production method as the most important purchase criterion, 1% religious consideration and 1% general animal welfare considerations: no respondents spontaneously mentioned animal welfare at slaughter as a purchase criterion. Those who purchase meat are also generally satisfied with the information available on meat and meat products (80%, 17% 'very satisfied' and 63% 'satisfied'). (Food Chain Evaluation Consortium, 2015: ii)

Products from higher welfare systems generally tend to cost more to consumers. Yet while that cost remains as the most important barrier to consumers (Brooklynhurst, 2010), higher welfare products can be higher priced, not necessarily because they are more costly to produce, but also because they constitute an important and distinctive niche within market specialization. Many higher welfare products are often sold in premium ranges, commanding higher prices largely because these can be obtained from discerning and committed consumers. Higher production costs (where they occur) are being passed on directly to certain consumers but additional revenues are also being generated on such products because of their premium status. Successive studies have demonstrated broad consumer approval of the intentions of specific welfare labelling (Hoogland et al., 2007) yet also identify relatively low levels of use and little broader impact on behaviour change among wider populations (Brooklyndhurst, 2010; Tawse, 2010; Grunert et al., 2014). Others report on consumer confusion over the exact meaning of welfare labels and criteria (QA Research, 2013) or on the expectation (sometimes frustrated) that higher welfare standard products will necessarily come with other additional qualities in taste and texture (Napolitano et al., 2010).

Arguably, a more effective approach to encouraging consumer choice for higher welfare products has been production system labelling. The 'model' to some extent for this type of approach is the EU shell eggs mandatory labelling regime that dates originally from 2004. Under that scheme, egg production systems are classified as:

- Free range
- Barn
- Eggs from caged hens (with cages redefined as 'enriched cages' in 2012)

The additional EU classification of 'organic' eggs adds a further element of production system classification. The only system that meets the requirements of the EU organic regulation and Soil Association certification is free range. In 2011, of the 347 million laying hens within the EU27, around 40 per cent were housed in non-cage systems. Of these, around 4 per cent were classed as organic, 12 per cent as 'free range' and 24 per cent as 'barn' (Compassion in World Farming, 2013)

A further EU-driven production system labelling scheme exists for broilers (the poultry meat marketing standards EC 543/2008). Under Article 11 of this scheme, poultry can be labelled as:

- Fed with (a specified foodstuff in a specified amount)
- Extensive indoor (barn reared) – where stocking rates and minimum slaughter age are specified)
- Free range – where indoor stocking rates and minimum slaughter age are specified and where birds spend 'at least half their lifetime' in continuous

daytime access to open-air runs comprising an area mainly covered by vege-tation of a specified size

- Traditional free range – where criteria include indoor stocking density, the maximum size and population of poultry houses, continuous daytime access to open-air runs, vegetation cover on runs, the use of slow-growing poultry strains, the amount of cereal in feed, minimum slaughter age

- Free range – total freedom – criteria are as for 'traditional free range' but with continuous daytime access to open-air runs of unlimited area

Production system labelling has been endorsed by a number of organizations, from the Farm Animal Welfare Forum (2011) to the British Veterinary Association (BVA). The advantages of system labelling are that it is theoretically more generalizable across different social or cultural contexts than a welfare-based label, within suitably robust assessment parameters. Moreover, it is an inclusive system, rather than an exclusive system, allowing all units to be so identified. Finally, it is flexible, permitting the use of new parameters to be brought into consideration.

Advocates of production system labelling maintain that it is prompting a shift in retail demands, in consumer behaviour and, as an eventual consequence, in production methods themselves. Compassion in World Farming assert that since shell egg production method labelling came into place in 2004, production, in the UK alone, of cage-free eggs (so barn and free range) increased from 31 per cent in 2003 to 51 per cent in 2011, beating caged systems as the dominant production method for the first time (Compassion in World Farming, 2013). Similarly, a number of major retailers stopped selling caged shell eggs altogether, making this an issue of retailer brand identity as well as direct consumer choice. Since then, as current Defra figures show below there has been a slowdown in free-range production and a slight regrowth in enriched cage production, which to a degree has been expected since the ban on intensive cages and the approved use of enriched cages. However, only around 48 per cent of the eggs produced in the UK go for sale as shell eggs on retailers' shelves. The other 52 per cent are used in food manufacture and food services. These sectors in general use far lower proportions of free range or barn eggs. Defra in their annual report on the UK poultry sector conclude that the proportion of eggs produced in the differing systems has changed little over the past four years (Defra, 2017, see Chart 4.3).

A second argument offered for production system labelling, drawing upon the experience of shell eggs, is one of raising awareness of animal production in general, in the belief that greater awareness, fostered by such immediate,

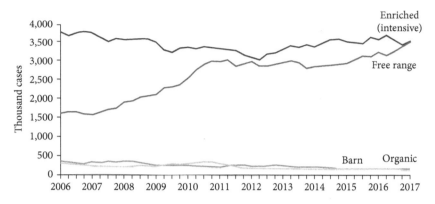

Chart 4.3 Egg production by type. Source: Defra (2017).

accessible and affective cues as 'free range', will bring greater support for enhanced welfare conditions, including those relating to other species in other production systems. To this end, the Farm Animal Welfare Forum, in their 2011 consultation document 'Labelling food from farm animals' (FAWF, 2011), suggest production systems should be classified across two parameters: first, 'intensive or extensive' and, second, 'indoor or outdoor'. Similarly, Compassion in World Farming has consistently argued that the EU voluntary poultry meat-marketing scheme should also include a category 'Intensive Indoors'. There are two concerns here. First, an overly simplistic focus upon what might be interpreted as more anthropomorphic indicators (such as outdoor access) in favour of more scientifically credible indicators derived from animal welfare science arguably shifts the goalposts of welfare assessment back to the environment and away from the animal itself. As many animal welfare scientists have argued, enriched and spacious cage systems can offer certain welfare advantages to individual animals though these may less immediately apparent (Sherwin et al., 2010). Second, retailers do not like labels that imply the product is of a lower standard than others available in the shop unless they can positively label alternative promotional characteristics, such as, most commonly, price (e.g. for 'value' ranges). For this reason, a number of high-end retailers no longer sell caged shell eggs – a process known as 'choice-editing'. Similarly, they might not specifically label as such individual products farmed under, for example, RSPCA assurance standards, preferring to incorporate the assurance into their own generic brand line.

A third, and broader, concern about labels and production systems is how they are differentially understood and interpreted both by consumers and by food chain actors. Despite the EU's clarification, the term 'free range' means widely different things to different people (QA Research, 2013, 2014), with many consumers believing free-range hens to be inherently 'happier' and 'healthier' and their eggs better tasting than those from cage systems (Pettersson et al., 2016). As Brooklyndhurst argue in their report to Defra (2010: 5–6):

> Welfare labels tend to emphasize the symbolic, altruistic aspects of the issue, which are a low priority for most consumers. In fact, it is the perceived tangible benefits provided by higher welfare foods that consumers are most interested in, motivated by, and willing to pay for.

For a number of food chain actors, animal welfare bodies and the European Commission, the solution to many of these issues could be found in the statement of a single welfare label at the European or international level that would simply identify products coming from recognized and certified higher welfare systems. If there are entire production systems that do not provide a life worth living for farm animals, then we might argue those systems should not be allowed to exist. If there is concern that there are measurable differences between an acceptable level of 'life worth living' (the minimum requirements for which are defined by statute) and a 'good life', then retailers/consumers – and of course producers – should be able to choose between them according to ethical commitment, to circumstance, business model, spending power, sensory preference and so on. The BVA has stated its wish to see: 'the development of a clear welfare label that consumers recognises as a mark of higher animal welfare' (BVA, 2010) while FAWC, in its 2006 report, also argued that 'the Government should press at EU level for a single, accredited, mandatory labelling system on animal welfare grounds to be agreed by stakeholders and used for all animal based products' (FAWC, 2006: 26). The European Commission too has long floated the possibility of an EU welfare label, along the lines of the current organic label (Commission of the European Communities, 2009), a possibility given impetus by a favourable feasibility study (FCEC, 2009). However, the fact that it hasn't happened yet is symptomatic of enduring issues with welfare-specific labels as identified above. Moreover, evidence, from both recent Defra-commissioned research (Brooklyndhurst, 2010) and the CIWF (QA Research, 2014), suggests two things. First, those who might choose products under such a label are likely to be those already seeking what they see as higher-quality products. The advantage of the label is that it would make their lives easier but would do little to increase their numbers. Second, buyers of such high-end-quality products (the ones that include higher-level welfare considerations) are also buying them for other reasons too and would perhaps not be prepared to give up on what they perceive as a broader sense of product quality for the specific sake of welfare. Finally, such a singular scheme would inevitably impact upon existing welfare labels and assurance schemes.

> Clearly any such EU scheme, which could avoid segmentation of the internal market as well as facilitating intra-Community trade, would need to demonstrate that it can add value both to existing private schemes and to the organic regulation without harming them. (Commission of the European Communities, 2009: 4)

Finally, and in conclusion, these debates over the visibility of animal welfare at the end point of the commercial food chain, the point of sale, all raise the question of labels and the demand-driven market they serve as a viable and additional form of both food chain and welfare governance. It is, for example, moot whether the EU ban on battery cages has done a great deal more for raising the capacity for improved welfare in egg production than labelling per se. As the graph above (Chart 4.3) shows, caged production was already falling fairly substantially in anticipation of the ban before the 2004 labelling rules were introduced. Labels, as we have argued throughout this chapter, are staged, assembled and carefully framed both in terms of content and presentation. They are designed to be persuasive rather than prohibitive, to encourage rather than to exclude. Moreover, they tell us what we want to hear. Can a production system label, for example, be credible as an indicator of individual animal welfare if it does not include parameters that assess welfare at slaughter? One of the arguments against a 'method of slaughter' label, which many concerned about the prevalence of non-stun slaughter have argued for, is that it would reveal how much meat from non-stunned products enters the conventional, rather than the specialist, food system.

In some ways, it seems a complicated route: to target consumers – to impact producers – to improve the lives of animals. As long as these animal lives are a marketable commodity, this has certain logic to it. Indeed, the competitive power of labels and brands has undeniably been a significant force in achieving market-based improvements in welfare standards in certain areas as retailers and food chain actors effectively compete to outbid each other in the quality and reach of their assurance, seemingly independently of the consumers themselves. On the other hand, consumers, certainly, of animal products need to be more aware of how those products are produced and of the connectivity the lives of consumed and consumer share. More should be done to actively challenge their reluctance to think about the workings of animal husbandry. Consumers are concerned about animal welfare, yet many do not feel responsible for it, preferring to exercise what Harper and Henson (2001) have called a 'voluntary ignorance' or to transfer those responsibilities to other actors. Indeed, a common survey finding is that consumers feel that responsibility lies predominantly with the food chain actors, including farmers and retailers and with government and the regulatory agencies. More and more though, the proliferation of market-driven schemes, culminating in labels and brands, marks a retreat from more regulatory forms of welfare governance. Yet, in this, labels, and the assurance schemes behind them, act as fetishes which, for Freidberg (2003b: 33), protect as much as reveal, shielding retailers and food companies from the glare of adverse media interest. On its own, ethical consumption is also a form of calculation that reinforces identity but arguably has little transformative power. Ethical consumption, if that is what this is, should 'be based not on ability, activity, agency and empowerment (Buller, 2010), but on a compassion that is rooted in our vulnerability and our passivity' (Wolfe, 2010: 141).

Chapter 5

Globalization and Farm Animal Welfare

This chapter and the one that follows address the geographical challenges of spreading ideas around farm animal sentience and welfare across different food production systems and cultures. We have seen in Chapters 3 and 4 how, in the UK, both the technologies and materialities of farm animal husbandry, along with wider cultural and social engagement with the welfare of farmed animals, have been differentially enrolled in the economization of animal welfare as food quality. In this and the next chapter, we consider how this process is taking place in other parts of the world. At the global level, bio-political and zoonotic concerns relating to the management of animal health are increasingly emerging as major drivers for broad concern about how animals are farmed. Yet, this focus on animal health shapes the economization of farm animal welfare less as a component of individual product quality and rather more as a component of international tradability and exchange. To explore these differential trajectories of farm animal welfare policy and practice, as well as the place of the animal welfare science in supporting both, we embark here on two specific case studies. The first of these looks at Hungary and how the Hungarian food sector and Hungarian society have responded to the need to meet European Union (EU) animal welfare rules and legislation following the country's accession to the EU in 2004. With very little consumer engagement around the welfare of farmed animals and no specific labelling scheme to help differentiate products, the economization of animal welfare at a domestic level in Hungary has proved challenging. The second case study, which follows in Chapter 6, is China, a nation that is increasingly coming to dominate the global meat industry initially as an importer but increasingly as a producer; a domination built on the rapid and large-scale intensification of livestock production. For both of these case studies, we draw upon fieldwork undertaken in Hungary in 2005 and in China in 2007 and 2008.

Animal welfare as a global imperative

Farm animal welfare has become a global phenomenon through the international trade in meat and dairy products. Demand-led consumer concerns for food coming from high welfare production systems impact progressively upon globalized food supply chains. In order to trade, producers and suppliers in exporting countries, with little domestic tradition of popular concern for farm animal welfare and little regulatory infrastructure to protect animals from suffering, can be increasingly obliged to meet the welfare standards and regulations demanded by consumers in other countries, whether these are set by corporate food chain actors, voluntary agreements or by global bodies such as the Food and Agriculture Organization (FAO) and the World Organisation for Animal Health (OIE). Many European retailers will trade only in meat produced to specifically European farm assurance standards, which has led countries like Brazil and Thailand, with a thriving export market to Europe, to show a greater interest in animal welfare standards (Bracke, 2009). Within South America and Southeast Asia, a growing number of farms and food-producing companies align themselves to meet European rather than the local production standards. In some of these regions, where a warmer climate and the lower cost of labour and of livestock housing combine to reduce production costs, EU standards can be met or even improved upon, yielding, for example, maximum stocking densities that are equal to or lower than 2011 EU Poultry Standards (Bracke, 2009). Moreover, to be even competitive in this global trade, producers need to meet and maintain healthy and productive animals that comply with the exacting quality control standards of the destination markets. Since farming practices that take into account high animal welfare standards guarantee greater productivity, better quality, more food safety and added value for farmers (FAO and Slow Food, 2012), welfare, it is claimed, emerges as a potential 'win-win opportunity by animals, farmers and consumers' in an increasingly global marketplace (FAO and Slow Food, 2012). In this manner, farm animals and their welfare become enrolled, on the one hand, within broader economic and political forces (Wolch and Emel, 1998; Johnson 2015) as a growing part of national and international public policy, commerce and trade (Bowles et al., 2005; Fraser, 2014) and, on the other hand, within an increasingly international animal welfare science as a framework for improving on-farm practices (Thiermann and Babcock, 2005; Fraser, 2008b). Significantly this geographic spread of welfare standards emerging predominantly out of Western Europe is taking place despite huge cultural variations across the globe in the sensitivity expressed towards different farmed species and in their acknowledgement as sentient beings.

At the global scale, diverse cultures perform different practices with, and give different meanings to, animals raised for food production. Even within the UK, the coexistence of different animal slaughter methods under distinctive religious observances with more mainstream slaughter regulations points to significant diversities and practices with respect to animals. Internationally, geographical, cultural and religious variations exist in the edibility of certain stock animals (most notably, cattle and pigs but also dogs and many wild-caught species). Poultry are legally recognized as sentient in Europe, but not in the United States. In Asia, shift in diet towards milk-based products is leading to the growth of highly intensive dairy cattle farming in areas long understood as unsuitable for dairy production because of the absence of pasture. In Hungary, a traditional breed of pig, the Magalitza (or woolly pig) is proudly and extensively reared, in contrast to more commercial and intensively reared pig breeds. These examples demonstrate how economic, cultural and social processes operate dynamically across the globe in response to the geographic spread and circulation of animal bodies and species-specific knowledges within local human communities. The comprehensive framing of a food animal species as a subject to care for, whose well-being or welfare is to be ensured, is thereby fraught with difficulty.

Yet, while there may be major differences in cultural relations to various animal species and husbandry practices, the development of an evidence-based animal welfare science is arguably a mode of knowledge production that can counter such culturally specific knowledges and practices to address more generic species-specific needs across geographical and cultural divides. This, for example, lay behind the European Commission's funding of the Welfare Quality® research project and its associated sub-projects. The goal of the project was to support the establishment of international science–based farm animal welfare measures and standards (Blokhuis et al., 2013) and to encourage the dissemination of animal welfare scientific knowledge to parts of the world both that supply European food markets and those that do not.

However, the task of developing a science around farm animal welfare is not driven solely by concern for the experience of the sentient animal. Its treatment and handling also shape the quality and health status of the food produced. In recent years, concerns over the health of farm animals have taken on a new urgency with the growth of zoonotic animal diseases and the threat of human antibiotic resistance caused, at least in part, by the overuse of antibiotic medicines in animal farming (O'Neill, 2016). That the same critically important antibiotics, such as Colistin, can be used in both animal and human treatment is seen as a major issue. Evidence of growing resistance to Colistin by *Staphylococcus* bacteria widely found within the farm animal industry has led to the banning of its use in Chinese animal husbandry as part of a global drive to limit its usage in farm animal populations. The international energy currently being invested in making improvements to farm animal health and welfare across the globe is a key strategy in seeking to reduce the dependence of the livestock industry on antibiotics. However, the successful adoption of policy responses either at the national regulatory level or within the mechanisms of international food supply chain governance, often, depends, at least in part, upon the engagement and sometimes mobilization of consumers and citizens. In demonstrating their support for actions to protect and enhance farm animal welfare, consumers and citizens represent a potential market, one which may well offset the costs of higher welfare production standards. This, as we have seen above, has been very much the European model of creating a market for higher animal welfare food products, in other words the economization of animal welfare as a food quality. It has developed within the context of public food scares, ethical consumerism, anxiety over the quality of food from certain production methods and clear alternatives being indicated through the work of trusted NGO sources. In other words, there is a model for achieving improvements in animal welfare through liberal trade-related economic strategies operating within a framework of responsive democratic government.

The role of the EU has in many ways been exemplary in this regard. EU animal welfare legislation, which dates from 1974, focuses predominantly (but not exclusively) on animals that are of direct relevance to trade between EU Member States or between the EU and third countries. The European Commission's website makes the following statement:

> In today's globalised food marketplace, European farmers and food producers face competition from many countries, some of which have lower animal welfare standards than those applied in the EU. This places EU farmers and producers at a commercial disadvantage, because they must invest more money in their businesses to meet the EU's stricter rules. (EU Commission website, 2016)

Unlike for domestic, wild or zoological animals, concern to create a level playing field for European interests in the globalized food marketplace lies at the centre of EU policy to improve, establish and meet farm animal welfare standards. Critical to this legislative commitment is the assumption that European food consumers, who are generally considered to be culturally engaged in the welfare of farm animals and supportive of policy interventions in the field, constitute a premium priced market for higher welfare. In reality, of course, there are major variations within the individual Member States of an enlarging EU in the specific sociocultural and economic mechanisms currently in place for supporting and selling products from higher animal welfare systems (Roe and Higgin, 2008; Food Chain Evaluation Consortium, 2009; Heerwagen et al., 2015).

This introductory discussion has begun to outline the global context in which the internationalization of farm animal welfare is taking place. Animal welfare is a politically significant topic at an international level, not only through the activities of campaigners and NGOs, but as a direct consequence of the international movement of meat and livestock and through internationally agreed global animal health pacts. In the development of standards for farm animal welfare, in the agreements that are reached, in the generation of knowledge that informs these debates and in the animal lives that pass through each, there is a politics too.

Hence, our aim in this and the following chapter is to reveal and articulate knowledges associated with farm animal welfare through the two case studies and through the analysis of specific encounters between humans, animals and food in the field. In many parts of the world, farm animal welfare is not a component of food quality for either consumers or food chain actors. Our interest here though is in exploring how the uptake and meanings associated with animal welfare are being shaped in specific places and specific cultures to provide a foundation from which consumer-driven market activity could emerge. There are questions here about how animal welfare knowledge travels across space. In approaching these empirically based chapters, we ask: Who are the spokesperson for animals? What do we know of the international geography of different representations of animal welfare? How are knowledges of animal welfare formed so they travel universally, or how and why are certain stories about animal welfare told in particular places, and not others? How is expertise and trust built around animal welfare in the local, national and global community? Whose or what knowledges are discounted/ignored in the roll-out of animal welfare through global trade/health bodies, international NGOs and the demands of concerned citizens?

Making morally and technically informed citizens: Animal welfare as knowledge controversy

Andrew Barry (2001) has developed the concept of a 'society of communication' to explain the reliance liberal governments place on making morally and technically informed citizens as vehicles for bringing about changes in society. Indeed we can see that the informed consumer citizen has been an important component for assembling a market that can drive improvements in farm animal welfare in Europe (as discussed in chapter 4). However, it is probably fair to say that European citizens are not as well versed as they might be in scientific and technical understanding of how the various farm animal species should be cared for at different stages of their life. Instead, public understanding of how to provide the best care for farm animals has tended towards largely anthropomorphic assumptions, such as that having more space is the route to a better life. Animal welfare science, by contrast, argues that to meet the welfare needs of selectively bred commercial food animals requires attention to a far more complicated set of species-specific biological needs that extend well beyond mere space allocations and include levels of stockperson attention.

As was discussed in Chapter 4, the question of who is responsible for ensuring improved animal welfare swings between the consumer and the food industry. Discussions about a mandatory animal welfare labelling system for European foodstuffs, and what information this should contain, directly connect with the debates about better informing European consumers about the standards currently in operation and passing responsibility therefore on to them. Barry's concept of a 'society of communication' is helpful to understand the significance of different communication channels around farm animal welfare. It is particularly valuable in the light of attempts to improve farm animal welfare in countries where it has historically been, or remains, more challenging for a 'society of communication' to be established due to a legacy of a less liberal politics. There is then, we maintain, a specific role for animal welfare science to play in the internationalization of animal welfare concern – as a mechanism for disseminating new scientific knowledges around the experiences of animals, and as an empirical tool for understanding and evaluating the implications for changes in farm animal management techniques. Again returning to Barry:

> The deployment of technology is often seen as a way of avoiding the noise and irrationality of political conflict. In those international political arenas in which consensus may be difficult to reach, it is thought that science and technology have a large role to play. (Barry, 2001: 7–8)

Yet we must be cautious here. It is increasingly evident that science and technology do not always lead to a consensus, the obvious example being the ongoing and increasingly vigorous debate over anthropogenic climate change (Demeritt, 2006; Hulme, 2008). The notion of animal sentience (that animals have feelings that matter to them and that they deserve legal protection to ensure their needs are met) is far from being universally accepted across the world, despite its scientifically supported legal establishment across the EU since 1997. In short, animal welfare is also, to use Barry's phrase, a 'transnational knowledge controversy' (2012). We might accept the scientific evidence for the demonstrable sentience of an increasing number of animal species, and this is surely shaping applied animal welfare science's understanding of ways to improve the living conditions of domesticated farmed species. However, there are often entirely understandable difficulties in applying the findings of these scientific studies, not only in Europe and America but elsewhere across the globe, due to the considerable challenges associated with embedding them within the local social, cultural and economic realities of food production. Even within the UK, the history of farm animal welfare over the last fifty years demonstrates a long-standing tension between those who believed industrial farming was simply incompatible with the well-being of animals and those others who argued that the productivity of the animals in these systems was in itself evidence of their good health and welfare (Kirk, 2014).

> This was a highly instrumental form of animal ethics; the provision of adequate environments was driven as much by the desire to maximise animal productivity as to preserve animal well-being, so much so that the (Brambell, 1965) committee entertained the idea of breeding animals better suited to economically designed environments as opposed to altering industrialised farms to suit the needs of existing animals. (Kirk, 2014: 255)

This tension is revealing and still relevant when considering the current spread of farm animal welfare concerns internationally and the harmonization of scientifically established animal welfare standards across different cultures. Today, knowledge controversies over what and which science to trust are soon scaled up to the international scale. Countries that want to rapidly increase output from livestock farming are often keen to use the latest technologies to drive forward efficiencies and higher productivity. Unfortunately, in their effort to 'catch up', many are turning to second-hand technologies that are no longer used in states where animal welfare concerns are higher up in the political and social agenda. A clear example of this has been various forms of animal confinement (such as sow stalls and egg-laying hen battery cages) that are now banned in the EU but are still being manufactured and sold (in some cases by EU manufacturers) to other countries. This history partly accounts for the interventions that international animal welfare NGOs are now making in non-European parts of the world where a process of animal production intensification, similar to that experienced by the UK from the mid-twentieth century onwards, is taking place.

In what follows, we discuss the development of an agenda to improve the lives of animals living in industrialized farm production systems outside of Europe. These are stories of technology transfer, idea transfer, of working with culturally and geographically specific food animal production practices and retail activities: stories of husbandry practices seen as acceptable and unacceptable from the perspective of Western-homed international NGOs. We return again and again to the importance of retail activities in raising minimum welfare standards for farm animals and particularly to the role that the European retail sector has (admittedly more so in some countries than others) in driving awareness and change through the technologies of product labelling and trading standards. The retail market's role is twofold, we maintain: disseminating information and driving real changes in on-farm management to improve welfare. Yet as we demonstrate, this is not universally suitable as an effective model for rolling out animal welfare improvements internationally.

Emerging countries: Case study Hungary

Hungary joined the EU on 1 May 2004. The juridical and trading rules that were consequent on that joining forced adaptations and changes in Hungarian animal health and welfare policy in advance of any engaged civil/consumer society being established. Consumer culture in Hungary at the time of accession was dominated by food price concerns and anxieties over the safety of imported food products. Even today, Hungarian wages remain relatively low within the EU, with Hungarians spending on average a third of their salary on food (Balasz, 2015) while subsistence agriculture continues to occupy around a third of the nation's population. Progress on farm animal welfare is driven by membership of the EU and the need to meet EU standards. In this regard, Hungary presents a rather different example of the alternative pathways and processes, beyond the core Western States, through which farm animal welfare and the science that supports it become enrolled as a societal and economic consideration in food production. It took much of Europe half a century to establish farm animal protection laws, yet, as Von Keyserlingk and Hotzel (2015) have argued, emerging countries do not have the same timescale to make changes to their farm animal production systems. We draw here upon fieldwork carried out in 2005 in Hungary to explore the establishment of farm animal welfare as a popular concern and as a political-technical achievement within livestock farming in a newly established EU Member State. The fieldwork consisted of interviews with key informants within Hungary – government officials, animal welfare NGOs, producer organizations, farmers and retailers. Some of the interviews were carried out in English, whereas for others a translator was used. The findings have previously been published as a report in 2007 (Roe et al., 2007).

Hungary has had to overcome challenges associated with land ownership, the structure of the retail sector, the infrastructure around food safety standard inspections and the availability of consumer information about animal welfare as a popular concern. These factors act as a barrier to developing a sector of the food retail market that can drive forward improvements in farming practice and address the needs of sentient animals by developing a culture of concern around farm animal welfare. However, Hungary does have the full support of a trade relationship with other EU countries that seek to buy food products meeting EU animal welfare trading standards.

Hungary has faced major challenges in meeting farm regulatory standards to address animal welfare concerns because of the speed of change required. As a new member of the EU, the country is under particular pressure to bring about changes despite, as the empirical material that follows demonstrates, an absence of substantial local culture and knowledge around farm animal welfare. Animal welfare NGOs and the Hungarian government in 2005 were interested in supporting the development of a 'society of communication' around animal welfare to develop both scientific and technical understanding of the issue among the population. Their intent was to replace traditional approaches to animal husbandry as mere shorthand for welfare with a more informed understanding and to promote the topic in general as an area for public debate. For example, a comment from Hungary's Advisory body on Animal Welfare[1] underlines the fact that the public's concern laid largely elsewhere:

> Stray dogs or the torture of dogs. If [the public] say something on farm animals, that is just in the interest of farmers and slaughterhouses. (Interview with Hungarian Advisory Board on Animal Welfare, 2005)

From what could be understood there was little attention to farm animal welfare in the media. Nevertheless, the Ministry of Agriculture did comment upon how caged poultry disturbed people and general animal cruelty was often reported in the press.

The only organization focusing directly on animal welfare was the Fauna Society, which received significant funding from the international nongovernmental body Compassion in World Farming (CIWF). Like many NGOs in Hungary, the Fauna Society was formally established in 1989, just after the transition, but, at the time of writing, was still little known in Hungary. Nevertheless, although animal welfare concerns were not widespread in Hungary, the Society acknowledged

---

[1]The advisory body has members from the Ministry of Agriculture and a representative of the ministers of environment, economics, education; scientific members; university representatives; medical representatives; breeders of laboratory animals; drug company representatives and NGOs.

that when the issue of farm animal welfare is raised with people, it is met with a lot of interest:

> I think the main thing is we are on a stand to talk to the public and meet the people. Our experience is that if someone is interested in animal welfare and all of the topics we deal with, the next question is 'what can I do', 'what can I buy?'. (Interview with Hungary-based Fauna Society, 2005)

The low level of general awareness, combined with weak media attention and scrutiny, meant that consumers could be easily misled about the welfare conditions of the products they were buying:

> We will make a report of that to the consumer agency, as on the picture [on a package of eggs] you can see free range hens, happy hens, but this is from battery cage system, so this is misleading for the customer. They think that this egg comes from a happy hen. (Fauna Society, 2005)

Farm animal welfare is a concept that needs establishing within the country and the national context has implications upon how this process takes place; what meanings of farm animal welfare are disseminated and how might a market that economizes farm animal welfare become established? These initial examples illustrate there is a need to develop a concern for farm animals as well as replace product advertising that misrepresents production systems. The discussion moves now to the complex issue of Hungarian tradition and Hungarian food provenance and how that can impede the uptake of interest in farm animal welfare by consumer/citizens, producers and retail brands.

Hungarian tradition and provenance

An important feature of the Hungarian food market, brought to our attention by a local consumer organization, was the degree of concern for the provenance of food, in short a strongly pro-Hungarian attitude towards food acquisition. This sentiment was accompanied by the very positive image of locally produced equated to safe, good quality food.

> Q: Do people think that when it is from Hungary it is okay?
>
> A: Yes, because we have a big tradition with food. Our first food law is more than a 100 years old. Hungary was always exporting. During the Communist period we exported a lot of food, and at that point it was very important to be trustworthy.

Q: Labels – So people will recognise it and know it … So you can see that it is really Hungarian?

A: We have in the shops a lot of imported chicken and there was a problem with this chicken so the association decided to have this label put on the Hungarian product. (Interview with Hungary's National Association for Consumer Protection, 2005)

The most common food labels on fresh meat products were those that stated the product was made in Hungary (see Figures 5.1 and 5.2). These labels appeared widely recognized and are used to support the market for Hungarian food products, which, as described by a representative of Hungary's National Association for Consumer Protection, are particularly sought after by the Hungarian public.

The key element of the public concern is to consume Hungarian product, not a free range egg, but a Hungarian egg. I would say 10 out of 10 persons would prefer to buy a Hungarian product. If you would ask whether organic food would be bought by the consumer, I would say 1/10 of the 10 would. This is the rate and the proportion. It is an approximation not exact. (National Association for Consumer Protection, 2005)

From our study it was nevertheless evident that, in 2005, Hungarian consumers had few shops available to them where distinctively animal-friendly products or organic-certified food products (often read as a proxy) were available. For

Figure 5.1 Hungarian poultry product with the 'Hungarian Quality Product' logo (middle left) and 'Made in Hungary' logo (middle right). Photograph: Roe

Figure 5.2 A second Hungarian poultry product by Gallicoop with 'Made in Hungary' labelling. Photograph: Roe

many consumers, it would appear that animal welfare was considered simply synonymous with Hungarian provenance. However, as we go on to discuss here, the challenge has been to develop an appreciation of animal welfare science that not only offers a critical perspective on existing traditional farming techniques but also offers the means to integrate higher welfare practices into the rapidly growing intensive livestock sector.

At the opposite end of the supply chain, Hungarian farmers were asked during the research where they felt good farm animal welfare existed in Hungary. Several among our interviewees drew attention to the traditional Hungarian breeds of the Mangalica pig and the Hungarian Grey cattle. These animals are considered to have a very high level of animal welfare as they are produced extensively with lots of room allowing for what is seen as being their 'natural behaviour'. Their specific needs, in terms of feed, grassland access, space and manual care, are all thought of as being met within traditional production systems.

> Mangalica is a semi-wild breed. It is not as domesticated as regular pigs. It just cannot tolerate to live close together, then they will fight. So because of this breed, we already have to offer conditions above EU regulations. (Interview: Farm no. 4)

The market niche for Mangalica pigs within Hungary is however very small. Their meat is expensive and is mainly exported.

> The Hungarian society is not yet rich enough for Mangalica meat. Mangalica is very expensive and not many Hungarians buy this. There is only a very narrow segment of the market that can afford it. But it is not too difficult to sell Mangalica since only few farms produce it. (...) You cannot buy it from a butcher. You can only eat it in the best, specialised restaurants. (Interview, Farm no. 4)

Nevertheless, despite its rarity and price, the Mangalica pig has significant cultural value in the Hungarian imaginary and, more importantly here, is considered as epitomizing good welfare. An extensive, 'free-range' conception of what constitutes good animal welfare is central to the associations that were made between good welfare and Mangalica pig production. As is so often the case in so many countries, the public imagination of good welfare can be largely at odds with the realities of managing good welfare within more intensive, industrial farming systems. This is a common challenge everywhere. More important is how to support ideas that good animal welfare can also be achievable within intensive, industrialized farming systems.

Of course, we can assume that today many farms in Hungary are practising good animal welfare and are effectively using novel technologies or breeds of animals in an intensive fashion. Contemporary claims of acceptable welfare standards should not be simply dismissed. During the course of our research, several farmers and informants made the explicit connection between good animal welfare and good Hungarian stockmanship:

> In Hungary the farmers traditionally love their animals; that is very, very traditional Hungarian. Hungarian farmers try to protect their animals, to love

them. So when we go to the farms, you will see that most people love their animals; there is a very strong connection between animals and people. But it is not in a quality assurance scheme, not formal. It is tradition. (Interview: Livestock and Meat Product Board)

Although such strong belief in an implicit and inherent welfarism that remains embedded in traditional practices and sensibilities may act as a barrier to the acceptance of a more critical animal welfare science, there was a lot of apparent cultural pride around good stockmanship and positive relations with farm animals in Hungary, as the above statement confirms. The place of animal welfare science as a voice of expertise to help manage expectations and realities about farm animal welfare is absent in these discussions. The Hungarian fieldwork reveals that gut feelings and personal reactions about what makes farm animals happy and live healthily come across as the norm. However, this may simply be because there has been little cultural messaging about alternative ideas associated with farm animal welfare, the very concept of which remains largely defined in terms of animal health and productivity.

Tackling an animal health approach to welfare within an industrializing livestock sector

At the time of the study, the approach to farm animal welfare in Hungary was firmly based in tackling animal health issues as a route to guaranteeing good welfare. This came through clearly in the language used by farmers, farm organizations, government officials and consumers who when asked to define farm animal welfare nearly always turned, on the one hand, to descriptions of animal health as a measure for the animal's productivity and, on the other hand, to issues of food quality and safety.

> Yes of course animal welfare is important. The farmer has the same interest as the animal. His interest is to make the animals feel comfortable, feel fine. Because – if the animal does not feel fine, the farmer will go bankrupt. Because – without good animal welfare, you cannot have good production. (Interview: Farmer number 4)

Another farmer links responsible farming practice to the perceived link between animal health and food safety.

> Animal health gets the most attention on the farm because it is the only way to produce safe food. It is directly connected to food safety. (Farmer number 6)

Yet, within contemporary animal welfare science, using simple animal productivity as a measure for animal health and welfare is considered both outdated and misleading for it pays little or no attention to the subjective life of the sentient animal, its needs or its feelings. Neither is it accepted as the basis for animal welfare improvements – where improved productivity might be simplistically associated with improved welfare. In Hungary, it would appear, work has been needed to technically and scientifically engage both consumers/citizens and the farming community in less productivist and more animal-centred notions of welfare. Moreover, it is clear that concerns around animal productivity are not an effective way of engaging consumer/citizens in the issue of animal welfare for they tend to privilege the commercial motives of a farmer, rather than the consumer/citizen's ethical responsibilities towards a sentient creature they eat. Nor, for the same reason, do they support the development of a market to support improvements in farm animal welfare.

During the Soviet era, Hungarian farming was largely structured into State and collective farms. By 2005, many of these were either managed by cooperatives or privately owned. Yet, a characteristic feature of Hungarian agriculture over the last decade has been the predominance of traditional, small-scale farming. A further concern, expressed by the Ministry of Agriculture, is the adaptability of such a sector to the global food supply market and the various standards that are increasingly required to operate within it.

> I think that the problem now is that we have too many farms. The small farms and companies, the animals on these farms are healthy but it is not economic. The farmers are on the streets in Budapest [protesting] because they cannot live off them. When you buy chickens from the village where your mother lived, …
> I know that there are not too many chickens on these farms, and they can manage to keep them healthy. (Interview: Representative of the Hungarian Ministry of Agriculture, 2005)

This comment illustrates the anxiety many felt in Hungary at the time over the need to manage the health and welfare of livestock on large-scale farmers, and yet also the need for structural changes to improve farm incomes. The structure of Hungarian farming was going through a process of substantive change in 2005, as the number of small farms diminished (Landbourwraad, 2005) and the larger farms increased, many as a consequence of foreign investment in the various livestock sectors.

From on-farm production standards (including organic standards) to the rules governing the slaughtering of animals for human consumption, EU regulations on animal welfare have had to be adopted and implemented with the accession of Hungary to the EU. Yet, although the formal legislation was in place, the full implementation of the new regulations appeared only patchily in 2005. For example, while EU approval was now required for all Hungarian meat processing plants that exported to elsewhere in the EU market, responsibility for the approval and inspection of those processing meat exclusively for the domestic market lay wholly under domestic quality and food safety control. The internal Hungarian market for cattle/beef products is not very large. Far larger is the export market for Hungarian beef to markets such as Italy. Consequently, many animals (particularly calves and beef cattle) were being transported live over long distances from Hungary to Italy. In contrast, the pig production market is very important to the domestic Hungarian market and the industry comprises both large and small production units. It seems that some animal production sectors will be able to move more quickly to address farm animal welfare legislation because of the importance of export sales, whereas those more reliant upon the domestic market may lag behind.

At the time of accession to the EU, Hungary had only a fragmented animal slaughter industry, essentially providing the domestic retail market, much of which – it has been suggested – fell below EU standards at the time. By way of contrast, the much larger export-oriented slaughterhouses and meat processing facilities were already beginning to introduce changes to meet European animal welfare standards. The consolidation and rationalization of the country's slaughterhouse capacity, much of which is now owned by multinational meat processing companies, has led to a notable drive to increase standards.

Developing a Hungarian market for higher welfare food products

In 2005, it was evident from fieldwork that concern for farm animal welfare was not a major driver of consumer food choice. One of the main reasons was the lack of a sizeable enough affluent Hungarian society.

> It is a social problem, the situation here. It is a problem of the society, the structure. Many people are poor and very price oriented. So, there is attention for animal welfare, but the consumer does not have enough money to buy it. (Interview with Livestock and Meat Product Board, 2005)

Observation revealed the limited presence of organic food products for sale in supermarkets and, at the time, there was only one dedicated organic store in the country, though this was oriented more towards healthy human lifestyles than animal welfare. One retailer did comment that some consumers asked for organic meat: 'They say to the butcher why is [organic product] not here?' (Interview with Provera/Cora, 2005).

Hungarian consumers were more concerned about the availability of food and at a price that was affordable, followed by anxieties over the safety of the food to eat. There was distrust of certain imported foods into Hungary following recent food scandals over pesticide residues found in paprika imported from Morocco. Consequently, consumers tended to seek out country of origin labelling where it could be found (see earlier discussion of Hungarian origin labelling). As new members of the EU, Hungarian consumers, according to the National Association for Consumer Protection, had some apprehensions about foreign-produced food appearing on their supermarket shelves. Yet, despite the dominance of these different concerns among consumers, there was evidence that the profile of improving farm animal welfare was on the rise. For example, one consumer magazine featured a major article on caged egg production, a topic of some relevance at the time as the EU ban on battery cages and the enforced move towards enriched cages, barn or free-range production systems was due to be implemented in Hungary in 2012, prompting a new degree of public awareness and debate (Figure 5.3).

Here, EU legislation has driven an emergent consumer information strategy. Another mechanism for engaging consumers is through the bundling of higher welfare considerations into broader product quality indicators. However, there were few identifiable food labels in Hungary that made specific claims that could guarantee higher animal welfare standards were being met. There was however one exception to this, the Hungarian *Mastergood* range of poultry products.

In 2005, *Mastergood* poultry products were available in a number of food retailers. *Mastergood* products combined animal welfare claims along with other 'quality' indicators, most notably as tradition and provenance. The *Mastergood*

Figure 5.3 Box of ten free-range eggs, found in supermarket, Budapest, 2005. Photograph: Roe

scheme mimicked the French *Label Rouge* and stood out as the only quality assurance scheme identifiable to the consumer. Although regional food quality assurance schemes could become a model within Hungary, the lack of a strong regional governance structure within the country was seen as a major barrier. At the time, food prices were rising, making it harder to create premium brands with higher prices. Where specialist premium meat products did exist they tended to be organic and were found only in specialist meat shops and not in the fresh meat sector in the Hungarian retail stores.

The pro-Hungarian attitude to food exhibited by the typical Hungarian food shopper indicates a loyalty and belief in the quality of Hungarian produced food over and above imported products. A challenge then is to engage Hungarian producers to diversify their production systems to enable citizens to make choices. However, this is not the principal barrier for as long as Hungarian wage packets remain low there may simply be insufficient numbers of Hungarian consumers who could support a diversifying food quality market. A new report by Balasz (2015) indicates that Hungarian incomes have remained low, with a third of household incomes still being spent on food (against an estimated 11 per cent in the UK in 2015, Office of National Statistics, 2017). In recent years, there has also been a fall in the amount of pork consumed in Hungary and there is still little sign of a consumer-driven market for quality food developing that might bundle in higher animal welfare. However, because of EU membership and being bound by EU regulation, farmers are receiving subsidies to support production systems that encourage higher levels of farm animal welfare in the cattle, pig and poultry sectors. In the case of Hungary, it appears that the model for improving farm animal welfare that has dominated Western European states – increasing the visibility and market for higher welfare food products – has not yet become economically viable or socially acceptable. Instead, it is the combined deployment of regulation and subsidies to support costly improvements in farm animal production to meet EU standards that has had most impact on the meat and dairy sector in Hungary.

In conclusion, this historical review of how Hungary was starting to orientate itself to farm animal welfare in 2005 identifies a greater emphasis on the economic and macro-political environment to support progress, rather than civil society's ability to engage ethical consumers with the topic of farm animal welfare. Hungary by becoming an EU member has little national influence in promoting their nation's position on farm animal welfare. Instead, the country must work with the dominant paradigm of approaches to farm animal welfare that is well established in Western Europe. This means accepting the regulations that have been imposed based on animal welfare science developed outside of Hungary. There is little scope for dissent or knowledge controversy between Hungary and the other long-standing EU members over the scientific basis for animal welfare. Equally, Barry's 'society of communication', raising the profile of farm animal welfare through the activities of animal welfare NGOs, at times working to promote certain food brands/products that meet more stringent animal welfare standards, has had less success in Hungary due principally to the structure of the Hungarian economy. Hungarian consumer/citizens have concerns about the price of food and there is not the collective buying power of a more affluent sector of Hungarian society to stimulate a market for quality food products (including animal welfare as a component) or create economically viable segmentation between products with higher standards and those without. Ultimately, farm animal welfare remains interpreted in terms of animal health and productivity while standards are met in order to trade with parts of the world which demand animal welfare standards. What is almost completely absent is any competitive market for improving farm animal welfare as a product quality within a quality-tiered food market.

Chapter 6

Emerging Welfare Concerns in China

In this chapter, we continue our analysis of farm animal welfare beyond the UK. We build on the theme of the previous chapter, that closed with a discussion of how farm animal welfare is becoming established as a food industry concern in Hungary, to develop a chapter-length analysis of how international animal welfare NGOs have worked to introduce and develop understanding of the concept of farm animal welfare in China. We begin, however, with an overview of livestock production in China.

China is a country that has experienced a very rapid increase in livestock production over the last two decades as the agricultural sector has moved towards increasing the number of animals produced in intensive, industrial-scale livestock production and reducing the number of peasant livestock farming practices (Li, 2009; Neo and Chen, 2009). China is now the largest consumer (Larsen, 2012) and the largest producer of meat in the world, pork being the most favoured meat product (Neo and Chen, 2009). To meet this demand, the country produces half of the world's pigs (United States Department for Agriculture in Larsen, 2012). In the middle of the second decade of the twenty-first century, global anxiety over anti-microbial resistance and the heavy reliance of the industrial-scale, intensive livestock production systems on antibiotics in China is a cause of great concern. Over the last three decades, there has been a dramatic uptake of the Western industrialized livestock farming models and associated technology in China. This has achieved rapid increases in agricultural productivity in stark contrast to traditional low-intensive Chinese farming methods (which characteristically would involve as little as two or three pigs per farm). Indeed since adopting a Western farming model and practices, livestock production in China has become the fastest growth sector in Chinese agriculture (Li, 2009).

In 1990, China produced 30.42 million tons of meat, doubling that of 1980. Fifteen years later, China's meat output reached a record high of 78 million tons representing 29.26% of the world's total. Per capita meat consumption in

China hit 63kg. Although peasant household-based production continues to dominate pig farming in sheet numbers, for example, factory farms contributed a higher and disproportionate share (27% in 2005) to the total pork output. Shortage of meat supply is history. (Li, 2009: 236)

The dramatic shifts in Chinese farming methods have not gone unnoticed by foreign animal welfare organizations. The export of Western farming models and technology to China has raised the concerns of Western animal welfare NGOs who see in this the prospect of deteriorating welfare conditions as traditional approaches give way to intensive production methods leading to a dramatic rise in the number of animals being produced. These organizations might, however, be heartened by the argument that:

[A] review of China's three main thought systems suggests that the country is not culturally inclined to animal cruelty. Daoism stands for the ideas of species equality. Confucianism advocates moderation and restraint, though it does propagate an anthropocentric world outlook. Buddhism condemns killing and calls for mercy towards animals. The many reported cases of animal cruelty in contemporary China run counter to Chinese cultural tradition. The nature of modern-day politics, especially government and corporate behaviour, motivated by the need for economic growth, may better explain many of the conflicts between people and other animals. (Li and Davey, 2013: 44)

Through a discussion of interview extracts with Western NGO personnel working in China and through ethnographic observations from spending time with them while carrying out their work in China, this chapter considers how the international dissemination of animal welfare science and technology, by Western animal welfare NGOs, is being received in China. The fieldwork and ethnography was carried out between 2007 and 2008. The various knowledges and understandings of farm animal welfare, among NGOs and scientists alike, have followed the growth of intensive agricultural production techniques to China to feed its rapidly expanding population. However, our attention here is not on the public-facing campaigning work of NGOs, which admittedly has not been very extensive in China. Rather, we look more specifically at how these bodies are working closely with livestock producers and meat processing companies to disseminate welfare knowledge and to lobby for the take-up of novel standards of livestock production that adhere to recognized welfare standards imported from the West. By following the NGO actors in their work, a multi-sited ethnography was undertaken as a means of sharing and participating in the pioneering encounters of international NGOs (INGOs) and their employees on a journey that included visits to farming communities in Inner Mongolia and livestock farms on the outskirts of Beijing as well as a conference in the heart of Beijing. In this sense the work obliquely connects to existing work by Hann (2007) on (post)-socialist Chinese everyday cultures, but the study focuses more on key stakeholders in the food industry, rather than common everyday food practices.

Methodologically, it is unusual for a multi-sited ethnographic approach to be used to study development-focused international NGOs (although this is encouraged by Bebbington and Kohari, 2006), and even more unusual in the field of animal welfare work (as opposed to human welfare work). Cultural geography's post-structural concerns with the body, practice and non-human agency are central to the ethnographic narrative of how new meanings and practices around farm animals are being exchanged; these are approaches that have been discussed elsewhere in the book (see Chapters 1 and 3).

Previously in this book we have described how animal welfare is assembled in relation to the commodification of farm animal bodies becoming food (Chapter 4), and understandings of animal welfare have also been modified alongside changes in scientific and public engagement with the topic (Chapter 2). Throughout this chapter the narrative weaves in and out of ethnographic description of the multicultural and multi-natural encounters in Inner Mongolia as we accompany agriculturalists, an animal welfare scientist, an NGO representative and a translator, all working for a Western NGO who were, at the time, beginning a conversation on animal welfare with Chinese farmers and meat processors. The following extract is from Roe's research notes.

> We pulled-up at a collection of single rise buildings with pens holding white goats, white sheep, and stylish black curly coated goats – this was a farm. There another group of Chinese men greeted us in suits, and standing silently around at a distance were two or three people who looked like they looked after the animals, whose faces we couldn't see, whose eye I could never catch, whose gender was sometimes hard to make out so swaddled were they in cloths and puffer jackets and woollens to protect their bodies from the cold and the dust (see Figures 6.1 and 6.2). In contrast, the sheep and the lambs, the goats and their kids look positively friendly, obviously relaxed with humans, at ease with the climate, and were as welcoming as any sheep or goat, on any UK city farm I've visited.

Figure 6.1 Inner Mongolian sheep and goat farmer. Photograph: Roe

Figure 6.2 Inner Mongolian sheep and goat farmer. Photograph: Roe

Where were we? I think we were at a showcase cashmere goat and sheep farm. I say think because it became evident as the six of us guests, that includes – the British farmer, the Canadian expert in knowledge transfer partnerships (KTP) between the West and China in livestock farming, the animal welfare scientist, the NGO lobbyist and myself, the social scientist with a research funding grant to study post-Mao natures through studying the work of western NGOs on farm animal welfare, started to realize that Peng – the translator – was struggling to understand the inner Mongolians, or he, after three days of conferencing and translating, was also struggling to speak to us in English.

This was an important trip for Peng the first time he has returned to Inner Mongolia in thirty years, where he lived for the first few years of his life. His Beijinger parents, who were considered as Intellectual Youth, were sent there to work the fields as part of Mao's anti-bourgeoisie scheme. Whatever, something wasn't working. We weren't getting much information from him, normally our tireless intermediary. Perhaps this was because we were standing on a vast cold, dusty and windy plain, which took the words out of your mouth and didn't effectively put them into someone else's ears. Being there felt like a struggle. Although apparently communication problems had been becoming evident in the men's car. Our Chinese host was a short, smiley, Han Chinese-looking fellow, rather than the tall Genghis Khan like Mongolians (later in the trip our tall British farmer was asked if he would hug a tall Mongolian lady because she rarely gets to hug and hold men her size). Size-aside, our Chinese host had a great laugh. He would just laugh and smile and slap the backs of the Western men. And it was this warmth and liveliness that our Canadian expert in knowledge-transfer partnerships in China also did with great ease and charm. The eyes of the Canadian and the Chinese man both sparkled effortlessly. What are we doing here? We were here to promote farm animal welfare. However animal welfare as a term, a conjunction of two words – animal- and -welfare – are novel in the Chinese language. (Extract from author's ethnographic research notes, 2008)

As You et al. (2014: 1) write: 'In China, animal well-being concerns can be traced back to ancient times in some literatures, such as "kindness to humans and other creatures" and "loving human and every creature", which have become prevalent quotations among Chinese people for generations.' And yet, a survey by You et al. (2014) of 5,983 respondents revealed that only 2,187 (36.6 per cent) had ever heard of 'animal welfare'. It is hard to say whether the use of the term 'animal welfare' equates with ideas established in the West about treating animals with kindness, when human practices shape their existence as they become pets, food animals or laboratory animals.

Table 6.1 Key statistics on Chinese attitudes to animals

Pigs and domestic fowls are only beast, and people can treat them as they wish.	72.9%
Humans should improve the rearing conditions for pigs and domestic folks to ensure the quality and safety of animal products.	19.2%
Pigs and domestic fowls should enjoy happy life and be free from troubles as humans do.	7.9%

Source: You et al. (2014: 4).

Table 6.1 presents Chinese peoples' feelings about farm animals from the research findings of You et al.'s (2014) study of the attitudes of Chinese people to farm animals. It has to be said that overall these figures indicate a relative lack of engagement with farm animal welfare as a major concern. Equally interestingly, only one in five of those interviewed makes any connection between the quality of animal products they eat and the conditions in which the animals are reared.

Comparative questionnaires in other parts of the world (e.g. in Europe, Kjaernes and Lavik, 2008 and the United States, Rauch and Sharp, 2005) use different questions so they can't be directly compared but they do indicate greater consideration of animal welfare among consumers when they purchase food. One possible suggestion is that for the Chinese, the act of killing and eating an animal is the act that culturally attracts their concern. By way of contrast, the life the animal leads before it is killed attracts less cultural interest. A Western NGO spokesperson commented in 2007 that in his discussions with the Chinese he often found that animal welfare was difficult to convey to them in the way it is understood in the UK. The response that kept coming back from the Chinese was 'but we kill them anyway'. In contrast, it is an interest in quality of life that is stronger within the Western concept of animal welfare and how in turn this is refracted through the quality of the meat itself (Evans and Miele, 2012).

Animal welfare NGOs

Animal welfare NGOs based in the UK started working in China in 1998. Up until then, the Royal Society for the Prevention of Cruelty to Animals (RSPCA) had done little campaigning work in that part of the world. Back in the late 1990s, the RSPCA representative was tasked with trying to make bridges and find contacts particularly in the Chinese academic community. During the first three or four years of actively trying to introduce the topic of animal welfare, they made no contact with officials, in any official capacity. Moreover, farm animal welfare per se was never discussed. Instead the conversations focused on environmental conservation and wildlife protection. It was not until 2004 that the topic of farm animal welfare was formally introduced. In 2004, two UK-based charities, Compassion in World Farming (CIWF) and the RSPCA, made contact with the Chinese ministry responsible for food safety and quality – the Ministry of Commerce. At that point, the NGO representatives raised concerns with them about the impact that livestock rearing and livestock transport to slaughter was having on meat safety and meat quality. This focus on how the welfare of farm animals had an impact upon the quality of the end meat product should be noted. From this beginning, an ongoing dialogue with Chinese officials was initiated.

One approach used by the NGOs to support the promotion and distribution of information relevant to farm animal welfare was holding conferences for the livestock industry, government food safety and farming officials and relevant scientists and academics. The first conference was held in 2005, hosted by CIWF and RSPCA and the Ministry of Commerce's *Meat Hygiene* Journal. The conference explored how improvements to farm animal welfare could be useful to the Chinese meat industry in terms of benefitting product quality. The title of the conference was *International forum on pig welfare and meat safety*. Notably, the language used was not of 'meat quality' but of 'meat safety'. Within the UK, mainland Europe and American context, farm animal welfare as we have argued above is frequently promoted as a meat quality concern, whereas within the Chinese context the introduction of the topic was through concerns about meat safety; the implication being that it would be safer to eat if the animal had 'good welfare' at some level. This type of conference was described as a way to 'open the door' although the RSPCA recognized that this approach to farm animal welfare:

> was limited because we're interested in the animal and they're interested in the point after the animal dies. We were playing the card, of course, that the quality of the meat, and the safety of the meat has a direct connection with the way the animal was handled and reared, which you know is true, up to a point. (RSPCA representative 2007)

By the time of a second conference in 2008, the onus had changed and the language of farm animal welfare was explicit: 'Farm animal welfare: science for the twenty-first century'. Four leading international organizations with an interest in farm animal welfare hosted this event: the World Society for the Protection of Animals (WSPA), RSPCA, CIWF and Humane Society of the United States (HSUS). An RSPCA representative described the reasoning behind this conference:

What hooks can we hang animal welfare on which will interest the Chinese government?; apart from the food safety issue, which was a bit too narrow, and didn't focus enough on the animal itself. We didn't want to go down the route of having a sentience conference per se because we thought that was not practical enough for the Chinese. And although sentience is very important to us – we all agree on that – it's not something that we want to push as the main thrust of our work in China because it's a little bit too 'fluffy'. (RSPCA representative 2007)

In this quote, we can clearly identify a certain self-consciousness regarding how a Chinese audience might receive caring for animal feelings. It is also clear how the Chinese officials' interests are being understood as concentrating on approaching practical solutions to challenges within the food industry, such as addressing their food safety history. In other words, this particular interlocutor assumes, from his experience of dealing with the Chinese, that they are not interested in being presented with the new challenge associated with farm animals being considered as sentient beings.

The RSPCA representative describes the Chinese perspective running through all discussions he had about Farm Animal Welfare as: 'if we're going to kill this animal for food, it seems really hypocritical to worry about, you know, how you cared for it. You're carrying out the most cruel act you can on the animal, robbing it of this life, producing it solely to kill it'. Thus to the Chinese audience it seemed paradoxical and hypocritical to show concern for details of how an animal lived its life.

In response, the NGOs shifted their attention to the science of farm animal welfare, arguing that China had lagged behind in developing a Chinese contribution in this established discipline. With Chinese interest in dramatically increasing the size of their livestock industry and their consumption of meat along with a strategy of having fewer, but much larger, farms in fewer places (Neo and Chen, 2009), the NGOs sought to emphasize the contribution of animal welfare science to improving their animal-rearing techniques and efficiencies. This involved a notable stepping back from arguments about morality and responsibility for animal lives. Rather:

We want to encourage research in China into animal behaviour in the Chinese farm context, we want to encourage the academics that are looking at production – animal production, livestock production – to branch into this area and look at what solutions are available locally to improve conditions for animals. (RSPCA representative 2007)

Thinking about what type of animal welfare is being promoted here, it is a sense of good animal productivity being achieved through good animal welfare. As we saw above in the Hungary case study, the effort there was to move on from understandings of animal welfare as achievable if an animal was productive. The concept of animal welfare was familiar in Hungary and was associated with animals living in a particular way. In China, the very term 'animal welfare' itself is novel, something we return to later in this chapter.

In recognition of the Chinese government's strong commitment to increase meat and milk consumption, the international NGOs suspended the part of their agenda that sought a reduction in animal-based food consumption. This meant refraining from advocating the health benefits of a reduced meat and milk diet, something that was in direct contradiction to Chinese government policy. In summary, the common thread of the 2008 conference, to which all four international NGOs could subscribe, was as follows:

> We look at the horror of what's going on in China and the danger of 'run-away' civilization which is actually what has been happening anyway in parts of the country. And the export of old rearing systems from European companies being exported to Asia. At Expos and Fairs in Asia all kinds of equipment are available that either are banned in Europe or coming up for total ban in the EU. They also discuss with the Chinese the environmental degradation that occurs through intensive farming and farm animal waste disposal. (RSPCA representative 2007)

Peter Li (2009) explains the Chinese relation to farm animal welfare in the following extract.

> In European Union nations, Western farming practices are criticised for their adverse impact on farm animal welfare. This criticism has been unknown to most if not all Chinese farmers. [...] Western Farming practices are hugely popular in China because of their value in promoting growth and productivity. Sow stalls are universally used in breeding farms. This equipment severely limits sows' freedom of movement and their ability to perform many natural behaviours. Confined sows are not only physically exhausted, but also mentally distressed. Being relentlessly milked by their piglets who have nothing to do in the barren pens, sows' immune system could drop thus creating the need for drug intervention. Similarly, mutilation causes long-term pain to the piglets making them susceptible to viral attack. Drug use is again necessary on the farms. Living in barren pens, piglets resort to fighting to overcome boredom. Injuries from fighting are an apparent reason for drug use. And, drugs are also

used before loading the livestock for the slaughterhouse to ensure that they do not die on the road. (Li, 2009: 237)

Li's description of pig production in China highlights many of the features of Western pig farming that much European animal welfare legislation has sought to redress. In many ways, therefore, it describes what is considered normal within intensive pig units where specific welfare legislation is not applied.

Over the last twenty years, support for the position taken by animal welfare NGOs across many countries has changed. Perhaps, most notable is the shift in position of the OIE, which, from a position where animal welfare barely featured in their policies and statements, has recently taken up a far more committed position on the relationship between good animal welfare and good animal health.

> Animal welfare means how an animal is coping with the conditions in which it lives. An animal is in a good state of welfare if (as indicated by scientific evidence) it is healthy, comfortable, well nourished, safe, able to express innate behaviour, and if it is not suffering from unpleasant states such as pain, fear, and distress. Good animal welfare requires disease prevention and veterinary treatment, appropriate shelter, management, nutrition, humane handling and humane slaughter/killing. Animal welfare refers to the state of the animal; the treatment that an animal receives is covered by other terms such as animal care, animal husbandry, and humane treatment. (OIE, 2016)

Furthermore, the links between a healthier livestock population and a healthier human population (including a reduction in less zoonotic disease and reduced use of antibiotics in livestock systems) are now high on the international agenda. It is against this background of the shifting international geopolitics of animal welfare that we return to our ethnographic study of the activities of those NGOs who, in 2008, were investing funds and energies into China in order to mobilize the otherwise unfamiliar concept of 'farm animal welfare'.

Agro-industrial expansionism

> The Chinese hosts were here because they were a group of farmers who had worked with the Canadian Knowledge Transfer Partnership expert in our party, some 5–6 years earlier in a programme of knowledge exchange between Canada and China, and who were now part of a successful local meat wholesale supply company. Later on in the trip we visited their abattoir. During those earlier years when they worked together, they had learnt from our Canadian

facilitator about improving the feed quality and the breeding programmes to increase their agriculture efficiency. This was a new opportunity to gather more knowledge from Western experts about how to farm efficiently. To learn how to improve their business organisation as a collective of farmers who were grazing cattle, sheep and goats extensively for half of the year. (Excerpt from author's ethnographic research notes 2008)

We find in this approach to animal welfare, which was central to the activity in Mongolia, strong echoes of the OIE message cited at the end of the previous section. That message sought to place animal welfare as giving attention to how well an animal copes with the conditions in which they live and to consider how high productivity can be achieved through better welfare. It brings together the goals of high meat production and cheap meat with the achievement of better animal welfare.

The appetite for eating meat and eating it cheaply is a clear feature of the developing market economy around foodstuffs in China (see Figures 6.3 and 6.4). Pork and chicken are the dominant meats in Chinese modern culture and typically all parts of the carcass are eaten. It is rare for lamb to be sold, but it is a product that is eaten by the Muslim population. Meat is typically bought from butchers rather than through Western-style supermarkets, although, as will be discussed later, there is a notable rise in the number of Western-style supermarkets in the larger cities. In many Chinese homes, meat cannot be bought too far in advance because of the lack of refrigeration or freezing

Figure 6.3 A supermarket board on the meat counter advertising that meat is cheaper. Photograph: Roe

Figure 6.4 Tesco advert on a bus advertising that meat is cheaper. Photograph: Roe

facilities. It is therefore fairly typical for people to buy a chicken, take it home, tie a string to its feet and there it will live for a few days until the household is ready to slaughter and prepare it themselves. Middle-age and older people are very familiar with this practice, less so the younger generations.

With the hopes and aspirations of the Chinese to increase productivity through industrialized livestock production, Western NGOs from 2008 onwards have been focusing their attention on a critical stage in Chinese society's progress towards Western lifestyles and the readiness of Western corporate brands to respond. The growth of the Chinese economy means that there is now an ever-expanding middle class with money to spend. But the distance between farm and fork is increasing, particularly in the big cities. As a consequence, anxiety about the safety of the food is rising in popular consciousness. Stories of food poisoning circulate, if not in the State-controlled popular press then through the internet and by mobile phone texts. Thus, the middle-class resident in Beijing, though now comfortably off, is often still struggling to buy food they are certain is safe to eat.

The Chinese government has been committed to a livestock agricultural expansionist programme since the 1990s. The size and scale of changes to the poultry, beef, pork and dairy sectors over the past three decades are immense. The US-based Institute for Agriculture and Trade Policy (IATP) have recently produced four detailed reports that outline the development of these three sectors and their current position (Schneider and Sharma, 2014 on pork; Pi et al., 2014 on poultry; Sharma, 2014 on animal feed; Sharma and Rou, 2014 on dairy). These reports highlight the Chinese government's prioritization of abundant and cheap meat and show how central government policy is a key factor in the ongoing transformation of the livestock sectors. There is a strong belief that economies of scale and the industrialization of production practices will lead to an adequate and safe dairy supply. Equally, there is a commitment to importing foreign livestock breeds with higher productivity than Chinese hybrids and local breeds, leading to higher yields. Yet, the industrial model of production continues to present significant challenges in China in the areas of food safety, public health, environment health and the maintenance of viable rural livelihoods (see Neo and Chen, 2009).

As Chinese cities have got bigger and bigger, the food distribution system has become more complex in the form of an increasing number of supermarkets and wholesalers that both vertically and horizontally integrate livestock industries within the poultry, pork and dairy sectors. In the cities, shifts among the diets of Chinese people is an ongoing trend as food acquisition habits shift towards using supermarkets and the purchase of packaged meat, rather than the wet markets (Pi, 2014). As the IATP reports reveal, red meat and dairy products are becoming evermore popular and with this has come the development of farming and food distribution systems similar to those in the West. Yet, to produce livestock at the scale and with the methods commonly used in the USA, particular challenges have to be faced related to the suitability of the environment, most notably the quality of the land and the availability of water (Emel and Neo, 2015). Indeed, in various regions of China these constraints place significant hurdles to progress. The densely populated Beijing region and surrounding area, for example, is devoid of grassy pastures. It is predominantly made up of cold desert suffering from water shortages.

Milk, cheese and yoghurt are essentially seen as non-Chinese foodstuffs, though the government is now actively encouraging consumption of these products. In the nineteenth century and early twentieth century, only the region of Shanghai, which had long been more strongly influenced by Western culture, possessed any dairies. As with lamb production, dairy production is culturally associated with the 'outer tribes' not with the Chinese themselves. The nomadic tribes, like the Mongols and those of Central Asia, had access to pasture as they moved animals around. However, over the last few decades milk-based products have increased rapidly in popularity driven largely by the policies of the Chinese government who are actively encouraging an increase in milk consumption by Chinese citizens. Figure 6.5 shows a government-sponsored pamphlet explaining to Chinese consumers the good that milk can do to strengthen bones as well as other health benefits.

Figure 6.5 Chinese pamphlet emphasizing the value of milk consumption. Photograph: Roe

The China School milk programme started in 2000 and plays an important part in advocating milk drinking with the aim to improve the health of students and develop the dairy business. Statistics prove that students who drink two cartons of milk per day grow distinctly taller than comparison group as in six months the milk drinkers are respectively 0.72 cm (seven-year group) and 0.46 cm (nine-year group) taller than their comparison groups. (Li, undated)

However, there is frequent concern about the safety of the milk as it is not uncommon for school children to fall ill after drinking school milk. In 2011 *China Daily* reported that

Dairy enterprises are impaired by suspected and real poisoning incidents and low profits. Schools stay out of the program because they do not want to be implicated in safety scandals. And the country has no unified management or supervision of the program it started in 2000. (China.org.cn, 2011)

In 2010, still only 1 per cent of Chinese school children were receiving school milk despite the government target of 30 per cent by 2010 (*China Daily*, 28 April 2011). The lack of pasture in China undoubtedly creates challenges for dairy farms to achieve good levels of animal welfare. Many dairies have been established where the cattle remain on concrete flooring which creates a range of cow welfare and health problems. Whatever the challenges, the Chinese commitment to dairy production demonstrates how the science of intensive agriculture is establishing itself despite the use of animals poorly suited for local environmental conditions, which in turn is leading to health problems in cattle and environmental problems in managing the waste from these farms.

Elsewhere in this book, we have shown how interest in farm animal welfare in twentieth-century Europe has been strongly linked to concerns about food quality and safety. As we have seen, one response to this anxiety has been the establishment of food quality assurance schemes. These have been used to forge consumer trust through identifiable logos, to help retailers and food processers demonstrate 'due diligence' in the safety of their food that they are required to in the UK under the 1990 Food Safety Act, and to introduce an industry-regulated system for meeting animal health, welfare and biosecurity conditions as laid down in legislation. In China, the circumstances for a similar response are complex.

> Individual meat processors may produce high-quality products but overall the situation here does not provide confidence or trust. That is why the Chinese are working hard on that and trying to improve their food safety system and encourage the industry to follow the good practice but unfortunately the economical benefits have to be considered by the private sector [to assess] if they are happy with the investment and returns, so it is not a kind of chicken egg who comes first; if you want to increase your exports so you have to do this, you have to invest in this area but who is going to invest? The private sector hesitates to invest because their prime market is the domestic market here. (Interviewee working in agriculture and rural development in China in 2008)

Nevertheless, following the Western model, the Chinese have developed standard industry schemes such as, most notably, a 'green agriculture' scheme and an 'organic' scheme. However, individual labels mean little in terms of improving the welfare of farmed animals if the actual practices carried out on the farm, in the abattoir and in the factory are not genuinely altered.

> China launched a Green Food certification program and a pollution free agri-food program a few years ago and right now the major agri-food producers meet that standard, so it can see some improvement in that sector but the negative side is that sometimes the private sector will play around with that policy by providing counterfeit certification. They may get a certification first but they will never follow that standard or only partially follow the standards, that's a problem. (Interviewee working in agriculture and rural development in China in 2008)

Those individuals interviewed in 2008 who did not work for the Chinese government admitted, first, that it was hard to say whether the inspection processes that accompany these schemes are rigorous enough and, second, that currently any product could carry these labels. Figure 6.6 shows an example of 'Green chicken' product found within one supermarket store.

For those with money to spend, it is thus difficult to find food that is guaranteed safe to eat and the market is only slowly responding to this emerging demand sector. One of the only 'assured' options for wealthy residents of Beijing is to get a table at Lejen's organic restaurant on the outskirts of the city (see Figure 6.7) or to purchase her organic vegetable box.

Figure 6.6 'Green chicken' product. Found on supermarket shelf of Tesco, Beijing, 2007. Photograph: Roe

Figure 6.7 Lejen's organic restaurant, called 'Mrs Shanen'. Photograph: Roe

Within a walled garden, Lejen grows organic lettuces, herbs and other vegetables and has a small flock of hens and a small herd of cows. She is committed to supplying organic product to her customers and to knowing its provenance. As someone who grew up in New York, moving to Beijing in 1989, she is fully informed in the culture of good and safe food and has had to do it herself to provide this type of food for her family. She reports that the majority of her customers are nonetheless from the expat community in Beijing, with far fewer Chinese families. However, despite her best intentions, communicating her animal welfare values to her staff is a challenge. Here she discusses the struggles of getting her stockperson to be attentive enough to the needs of the farm animals (though as Chapter 3 has already shown, this is not an unfamiliar problem in the UK either).

> *Lejen*: I say we want the cows out in the pasture every single day unless it is raining heavily but it's not always the case. With the large older cows [...] they just don't see the importance. [...] And then for the bull calves that we just got, that's been more of an issue because you have to kind of get them to go to the pasture because there is an electric fence and they don't really want to go in that direction [...]. So my staff, the guy who is in charge of the cows would rather not do it because it's easier to feed them when they are in the pen, so I have to go there and I have to

say to him I am going to give you a fine today, […] I said I am fining you for what happened yesterday, […]. Then I would hear all these excuses – oh they didn't want to go in. It was too cold. It was … but I've seen farms where the cows are at pasture and it's snowing and there is snow on the ground and they are just giving birth, so it's OK but they don't really understand. They might think I'm a little crazy.

Roe: But do you think you are making any progress with them? Do you think their relationship with the animals is changing by having someone like you telling them do this, or?

Lejen: I would hope so; I would hope so you know. Just like getting them to change the water, just to make sure that there is water 24 hours a day is tough because they will say well they don't like to have cold water, they will never drink cold water so I give them warm water when I feed them, so they are getting water 3 times a day is OK. No it's not OK, these are dairy cows, they need more water and they will be like well if I leave it out there and then it gets cold or it freezes they are not going to drink it anyway. I'm like I don't care, if they get thirsty enough … if I'm thirsty enough I will drink it. So put it out there and so finally we took a tub, a bathtub and was able to fill that up with water and unplug the dirty water and clean water in and have to get them to understand that that water has to be so clean that you will want to drink it and not have brown water. It's just these things I am learning and then I have to make them understand and I have to always check, like I have to call up another staff who is not in charge of the cows and say OK are they out in pasture? OK do they have water? To them it's like the animals are not really so important.

Lloyd is a Chinese poultry farmer who recognizes the preciousness and heritage not only of historic Chinese artefacts but also of native Chinese livestock breeds. In the Shandong province, he is regarded as something of a hero; having originally been given five birds in 2003 he has successfully built up a number of flocks of the native Loopa chicken. The animal welfare NGOs are impressed with how Lloyd is rearing his chickens and his poultry farm has become the first to be assured under the World Society for the Protection of Animals Model Farm Project assurance scheme: though to achieve this some tweaking was required, such as cutting the number of cocks to reduce the mating stress on the hens, which was, apart from anything else, leading to unacceptable feather loss (see Figure 6.8).

This is how Lloyd describes his approach to animal welfare.

Figure 6.8 Sign to advertise the chicken farm's participation in the Model Farm Project. Photograph: Roe

Yes. It is a way of attitude towards life, yes, including animal welfare. Yes, man has to think about himself, think about the environment, think about the friend. Animals is man's friend and they have to think about that. Only if you do always take all your mind to think about money everything will go wrong. [...] For Chinese people for many years they have the mind to treat the animal well but the point is right now the people think economy is the most important. (Interview with Lloyd, 2008)

In the following conversation, he explains how and why Chinese people seem to not understand animal welfare.

Lloyd: I think right now in some areas farm animals is a very important way for the farmers to make money. [...] They can sell the eggs and turn it into money and buy food or buy various things – clothes or washing machinery.

Roe: And is there good money in producing food in China?

Lloyd: Yes, in southern China some farm animals raised by the farmers are very, they can sell a very good price because people think they are organic, yes. Right now people here take great emphasis on the importance of food safety very much.

Roe: The idea of animal welfare who do you think has any idea what that means here in China? You kind of know a bit about it, animal welfare?

Lloyd: Yes, I know what you're talking about. Some people, most of the people they do not treat farm animals good. For example when it is slaughtered, the ox they pour water from the mouth into the stomach and make the ox die and then they can sell more meat, the weight will be higher ... they can sell for more money. But it is the torture of the ox, yes and for the pigs they inject the water into the meat ... [...] Yes, many people do that.

Roe: Is this in the backyard though? It's not in ... in the big intensive pig farms they do that?

Lloyd: I don't know whether it is big or small but in many provinces, especially in the remote areas, well sometimes even in some big cities most people when they slaughter the animals will use that way. They only focus on the money. They do not pay attention to what the animal feels, what the animal will feel.

Roe: They don't have a conception of animal feelings at all.

Lloyd: No, they do not know. They thought the animal is a means for me to make money, yes. I do not care whether it is comfortable or uncomfortable, no.

Roe: So when they like scream out in pain do they not ... they just?

Lloyd: They ignore that. Yes, many people they eat the meat and they forget the cry. Many people. (Interview with Lloyd, 2008)

Lloyd expresses delight at getting the support of Western farming knowledge and animal welfare science. The NGOs have put Lloyd in touch with Lejen so his chickens can supply Lejen's restaurant and the first stages of developing a new assurance scheme can commence. For this is the goal of the NGOs; if the Chinese people don't trust their home-grown schemes, perhaps the NGOs can capitalize on their Western credentials and position themselves at the forefront of a farm assurance scheme that encompasses higher standards of farm animal welfare. In the meantime, Lloyd for one is clear about the role of the government in promoting animal welfare and doesn't discuss the food market as a place for educating the Chinese people.

Yes, I think the government should play a very important role in this great job, yes. They must teach the people. In China teaching is important. It is very necessary, not like the way in the Western countries. In China you must teach people what you should do or what you should not do is very important and then the government shall give loans to encourage, yes. They have to give actual support, yes. (Interview with Lloyd, 2008)

Lejen and Lloyd are two Chinese farmers who are unusually attuned to farm animal welfare. What is significant is the challenge they face in their own livelihoods. To a certain extent, both characterize the Chinese attitude to farm animals, one framed entirely by the economic drive to make money (rather than holding a set of values that the retail market encourages farmers and consumers to pursue which is characteristic of the European model for raising animal welfare standards). Again, we observe the absence of a strong engagement with the animal per se as a sentient being having needs that should be met to improve its well-being. When it comes to how to change opinions, Lloyd points to the important role of the government, rather than the market. There is a sense here that those more traditional Chinese philosophies that hold different values about animal–human relations are held very much in the background as economic imperatives become increasingly influential in shaping attitudes and ultimately practice. Returning to Barry's conceptual themes of a 'society of communication' and the place of science and technology for approaching culturally controversial topics, it is difficult to see how either can be effective in China without the support of the Chinese government as gatekeepers for any initiative either for changing attitudes to animals and promoting farm animal welfare or for promoting the establishment of farm animal welfare science through specifically targeted research funding. It would be in the Chinese government's gift to support the development of what Barry calls 'a morally and technically informed civil society' around the topic of farm animal welfare, which, for the moment, has not been high on the political agenda. Indeed, heightened popular concern for farm animal welfare may well be something the State seeks actively to avoid because of tensions around what is deemed moral behaviour within Chinese society as it struggles with both its ancient traditions and its current direction of travel.

Introducing 'animal welfare'

Returning back to that late afternoon in Spring in Inner Mongolia in 2008. The farmer in our party felt at home up there on the Mongolian planes, it reminded him of a time as a young farmer when he sheep-farmed in New Zealand. He kept announcing how he would love to farm here. He confidently approached a sheep and restrained her, while he felt her body for fat content, showed a method for testing the strength of the wool, and parted the greyer outer wool for us to feel the soft white wool beneath. These were all for him ways to know that these animals were well cared for and which one could therefore say meant the animals had good welfare. Or, to put it another way there was nothing evident from this survey of the animals to suggest any unacceptable treatment of these animals was happening that would undermine attempts to support good animal welfare by the NGO. The farmer then selected a lamb, picking it up he showed us all that this lamb was going blind [see Figure 6.9]. (Extract from author's ethnographic research notes, 2008)

Lambs may suffer from a congenital disorder that means that as they get older their eyes turn inwards, perhaps exacerbated by the dusty conditions there. He showed how to turn the eye outwards and instructed it should be

Figure 6.9 British farmer identifies congenital eye disorder in lamb. Photograph: Roe

done daily and drops given. He identified that this was an area that they could help the Chinese with, the treatment of animal diseases that Western farmers were well accustomed to. Overall, the assessment was that these animals were in good shape and would require little adaption to farming practice to invite them in to the Model Farm Project, a food assurance scheme that the NGO was trying to establish and develop in China and other emerging economies, namely Brazil.

I got the impression that the Chinese hosts and colleagues were excited to show off their animals to people from the West. They laid on an extraordinary banquet for us in a gaudily painted concrete yurt that evening with live Mongolian singing, ceremony and excessive levels of Bijou the Chinese celebratory spirit. We each sang a song to them, and had a cross-cultural sing-a-long to Jingle Bells! As a researcher I struggled to communicate to our hosts to gain information, their story, insight about what they thought about what the NGO were doing (I wondered, did they know we were from an NGO?, or did they think we were business people?, I'm really not sure) what were their relations to farming, what importance did they place on their animals, how would they put it in their own words etc? Although in another way it was easy through expression and gesture to have a lot of fun with them, and share reactions to what was going on around us at the party. When dialogue was taking place between the NGO group and the Chinese the term 'animal welfare' was never offered for translation to Peng, for example in the pre-dinner introduction and speech by our party, the words 'organic' and 'sustainability' were used, not animal welfare. (Excerpt from author's ethnographic research notes 2008)

Animal welfare is used in our culture to confer a responsibility to care for animals. International animal welfare NGOs are increasingly working in collaboration with the Chinese meat and farming industry to explore how to improve the interactions between humans and farm animals, first, by introducing the concept of 'animal welfare' and, second, by encouraging stockperson practices leading to better welfare. NGOs are nevertheless cautious about using the term 'animal welfare' in certain contexts for not only may Chinese farmers not comprehend the term but equally an approximate understanding of the term may seem irrelevant to the farming values they subscribe to.

For all that, it is important to acknowledge – or give credit to – the many Chinese farmers who do recognize and comprehend good animal husbandry but may not connect their activities with the notion of good animal welfare. It continues to be the case that 'animal welfare' remains a term with little or no popular understanding in mainland China (Li, 2009; You et al., 2014). In 2008, the phrase *Dongwu Fuli*, which translates as the words 'animal' and 'welfare', would likely be met with incomprehension in the streets of Beijing. The words together don't make sense to regular Chinese citizens. And the research findings of You et al. (2014) indicate, there is still a long way to go for the term to have widespread cultural meaning. In the words of one translator: 'Well I think the Chinese translation is OK, it's very clear. It's the same word as human welfare and it's the same word in Chinese too.' It is the juxtaposition of the word 'welfare' as used for humans with the word used for 'animals' that draws a blank from the majority of Chinese.

The NGO initiative, called The Model Farm Project, sought to encourage the sustainable, welfare-friendlier farming practices of certain Mongolian farmers as well as Lloyd and Lejen in the periphery of Beijing, and to connect them to Chinese consumers sympathetic to their ways of farming food of a higher quality. Yet these are rare and isolated examples, very distinct from the bulk of livestock production in China. The mission of the Western NGOs is nevertheless to see this change, to get the Chinese public engaged with the fortunes of farm animals, to create a discourse and to promote an understanding among Chinese farmers and scientists of what this means. Since 2005, other Western NGOs working in China, including the RSPCA, CIWF and the Humane Slaughter Association, have started to introduce the term 'animal welfare' more and more.

As mentioned above, the 2005 conference organized by a meat science journal and Western animal welfare organizations, with the support of the Chinese Ministry of Commerce, tentatively introduced farm animal welfare to a Chinese meat industry audience. In March 2008, a similar team of NGOs organized a second conference in Beijing with the title *The importance of farm animal welfare science to Sustainable Agriculture*, a clear indication of the direction of thought at the time. At that event, Joyce d'Silva, ambassador for CIWF, commented: 'Its quite exciting because we are actually changing the language, at the conference in March even I know enough Mandarin to hear everyone using that term *Dongwu Fuli*' (personal communication). But what was evident at the 2008 conference was that the emphasis was not simply about using the term in conversation but about letting farm animal welfare science become authoritative in defining the need of animals and encouraging Chinese scientists to develop their own animal welfare science. The conference closed with an invitation for delegates to raise their hands in support of the statement: 'This conference acknowledges that science has shown that farm animals are sentient beings, and that protecting the welfare of farm animals is indispensable to sustainable agricultural development' (see Figure 6.10).

Agricultural science from the West has brought high productivity to Chinese animals and crops; farm animal welfare science is sold as an extension of that science. Rather than trying to promote Western cultural values or connect with historic Chinese values that appear to have been buried by Maoism and what has followed it, science can provide a less contested way of approaching politically and ethically sensitive topics. Yet, although scientific knowledges might be seen as culturally desensitized, there is always the charge of this process, by which Western values are disseminated, might be perceived by some as a form of 'civilizing' process. Indeed, 'civilizing' was what the nascent animal welfare bodies saw themselves as doing in nineteenth-century Britain (Ritvo, 1987). Might we see the activities of these current animal welfare NGOs operating in China (and elsewhere) in a similar light, working to develop a 'Chinese civil society' (Crossick and Reuter, 2008; Ma, 2008)? We don't think so. An important component of animal welfare engagement in the West has been public campaigning to encourage consumer choice for higher welfare products, an activity that in China has to be left to the State-run media (Turner

Figure 6.10 A photograph of delegates raising their hands to support the statement at the close of the conference *The Importance of Animal Welfare Science to Sustainable Agriculture*, Beijing, March 2008. Photograph: Roe

and D'Silva, 2005). Equally, charitable funds are flowing into the country, rather than being drawn from local fundraising. Increasingly, it would appear there is a willingness for partnership between Chinese commercial partners and animal welfare NGOs.

Over the last ten to fifteen years, the Chinese government has been committed to increasing dairy and meat production and consumption in China. As Li (2009) has argued, developmental states like China have been criticized for rapid 'industrialization without enlightenment'. The reforming Chinese government is a post-socialist developmental State (Low, 2004: 133–46), for which, in Deng Xiaoping's words, 'developing productivity' is the primary objective. The efforts of the NGOs are supporting the Chinese government's objectives to draw upon Western science and technology to advance Chinese modern society towards a more sustainable, harmonious relationship with the environment (Keping and Herberer, 2008). These activities strongly orientate nature–society relations around farm animals towards technocratic notions of animal productivity, an ideological legacy of the agro-industrial modernizations of the mid-to-late twentieth century (Brambell, 1965; Rushen, 2008) in Europe and America. Yet, these activities and interventions are also supporting them in innovating livestock production systems more rapidly to include animal welfare measures from the outset, rather than enter a long period of catch-up, employing methods that have since become illegal in the West. In this sense, although the farm animal as a sentient subject is not directly evoked, the work of the animal welfare NGOs is one of helping to assemble in China the figure of an edible, industrial-scale 'farm animal', whose improved care can lead to a healthier animal, one that is safer to eat and more agriculturally sustainable. In this, it is not so surprising that the term 'sentience' was almost entirely absent in discussion with the Chinese, likewise, in many circumstances, the term 'animal welfare' (a neologism in Mandarin). And yet, as interest in the quality of food grows in China, so too might it come to embrace, indirectly or directly, increasing care for the sentient animal.

Postscript

Since our visits to China in 2007 and 2008, the Model Farm Project funded by WSPA has been completed, but it has been hailed a success through a short film explaining what was achieved (Benchmark Holdings, 2013). This short documentary film tells the story of the Model Farm Project China through the voices of Chinese farmers who have benefitted from the animal welfare expertise that was shared with them throughout the project. It features some of the people and their businesses that we met back in 2007–2008. The message given in the film is that those farms that have invested in higher welfare standards, and those that have been open to Western animal welfare expertise, are experiencing many benefits, as are the Chinese consumers who accept higher welfare food as healthier for them. Not only do these farmers speak of the high demand for their higher welfare animal products, which include pork, poultry and cashmere, but they have also learnt how to farm more sustainably, for example through improved pig waste management, or by tackling over-grazing problems. Furthermore, they now appreciate seeing happy animals on their farms. These farms, and the supply chain that markets higher welfare food, nevertheless remain only a handful of isolated examples. Yet, they prove that there are serious possibilities and potentials in developing higher welfare foods in China with willing farmers and engaged consumers who want to invest their time and money in foods coming from systems where welfare standards are higher.

A recent, and significant, development that continues the involvement of Western animal welfare NGOs in driving improvements in farm animal welfare is a new funding award made to the RSPCA, to continue their work in China. In the spring of 2017, the UK-based animal welfare charity RSPCA announced they had received funding by US foundation the Open Philanthropy Project to support a two-year project to develop the RSPCA's farm animal welfare standards and higher welfare labelling scheme as a model for a similar assurance and food labelling programme in China (Dann, 2017). The money will also allow it to work closely with the official International Cooperation Committee of Animal Welfare – a key institution in bringing together Chinese stakeholders in the livestock farming and food retail sectors (Dann, 2017).

The position of farm animal welfare in contemporary China following the efforts of the NGOs discussed in this chapter is still evolving. Back in 2012 a group of vets who attended a forum on Animal Welfare Development at the Chinese Veterinary Conference, held in Suzhou, China, wrote a letter in the journal *Science* calling for China to develop and enact national animal welfare legislation and policies. Xiuxiang et al. (2012) identified the need for government institutions to be established to effectively implement legislation and for effective community education among those who work professionally with animals 'to accurately convey the concepts of animal welfare and the need for animal welfare standards' (Xiuxiang et al., 2012: 1151). Moving forward, the 'Animal Protection Index' report for China in 2014 (World Animal Protection, 2014) identifies the developing legislative protection for farm animals in China. Although it acknowledged that, at the time, humane slaughter legislation only applied to pigs, there was a declared hope that the General Principles of Animal Welfare that were under development would enable improvements in other areas

(World Animal Protection, 2014). Indeed, that same year, the first national Animal Welfare Standard for pigs was published while other welfare standards for beef cattle and mutton sheep were in the course of being drafted. But perhaps even more significantly, it was also announced in 2014 that a national standard of the General Principles of Animal Welfare Assessment had been drawn up and was under approval.

> It focuses on the welfare of various categories of animals including farm animals, and aims at raising the profile of AW within the livestock industry and improving awareness and concern over farm animal welfare nationwide. (Xiao, 2014: unpaginated)

Against this legislative expansion, Barber (2015) has studied the rhetorical strategies used to promote animal welfare in China through regulation and policy. She identifies 'empathetic narratives' whose intention is to evoke an emotional and sympathetic response. She goes on to show how these 'empathetic narratives' around non-human animal welfare are localized within a rapidly modernizing China that looks to a future where animal advocacy is warranted. What these narrative techniques might achieve is succinctly revealed by Barber:

> A powerful message for the potential of harmonious Chinese human and nonhuman animal coexistence emerges. This message is being skilfully presented through a variety of sophisticated media in China not just as what could be but also as what ought to be in the Chinese context. (Barber, 2015: 320–1)

This positive message about what is possible is in contrast to Lu et al. (2013) who exclaim that:

> There is no good soil in which to cultivate the awareness of animal welfare; people tend to ignore animals feelings and consider that animal rights are just luxury propaganda … there remains resistance to the implementation of laws and policies for the protection of the welfare of animals in China. (Lu et al., 2013: 355)

Finally, in 2016 the Chinese Health Ministry announced dietary guidelines to the Chinese public, as part of public health advice for its 1.3 billion population, exhorting them to halve their meat consumption (Milman and Leavenworth, 2016). The Ministry advises the consumption of between 40 and 75 grams of meat per person each day. This headline has attracted the attention of climate campaigners in particular but it may also have implications on how Chinese individuals value the meat they eat on a daily basis. Will eating less meat prompt a willingness to pay more for higher-quality meat, perhaps including higher animal welfare as part of that food quality?

This chapter and the one before it have illustrated processes by which animal welfare concerns, actions and policies are internationalized beyond Europe and North America, regions that have hitherto tended to dominate not only the welfare and food agendas but also much of the scientific literature. Both chapters have shown the difficulties associated even with the term 'animal welfare', with both Hungary and China preferring instead at times the terminology of environmental sustainability, thereby integrating the animal into environmental thinking. However increasingly it is the connection being made between human health and animal health, where the latter is seen as a critical component of the former, that is emerging as the more important message. Raising broader awareness about farm animal welfare is nevertheless challenged by the difficulties of open and unrestrained communication.

The government-controlled media in China effectively means that it is government who must lead and educate the public on the topic of farm animal welfare. By contrast with what we have seen in earlier chapters, there is a far lesser role for civil society engagement in either raising awareness about inhumane treatment of animals or direct campaigning work. This means that NGOs can effectively operate only by lobbying government or those with influence over government rather than through consumer- or citizen-focused campaign strategies. On a comparative note, the subsidized improvements to production systems in Hungary are a consequence of government-led initiatives that could be accompanied with government-led information campaigns. The effectiveness of local food safety and food inspection processes are central to implementing trusted improvements in farm animal welfare. Where these are absent, where State-led or private sector assurance does not exist, there are particular challenges. For where it is shown that science and technology can be the arbiters of controversy, as Barry (2001) writes, there needs also to be the infrastructure to support the effective implementation of technologies such as inspection processes and auditing techniques. Otherwise any attempt to create added value within supply chains may well fail.

Chapter 7

Future Food Animals,
Future Protein

Farming, part of every child's education. They learn the principles of agriculture at school, and they're taken for regular outings into the fields near the town where they not only watch farm-work being done, but also do some themselves, as a form of exercise.

Just think how dreary life would be if those chronic ailments, hunger and thirst, could only be cured by foul-tasting medicine, like the rarer types of disease.

They've beaten all records for the production of corn and livestock, their expectation of life is the highest in the world, and their disease rate the lowest. Thus by scientific methods they've done wonders with a country that's naturally rather barren.

They eat a lot of meat, because they think it enables them to work harder. (Thomas More's *Utopia*, 1516 [1965]: 75, 98, 99 and 122).

More meat

In one sense, the future of the livestock farming industry is rosy. The world population continues to grow with a projected 9 billion people living on the planet by 2050. Accompanying this growth is the continual expansion of animal-based protein consumption that is spreading in popularity to parts of the world where traditionally dairy was seldom if ever consumed and meat was a rare luxury. Global retail-driven meat supply chains (as distinct from subsistence production) have become ever more extensive and profitable (Shukin, 2009). More sophisticated meat and dairy distribution networks have meant that animal-based food products travel vast distances across the globe (most often as chilled carcasses and body parts, but sometimes as live animals). Meanwhile the dissemination of the science that drives livestock productivity has also found a global audience, keen to maximize the yield of meat, milk or eggs in relation to the inputs – feed, water, labour and number of animal bodies grown. Undeniably, for an ever-increasing percentage of the global population, achieving their dietary need for protein in the form of animal-based products is a highly desirable prospect. Moreover, alongside this dramatic expansion of land-based animal production, recent years have seen a highly significant growth in, and intensification of, aquaculture and, more recently, experimental forays in in vitro meat production and altogether new sources of protein for human consumption such as from insects. The model of intensive, industrialized land-based animal production continues to expand across the globe (Harvey et al., 2017).

At one level, this expansion is reinforced by the growing internationalization of cultural beliefs and aspirations around eating meat and dairy products. For consumers, animal-based proteins become associated with wealth as well as superior bodily strength, growth and well-being and are frequently marketed as such. However, at another level, it is also strongly encouraged and driven by global food companies who are increasing their influence in parts of the world new to large-scale animal-based protein consumption. In other words, the global political economy supports livestock production and in turn encourages meat and dairy consumption. The corporatized food and farming lobby, across the globe, has invested deeply in promoting animal-based protein consumption through a vast variety of food products. It is highly competitive about securing new markets and is continually innovating new ways to incorporate parts of animal bodies that have traditionally been dismissed as waste into sellable product.

Key to the efforts of the food industry to increase profit margins has been segmentation and the complex pricing of meat and dairy products. Competition between food industry actors, over-supply in certain sectors (notably milk), faster growing animals and new processing and manufacturing technologies, enabling more of the animal carcass to be rendered edible, results in a continued supply of cheap meat and dairy products, often sold at a lower price than non-animal-based protein alternatives particularly when in a form that suits the culinary habits and cooking time commitments of Western consumers. Inversely, the variability of husbandry systems and parameters for differential meat quality (provenance, breed, growth, cut, etc.) within the marketplace also supports a distinctive quality-driven meat market in which higher animal welfare is actively marketed to discerning consumers as a distinctive component.

As we have seen, the policy approach to improving farm animal welfare has relied heavily upon market differentiation and segmentation as a means of both addressing and encouraging 'ethical' consumption practices This has been a material-aesthetic practice that bundles together politics, ethics and norms in various ways to engage consumers at a personal level. This has had some success in raising the visual profile of higher welfare products in stores and in driving certain standards upwards. However, as a component of the quality of a value-driven and high-end food production system welfare runs the risk of becoming exclusive to only those who can afford it within an ethically driven and elite-driven food market. The reality of the animal health and welfare concern globally is that the changes need to be widespread across the majority, not limited to the minority of farm animals living within more exclusive high welfare production systems. The animal welfare NGO community has become increasingly effective at drawing attention to how industrialized farm animals are actually living their lives, rather than focusing attention on an open policy-informing discussion around the complexities and tensions of feeding a human population with animal-based products farmed according to regulatory minimum standards. Animal welfare must be meaningful and fully integrated into both farming systems and to wider animal-based protein policy. The rationale for explicitly conjoining expectations of animal welfare policy with animal-based protein policy draws directly from the multiple entanglings between animal production and human consumption discussed in this book. It is easy to ignore the distant lives of sentient animals and to focus instead on the desired food product, but, as we go on to explain, crucial to this manoeuvre is establishing and reiterating the connection between, on the one hand, the lived sentient animal and, on the other, the material food product; the latter being both the product of, and yet continual embodiment of, that sentience.

Farm animals are still sentient beings when the effects of consuming and producing animal based-products are discussed in macro-food policy issues. Some have linked the growth of cancer to the consumption of processed red meat (Rohrmann et al., 2013). Many have stressed the links between livestock production and environment damage – on a global scale and a local scale (FAO, 2006). The amount of land required by livestock production, for the animals and for their feed, raises considerable concern over food security between different global players as land that could feed (often local) people is given over to growing crops for animals to be eaten often by more distant populations (Benton and Bajzelj, 2016). Recently, the heavy use of antibiotics in livestock farming has raised a growing global concern over the possible transmission of resistant genes to human pathogens (O'Neill, 2016) along with other zoonotic threats of disease transmission from intensively farmed animals to human populations. Most notably the link between global climate change and the agri-food industry, and especially being the livestock industry sector, is being made ever more forcefully.

> Producing our three square meals a day causes emissions of CO2 through agricultural machinery and transporting crops and animals, nitrous oxide from the use of fertilisers (synthetic and manure), and methane from livestock and flooded paddy fields for rice. Furthermore, the demand for food has led to global expansion of farmland at a rate of about 10m hectares per year during the last decade. Some of this cleared land is – or was – tropical rainforest, adding more emissions and reducing the capacity of land to absorb and store carbon. When you consider emissions according to the services we use on a day-to-day basis, agri-food accounts for approximately 30% of all greenhouse gas emissions. (Benton and Bajzelj, 2016: unpaginated)

Counter-movements to the continual expansion and intensification of livestock production certainly exist. Joining the established ranks of animal liberationism, veganism and vegetarianism are a growing number of organizations and individuals seeking, for multiple reasons that include public health, environmental sustainability and ethics, to encourage consumers (variously described as 'reducetarians', 'flexitarians' or simply 'temporary' or 'part-time' vegetarians and vegans) to reduce meat consumption (and thereby its production) through the expanded use of non-animal-based proteins (Friel et al., 2009; De Bakker and Dagevos, 2012; Westhoek et al., 2011). Campaigns by Western animal welfare NGOs include 'meat-less days' or the encouragement to eat 'less but better' (de Boer et al., 2014) in attempts to shift downwards the numbers of farmed animals and their impact upon the environment. There is also potential innovation in growing meat without having to raise and produce an animal – namely through cultured, 'clean' or 'in vitro' meat (van der Weele and Driessen, 2013). Although this is far from achieving any sort of viable commercial status (and, for the moment at least, the resources currently required to produce 'clean meat' greatly exceed those required for more traditional methods), there is growing interest among larger corporate food groups in the future potential of these alternative meat products. Increasingly, non-meat alternatives are available in supermarkets, such as vegetable-based protein products like *Quorn*, soya meat and tofu, or non-dairy milk products like soya, rice or wheat milk (Sexton, 2016). One global institution's response to raising awareness about alternatives to animal-based protein is the United Nations declaration of 2016 as the International Year of Pulses which:

> Aims to heighten public awareness of the nutritional benefits of pulses as part of sustainable food production aimed towards food security and nutrition. The

year will create a unique opportunity to encourage connections throughout
the food chain that would better utilize pulse-based proteins, further global
production of pulses, better utilize crop rotations and address the challenges
in the trade of pulses. (FAO, 2016)

Nevertheless, despite the growing number of meat replacements of various
types, whether pulses or vegetable-based protein products, data suggest that
for the majority of consumers this market is having little impact on reducing the
ineluctable consumption of meat or cheese globally (Hoek et al., 2011), first,
because of the consistently high meat consumption levels in the 'developed'
countries and, second, because of the rapidly expanding growth in animal-
based protein consumption in emerging economies (FAO, 2013).

Consumers of animal-based proteins are a globally diverse, increasingly
urban population more distanced than ever before from the practical realities
of raising food animals. Farming skills are not part of formal education yet
certain agricultural and agrarian discourses and narratives – associated with
an age when the agricultural population was proportionally far greater, rural life
more familiar and food costs a more significant component of family budgets
– remain strongly embedded in consumer culture. Hence, Thomas More's
Utopian world as described 500 years ago still shares surprising similarities
with the world we are in today. The science of livestock productivity is highly
praised and valued, while the cultural value of tasty food and beliefs in the
superior value of meat to the consuming body continues to this day for the
majority. The critical difference is that the proximal connection with the practical
tasks of farming has largely disappeared, though paradoxically, of course,
the ideology of reconnecting with our food through the practical endeavour
of growing your own – whether vegetables or animals – or sourcing one's
food from short, local supply chains is a persistent and remedial reference
point for those seeking to redress the health, economic, social and ethical
concerns associated with global food supply chains (Carolan, 2011). Many
consumers thereby feel poorly informed about what is implied by the higher
welfare claims that emerge from these industrialized systems of production.
Miele and Evans recount consumers':

> surprise and the sense of dismay at the realization of their lack of understanding
> of what contemporary animal farming entails and the difficulties in accessing
> the sites where relevant information about the lives of farm animals was
> circulated (e.g. the internet, NGO leaflets, technical magazines, certain
> dedicated television programmes etc.). Access to those sites and to that
> information was considered crucial for making sense of the 'standardised

messages' offered by food labels and also for perceiving what information was missing from labels. (Miele and Evans, 2010: 183)

In the above quotation, these are EU consumers. In many other countries of the world, consumer–citizen concern is a long way off the public agenda. While such major knowledge gaps persist around the entanglings of animals, humans and food, progress towards investing in animal welfare and health improvements will be hindered.

For many consumers, there are obstacles in overtly making connections between the food they eat and the life of the animal involved in producing that item of food. The change in state and form as a consequence of the material transformation to the farm animal's body from living animal to dead carcass to cooked/processed meat/egg/milk and so on challenges how we communicate the practices and processes of what contemporary animal farming entails and the process of 'becoming food'. Yet ironically, while there is often a greater ethical emphasis placed on the quality of life of companion, wild and research animals, the quality of a farm animal's life might arguably be more important to us as it becomes the meat, milk or eggs that we ultimately consume. It is, however, so easy to ignore a farm animal's life through all its stages from birth, rearing, fattening or period of production through to slaughter at the point at which either the ideal weight/meat/fat balance is reached, or its productivity as an egg layer or a milk-giver starts to fall. Consumers encounter meat, milk, eggs or cheese far more frequently than they encounter living industrially reared farm animals in food production. Indeed, the representations of farm animals most familiar to people are cartoon-like anthropomorphic drawings in children's books (Cole and Stewart, 2014). Where encounters with farm animals do occur, it is often in a 'petting farm' or through textual or visual descriptions on food packaging, both of which appeal to a naturalistic sentimental imaginary about how they live which, of course, bears little if any relevance to the reality of farm animal lives. The Meatrix is one example of a cartoon that tries to address this tension (The Meatrix, 2017) between the family farming idyll and agro-industrial, intensive farming. Another is the film Cowspiracy (Anderson and Keegan, 2014), which investigates animal agriculture as the most destructive industry facing the planet. Finally, and most recently, Carnage (Amstell, 2017) is a mockumentary set in 2067, when the UK is vegan but older generations are suffering the guilt of their carnivorous past. Both of these latter films offer alternative readings of contemporary and future animal agriculture.

Intensive livestock production is not only the norm; it is now shifting into a new gear of global intensification partly in response to concern over global food security, partly because technological and biological/genomic innovations are making new levels of intensification both possible and profitable. Yet, there is a rising awareness among consumers, citizens, governments and food chain actors about animal welfare as food quality and a growing commitment within supply chains in many parts of the world for animal welfare standards. Consumer concern and market opportunity have both driven the growth and extension of farm animal welfare science whose task must be to continuously improve the ways in which we identify and assess the needs of farm animals in different production systems across more and more countries. Equally, the work of farm animal carepersons and the role they play in delivering good care for the farm animal are being increasingly recognized and supported, although many misunderstandings prevail about the realities of what this work can entail in practice. All of this is positive and deserves recognition, yet there is, we feel, a persistent and perhaps growing fragility here in the concerns and mechanisms for protecting (and perhaps even enhancing) the welfare of farmed animals.

Throughout the book, a qualitative analytical approach, drawing upon interviews and ethnography, has informed our study of farm animal welfare; one attentive to what and how the ideas, meanings and practices that circulate around the food animal through the material process of the animal becoming food, are framed as a process of economization. We have shown how this process informs care practices, animal welfare scientific knowledge–making practices, labelling practices and ultimately the drive to construct a market that retails and regulates animal-based proteins. Accepting that growth in the production and consumption of animals and their products is, in the short and medium term at least, inevitable – and for many, desirable – at the global scale, we want to end this book by exploring opportunities for moving forward. Throughout our analysis, we have emphasized the importance of seeing food production and food consumption, not as distinct arenas of policy or practice, but rather as connected and interrelated two-way processes, involving the co-presence of the sentient animal, whether in living body or in final product and the sentient human, whether carer or consumer. How those presences are intertwined, performed, communicated and given value has been the core matter of this book. To end, we open up three interrogations around extending this sense of connectivity. The first is conceptual, a different way of thinking through the 'material currency' (Shukin, 2009) in which sentient animals become the material of food. The second is more empirical, suggesting new ways of knowing the animal and of using and communicating that knowing within the food sector. Finally, the third offers a novel policy framework for joining up human health and welfare with food animal health and welfare in a more holistic and arguably mutually reinforcing way.

Connections 1. Sentient materialities: An animal-based protein approach to animal welfare and food

The first way of thinking we wish to explore is the idea of 'sentient materialities'. Sentient materialities is a concept that properly addresses the challenges of economizing animal-based protein production, processing and consumption by fully engaging with the animal as a sentient material body, rather than ignoring the qualities of the animal as anything other than a body which converts feed, to increases in body mass or product, and thus meat or egg/milk. It is a concept that is sensitive to the events of encounter between humans and animals, and human eater and animal-based food protein. It is sensitive to these events of when and how the agro-food network assembles technologies, bodies and knowledges that respond to and create sentient materialities, as things become food. Finally, sentient materialities is a concept which brings together interests in agro-food studies and animal studies to tackle global challenges that entangle feeding humans, growing animals and sustainable planetary environmental management in an uncertain future.

We pursue the notion of sentient materialities because we feel it offers particular investigative potency as an approach to the study of animal-based food protein networks and the types of events that are prominent within such networks. Two events stand out: the encounter between human and food animal, and the inter-corporeal event of eating and digesting. Investigating the first is informed not solely by facts about animal lives but instead through the study of moments when and where people encounter food animal lives: whether represented on a poster or on food packaging, a piece of descriptive text, driving past a herd of food animals, touching a food animal at a petting farm, or auditing farms for animal welfare standards for a corporate retailer, or slaughtering a lamb every minute, or stocking a shed full of 20,000 broiler chickens, or a vet treating an injured sheep. Whichever form it might be, they each open up the prospect of knowing food animals differently, if the concept of sentient materialities is used to draw out different ways to analyse these encounters.

The inter-corporeal event is forged in the need to care about the quality of the food we eat. The food needs to be safe to eat so the eater won't die or become ill as a result of eating it. When we eat, animal-based protein matter from the animal's body is digested within another body. What is folded into and out of this intimate inter-corporeal event can be mapped out more widely as a single food animal body frequently feeds not just one person, but many people; though the resulting food might not be of equal cultural or dietary value as different parts of the carcass are distributed across different – often global – markets. Equally, the animal body itself is part of a complex selective-breeding programme that brings the lives of other animals into consideration, demanding attention be paid to alternative inter-corporeal events such as, for example, artificial insemination, and the sentient materialities of the other animal lives involved in this practice. Paying closer attention to these inter-corporeal ethical connectivities, to not ignore either the body of eater or eaten, brings new approaches to tackling the cultural, environmental and health implications tied to what bodies or body parts are eaten? What sort of life did both eater and eaten experience? What are the implications of that food animal's lived and experienced existence in the broadest terms, and ultimately how is that filtered to address how these events relate to the suite of global challenges linked to animal-based protein consumption?

With the concept of sentient materialities, we can develop food and animal studies to embrace the making of the sentient corporeality of the animal bodies grown and eaten, as well as the sensibilities of the human bodies eating with ethical and/or biological eating allergies/intolerances and desires. These appetites are in part assembled through economization processes including pricing and marketing strategies, and the global politics of demand and supply economic practices by corporate livestock producers and regulators. Across the geography of ethical, economic and political practices that are enrolled into the economizing of sentient materialities, sentient materialities both afford and are afforded in specific forms *how* they are made and *how* they can be known. Sentient materialities include everything harvested from the animal's corporeal form, including body parts (legs, livers, muscle) and products (milk, cheese, eggs), as well as engaging directly with the living animal body's sentient experiences. Acknowledging these materialities and lives as sentient emphasizes the lived experiences of the animal and the ethical significance of engaging with food animals in these terms. In this way, the terminology of sentient materialities allows us to entangle food animal welfare concerns with human food–related concerns, through what becomes manifest as body eats body, and thus enables the more intentionally joined-up study of the assemblage of practices and processes that surround both the lives of animals that produce protein and the lives of those humans who eat, sell and farm them. To conceive the topic in this way emerges from post-structural work that has established the need to go beyond dichotomous approaches to the study of food production and food consumption and to engage in the human–non-human animal relations that exist within agri-food networks.

Finally, to think about the production–consumption exchange in terms of sentient materialities allows us to think differently about food politics and to use Goodman and Dupuis' (2002: 19) words: 'the contested material and discursive orderings of the social and the ecological which articulate every day bio-political contestations and connections'. Sentient materialities, their production and their consumption shape the debate, raise global challenges and underscore the role, place and liveliness of the sentient food animal, its products and its needs. This, we maintain, is constructive for working across the research arenas of animal welfare studies and agri-food studies, for attending to 'sentient materialities' opens up opportunities to know differently the farm animal alive in the barn or dead as foodstuff. The hope also is that this approach will inspire methodological innovation at the forefront of animal and food studies. We strongly believe that animals (farm animals in this case, but other animals in other circumstances) need to be conceived and engaged as active research participants, co-producers of knowledges both about how human and animal lives are entangled within the area of animal-based protein production and consumption and about how animal-based proteins can and do shape the lives of people and environments, connecting communities in villages, towns and cities, nationally and internationally.

Connections 2. Innovating animal welfare science: Valuable lives

Farm animal welfare science has been both an enabler and a critic of intensive livestock production. It has provided the scientific basis upon which production parameters have been established, yet has challenged many formerly established practices as being unacceptable to the animal. In this, farm animal welfare science provides a common currency for the establishment of comparable standards across widely differing cultural and economic contexts. Recent developments in farm animal welfare science, however, offer new possibilities for the sorts of more holistic connectivity between human and farmed animal that we seek to advocate here. The growing extension of animal-based assessments of welfare, which focus attention on the body and behaviour of the animal rather than on its environment or the resources available to it (food, water, etc.), marks an important shift, first, in the acknowledgement of animal sentience and subjectivity as being relevant and worthy of consideration within both husbandry practice and in consumer choice and, second, in the recognition of the critical role of human–animal relations within animal care.

Linked to this has been the new emphasis placed not only on identifying the capacity for farmed animals to experience positive emotions (rather than on identifying the causes of animal suffering) but also on providing the means for those positive emotions to be encouraged through specific interventions. 'Welfare' begins to take on a different meaning as the science shifts from a paradigm of protection to one of active enhancement. The notion of a 'life worth living' or even a 'good life', introduced by the Farm Animal Welfare Council (2009) and recently developed by Mellor (2016b), further extends the conceptual reach of farm animal welfare science to the individual animal's quality of life. Defined by Mellor (2016b: 16) as 'lives where they can and do avail themselves of opportunities to have positive experiences', a 'life worth living' takes forward not only the manner in which welfare is assessed (FAWC, 2009) but also its reach; a whole life and the balance of experiences during that individualized, lived life. The concept of 'integrity', which Rocklinsberg et al. (2014: 65), citing Rutgers and Heeger (1999), define as 'the wholeness and intactness of the animal and its species-specific balance, as well as the capacity to sustain itself in an environment suitable to the species' brings what is arguably an additional, embodied dimension to a more holistic understanding of farmed animal welfare for embodied, sentient subjects. Finally, we note that the technological development of precision livestock farming systems, which offer the potential for continuous biometric health and welfare monitoring both of individual farmed animals and of group, flock and herd behaviour, provides some of the possible mechanisms that might respond to these new conceptual approaches to welfare that increasingly pay attention to the individual and social lives of the animal concerned.

These various advances in animal welfare science share an emphasis not only on what matters for the animal but on what is valuable for the animal per se. In this, they shift attention, at least in part, away from the value of the animal as potential food product and towards the value the animal may place in a sustained life that is lived and experienced. Defining an animal's interest in this way is, one might argue, a step towards acknowledging the eventual entitlement of animals to having such interests represented in political and policy processes that extend beyond the human as the only political subject (Garner et al., 2016).

That these considerable advances in animal welfare science should take place at a time of renewed emphasis on intensification and industrialization in food animal production presents a very real challenge for animal welfare science. The growth of 'zero-grazing' systems, in which ruminant animals are kept indoors throughout their entire lives, and the multiplication of what the British media refers to as 'mega farms' (Wasley et al., 2017), housing as many as 1.7 million birds or 23,000 pigs (though establishments of similar or indeed larger size are far more common in the United States), are seen by many welfare scientists, consumer/citizens and welfare NGOs as inherently bad, particularly when it comes to the animals' or birds' ability to exhibit natural behaviours. Other welfare scientists and proponents within the food industry tend to argue that such establishments, if correctly designed and operated, offer the opportunity for significant welfare gains, particularly in environmental control, specialized veterinary access and improved animal health monitoring. However, these are not gains that are easily commercialized through labelling or product advertising. For some, of equal concern are the potentialities of contemporary breeding and genomic technologies (FAWC, 2012b). While researchers point to the positives that current developments hint at (such as better resistance to certain production diseases, improved tolerance of certain production conditions and reduced stress during domestication, e.g., Jensen, 2014), this too fails to translate readily to a commercialization strategy into which discerning consumers can buy. In contrast to the more anthropomorphically recognizable behaviours associated with positive welfare states, the risk here is that some of these new harder and scientific welfare parameters will become increasingly hidden from view, rather like the animals themselves. One response of the wider welfare community (which – periodically – enjoins welfare science with producers, NGOs, interested consumers and discerning food chain actors) to this challenge has been to promote a more nuanced understanding and definition of 'sustainability', one that gives animal welfare a more symmetrical footing with the more traditional concerns of 'society', 'economy' and 'environment' (FAWC, 2017). The advantage of this, apart from bringing the animal welfare constituency to a bigger policy table, is that it enables the less commodifiable yet achievable welfare advantages associated with larger, more intensive and technologized systems, or with genomics, to be enrolled into viable commercial strategies for eventual food products.

Connections 3. One Health/One Welfare

If the notion of sentient materialities offers us a way of constructively approaching the corporeal connectivities between the body of the consumed and that of the consumer and if new developments in farm animal welfare science allow us to place greater emphasis on the lived whole-life experience of the farm animal, the recent emergence of the One World/One Health agenda, and associated with it, the One Welfare agenda, offers one possibility of a more holistic (inter-species and interdisciplinary) policy framework that brings animal health and human health organizations and practitioners (together with environmental 'health') into a closer assembly. One Health has been described as: 'a worldwide strategy – a paradigm shift – for expanding interdisciplinary collaborations and communications in all aspects of health care for humans and animals' (ACVPM, 2009, quoted in Monath et al., 2010: 193). Although Woods (2014) reveals that animal and human health have long shared a close collaborative history (see also Osburn et al., 2009), a distinctive One Health agenda has established itself in recent years largely in response to a series of global health crises in part driven by the growing international trade in farm animals and farm animal products. The different and often uncoordinated responses of the veterinary and animal health sector on the one side, the human medical sector on another and the environmental and wildlife conservation sector on a third side, to a series of emerging and potential zoonotic disease pandemics such as SARS and HPA1H5N1 in the first two decades of the current century, demonstrated the important need for the different sectors to find ways of working together (Gibbs, 2014). The term 'One Health' has stuck and is now widely used though, as a number of commentators have pointed out, what this actually means in terms of a significant, or paradigmatic, shift in the conceptualization of the relationship between human and animal health remains unclear.

More recently, the issue of antibiotic resistance and the potential crossover of resistant pathogens from animal environments to those implicating human health has given the One Health agenda a renewed relevance though the stark differences between the possible responses to the human and the animal as patients remain. There is, as Hinchliffe (2015) observes, a certain 'triumphalism' in the 'One World/One Health' discourse, which, despite its purported holism and universalism, remains entirely modernist in its ontology and anthropocentric in its ethics. The primary goal here, as countless scientific papers make clear, is the protection of human health though, perhaps somewhat paradoxically, it has undoubtedly been the veterinary and animal health sector that has invested most time and effort in its promulgation. So why do we offer it here as part of a new connectivity? One answer is that, rightly or wrongly, One Health raises the profile and reach of veterinary and animal health and welfare concerns, allowing them some additional access to increasingly global political forums. Another is that within the broader remit of One World/One Health has emerged the parallel concept of 'One Welfare' defined as a recognition of the interconnections between animal welfare, human well-being and the environment (Pinillos et al., 2016). The increasing emphasis in One Welfare placed upon mutual human/animal care relationships, and the various factors that can impact both positively and negatively on these relationships, offer, at one level, the potential for greater interdisciplinary understanding of the power and value of such connectivities, particularly, as Fraser (2016) points out, within the farm animal sector. Yet, we wonder, is the optimism and singularity of 'One Welfare', like the 'One Health' project, misplaced? As Craddock and Hinchliffe (2015: 2) point out:

> No amount of persuasion or enhanced understanding or indeed engagement will be possible if we don't recognise, for example, the severe conditions that many people and animals are subjected to through their differential positioning or placement in social settings and economic markets.

For the farmed animal food sector, the 'One Health' and 'One Welfare' agendas offer a mechanism for mobilizing the notion of 'sentient materialities' that we evoked above. 'Eating well', in Derrida's terms, is to eat what is good and what is 'good' is increasingly seen in terms of the health and welfare of both consumer and consumed. If 'One Health' achieves anything, it will be through the collaborative endeavours of veterinarians and doctors who interpret food (and, in particular, animal products) as a mutuality of human/animal health/welfare.

For most of us, meat-eaters or users of animal products, our connection with farm animals is almost entirely post-mortem. Yet there is no meat or animal product for which there is no life behind. Given the ineluctability of the continued expansion of farmed animal production, making connections with those lives and making something of those lives knowable seem, at the very least, an essential endeavour.

Bibliography

ACVPM (2009), *'One Health–One Medicine': linking human, animal and environmental health*, American College of Veterinary Preventive Medicine News and Views 87.

Adams, C. (2000), *The sexual politics of meat*, New York: Continuum Press.

Agriculture and Horticulture Development Board (2014), *BPEX pig pocketbook 2014*, Warwickshire: BPEX.

AHDB (2017), farming data, available at: https://dairy.ahdb.org.uk/market-information /farming-data/#.WAH7BxSNIII, last accessed 19 March 2017.

Alworth, D. (2010), 'Supermarket sociology', *New Literary History*, 41(2): 301–327.

Amos, N. and R. Sullivan (2014), *The business benchmark on farm animal welfare*, London: BBFAW.

Amstell, S. (2017), *Carnage*, London: British Broadcasting Corporation.

Anderson, B. and J. Wylie (2009), 'On geography and materiality', *environment and planning A*, 41(2): 318–335.

Anderson, B. and P. Harrison (2011), *Taking Place: non-representational theories and geography*, London: Ashgate.

Anderson, K. and K. Keegan (2014), *Cowspiracy*, Santa Rosa, CA: A.U.M. Films & Media.

Anthony, R. (2003), 'The ethical implications of the human–animal bond on the farm', *Animal Welfare*, 12(4): 505–512.

Araujo, L. and H. Kjellberg (2009), 'Shaping exchanges, performing markets: the study of marketing practices', in P. Maclaren et al. (eds) *The SAGE handbook of marketing theory*, 195–218, London: Sage.

Ashley, B. et al. (2004), *Food and cultural studies*, London: Routledge.

Assured Food Standards (2015), *Red tractor assurance, annual review*, Kenilworth: ABS.

AssureWel (2015), *Improving farm animal welfare through welfare outcome assessment*, London: Tubney Trust.

Atkins, P. J. (2011), 'The material histories of food quality and composition', *Endeavour*, 35(2–3): 74–79.

Atkins, P. J. and I. Bowler (2001), *Food in society: economy, culture, geography*, London: E. Arnold.

Baines, R. N. and P. Ryan (2002), 'Global trends in quality assurance', unpublished paper presented at the Trade Partners UK and Ministry of Agriculture 'Modern Food Chain' Seminar, Kuala Lumpur.

Balasz, B. (2015), *Analysis of stability and tensions in incumbent socio-technical regimes*, Regime analysis of the Hungarian food system. FP7 PATHWAYS project. Exploring

transition pathways to sustainable, low carbon societies. http://www.pathways-project
.eu/sites/default/files/Country%20report%209%20Hungarian%20agro-food%20
regime.pdf, last accessed 21 August 2016.

Barad, K. (2007), *Meeting the universe halfway: quantum physics and the entanglement of matter and meaning*, Durham: Duke University Press.

Barber, S. (2015), 'Nonhuman animal welfare in China: evolving rhetorical strategies for changing law and policy', *Journal of International Wildlife Law & Policy*, *18*(3): 309–321.

Barker, Z. E., K. A. Leach, H. R. Whay, N. J. Bell and D. C. J. Main (2010), 'Assessment of lameness prevalence and associated risk factors in dairy herds in England and Wales', *Journal of Dairy Science*, *93*(3): 932–941.

Barnett, J., F. Begen, S. Howes, A. Regan, A. McConnon, A. Marcu, S. Rowntree and W. Verbeke (2016), 'Consumers' confidence, reflections and response strategies following the horsemeat incident', *Food Control*, *59*: 721–730.

Barry, A. (2001), *Political machines: governing a technological society*, London: Athlone.

Barry, A. (2012), 'Political situations: knowledge controversies in transnational governance', *Critical Policy Studies*, *6*(3): 324–336.

Bastian, M., O. Jones, N. Moore and E. Roe eds (2017), *Participatory research in more-than-human worlds*, London: Routledge.

Bayvel, A. (2005), 'The use of animals in agriculture and science', *Revue Scientifique Et Technique (International Office of Epizootics)*, *24*(2): 791–797.

Beardsworth, A. and T. Keil (1997), *Sociology on the menu*, New York: Taylor & Francis.

Bebbington, A. and U. Kohari (2006), 'Transnational development networks', *Environment and Planning A*, *38*: 849–866.

Bekoff, M. (2006), *Animal emotions and animal sentience and why they matter: blending 'science sense' with common sense, compassion and heart*, London: Earthscan.

Bekoff, M. (2007), *Animals matter: a biologist explains why we should treat animals with compassion and respect*, San Francisco, CA: Shambhala Publications.

Benchmark Holdings (2013), Model Farm Project. A success story. http://www
.benchmarkplc.com/articles/model-farming-in-china/, last accessed 30 July 2017.

Bennett, J. (2001), *The enchantment of modern life: attachments, crossings, and ethics*, Princeton, NJ: Princeton University Press.

Bennett, J. (2002), *Thoreau's nature: ethics, politics, and the wild*, New York: Rowman & Littlefield.

Bennett, J. (2009), *Vibrant matter: a political ecology of things*, Durham: Duke University Press.

Benton, T and B. Bajzelj (2016), Guest Post: Failure to tackle food demand could make 1.5C limit unachievable. 23.3.2015. *Carbon Brief Clear on Climate*. http://www
.carbonbrief.org/guest-post-failure-to-tackle-food-demand-could-make-1-point-5-c
-limit-unachievable, last accessed 18 September 2016.

Benton, T. and S. Redfearn (1996), 'The politics of animal rights: where is the left?' *New Left Review*, *215*: 43–58.

Berger, J. (1979), *Pig earth*, London: Bloomsbury.

Bergeron, H., P. Castel and S. Dubuisson-Quellier (2014), *Governance by Labels. Max Planck Sciences Po Center on Coping with Instability in Market Societies*, MaxPo Discussion Paper 14/2. Sciences Po, Paris.

Bermond, B (1997), 'The myth of animal suffering', in M. Dol et al. (eds) *Animal consciousness and animal ethics*, 125–143, Wageningen: Van Gorcun Press.

Bernués, A., A. Olaizola and K. Corcoran (2003), 'Labelling information demanded by European consumers and relationships with purchasing motives, quality and safety of meat', *Meat Science*, *65*(3): 1095–1106.

Best, S., A. J. Nocella, R. Kahn, C. Gigliotti and L. Kemmerer (2007), 'Introducing critical animal studies', *Journal for Critical Animal Studies*, *1*(1): 4–5.

Blokhuis, H. J., I. Veissier, M. Miele and B. Jones (2010), 'The Welfare Quality® project and beyond: safeguarding farm animal well-being', *Acta Agriculturae Scand Section A*, *60*(3): 129–140.

Blokhuis, H. J., M. Miele, I. Veissier and B. Jones (2013), *Improving farm animal welfare*, Wageningen: Wageningen Academic Publishers.

Bock, B. and H. Buller (2013), 'Healthy, happy and humane: evidence in farm animal welfare policy', *Sociologia Ruralis*, *53*(1): 390–411.

Boissy, A. et al. (2007), 'Assessment of positive emotions in animals to improve their welfare', *Physiology and Behavior*, *92*(3): 375–397.

Boivin, X. et al. (2001), 'The farmer and the animal: a double mirror', in M. Hovi and M. Bouuilhol (eds) *Human-Animal Relationships: Stockmanship and Housing in Organic Livestock Systems*, Proceedings of the 3rd NAHWAO Workshop, Clermont Ferrand, NAHWAO.

Boltanski, L. and L. Thévenot (1991), *De la justification les économies de la grandeur*, Paris: Broché.

Bonanno, A. and R.A. Lopez (2005), 'Private label expansion and supermarket milk prices', *Journal of Agricultural and Food Industrial Organization*, *3*(1): 2.

Bonne, K. and W. Verbeke (2008), 'Religious values informing halal meat production and the control and delivery of halal credence quality', *Agriculture and Human Values*, *25*(1): 35–47.

Botreau, R. et al. (2007), 'Definition of criteria for overall assessment of animal welfare', *Animal Welfare*, *16*: 225–228.

Bourke, J. (2011), *What it means to be human*, London: Virago Press.

Bowles, D. et al. (2005), 'Animal welfare and developing countries: opportunities for trade in high welfare products from developing countries', *Revue Scientifique Et Technique (International Office of Epizootics)*, *24*(2): 783–790.

Bowman, A. et al. (2012), *Bringing home the Bacon*, CRESC Public Interest Report, University of Manchester.

Bracke, M. ed (2009), *Animal welfare in a global perspective*, Wageningen: Wageningen University Press.

Bracke, M. B. M. (2007), 'Animal-based parameters are no panacea for on-farm monitoring of animal welfare', *Animal Welfare*, *16*(2): 229–231.

Brambell, R. (1965), *Report of the technical committee to enquire into the welfare of animals kept under intensive livestock husbandry systems*, London: Her Majesty's Stationary Office.

Brandth, B. (2002), 'On the relationship between feminism and farm women', *Agriculture and Human Values*, *19*(2): 107–117.

Brandth, B. (2006), 'Agricultural body-building: incorporations of gender, body and work', *Journal of Rural Studies*, *22*: 17–27.

Breuer, K., P. H. Hemsworth and G. J. Coleman (2003), 'The effect of positive or negative handling on the behavioural and physiological responses of nonlactating heifers', *Applied Animal Behaviour Science*, *84*: 3–22.

British Pigs (2016), Mangalitza pig. http://www.britishpigs.org.uk/breed_mg.htm, last accessed 21 August 2016.

British Veterinary Association (2010), *Welfare labelling*, Press release, 3 August 2010.

Brooklyndhurst (2010), *Are labels the answer: barriers to buying higher welfare products*. *Brooklyndhurst*, Report to Defra, London: Brooklyndhurst.

Broom, D. (1991), 'Animal welfare concepts and measurements', *Journal of Animal Science*, *69*: 4167–4175.

Broom, D. M. (1968), 'Behaviour of undisturbed 1 to 10 day old chicks in different rearing conditions', *Developmental Psychobiology*, *1*: 287–295.

Broom, D. M. (1988), 'Concepts about the evaluation of behaviour in relation to welfare', in J. Unshelm, G. Van Putten, K. Zeeb and I. Ekesbo (eds) *Proceedings of the International Congress on Applied Ethology of Farm Animals*, 145–146, Darmstadt: K.T.B.L.

Broom, D. M. (2001), 'Assessing the welfare of hens and broilers', *Proceeding Australian Poultry Science Symposium*, *13*: 61–70.

Broom, D. M. (2010), 'Animal welfare: an aspect of care, sustainability, and food quality required by the public', *Journal of Veterinary Medical Education*, *37*(1): 83–8.

Broom, D. M. (2011), 'The history of animal welfare science', *Acta Biotheoretica*, *59*: 121–137.

Broom, D. M. (2014), *Sentience and animal welfare*, Wallingford: CABI.

Buller, H. (2010), 'Palatable Ethic's', *Environment and Planning A*, *42*: 1875–1880.

Buller, H. (2012), 'Nourishing communities: animal vitalities and food quality', in L. Birke and J. Hockenhall (eds) *Crossing boundaries: creating knowledge about ourselves with other animals*, London: Brill.

Buller, H. (2013a), 'Animal welfare: from production to consumption', in H. Blokhuis et al. (eds) *Welfare quality: science and society improving animal welfare*, Wageningen, NL: Wageningen Academic Press, 49–70.

Buller, H. (2013b), 'Animal Geographies 1', *Progress in Human Geography*, *38*(2): 308–318.

Buller, H. (2013c), 'Individuation, the mass and farm animals', *Theory, Culture & Society*, *30*(7/8): 155–175.

Buller, H. (2014), 'Animal geographies II Methods', *Progress in Human Geography*, *39*(3): 374–384.

Buller, H. (2015a), 'Animal geographies III Ethics', *Progress in Human Geography*, *40*: 422–430.

Buller, H. (2015b), *We've got to keep our antibiotics for ourselves: antimicrobial resistance and the veterinarian's dilemma*, Paper to the Veterinary Anthropology Workshop, University of Edinburgh, 18–19 April 2016.

Buller, H. (2016), 'Closing the barn door', in K. Bjorkdahl and T. Druglitro (eds) *Animal housing and human-animal relations*, London: Routledge.

Buller, H. and C. Cesar (2007), 'Eating well, eating fare: farm animal welfare in France', *International Journal of Sociology of Food and Agriculture*, *15*(3): 45–58.

Buller, H. and E. J. Roe (2008), *Certifying welfare: integrating welfare assessments into assurance procedures: a European perspective: 25 key points*, Welfare Quality Report 17, University of Cardiff.

Buller, H. and E. J. Roe (2010), *Certifying quality: negotiating and integrating welfare into food assurance*, Welfare Quality Report 15, University of Cardiff/Welfare Quality, Cardiff.

Buller, H. and E. J. Roe (2012), 'Commodifying welfare', *Animal Welfare*, *21*: 131–135.

Buller, H. and E. J. Roe (2013), 'Modifying and commodifying farm animal welfare: the economization of layer chickens', *Journal of Rural Studies*, *33*: 141–149.

Burch, D. and G. A. Lawrence (2005), 'Supermarket own brands, supply chains and the transformation of the agri-food system', *International Journal of Sociology of Agriculture and Food*, *13*(1): 1–18.

Burch, D. and G. A. Lawrence eds (2007), *Supermarkets and agri-food supply chains: transformations in the production and consumption of foods*, Cheltenham: Edgar.

Burch, D. and G. A. Lawrence (2009), 'Towards a third food regime: behind the transformation', *Agriculture and Human Values*, *26*(4): 267–279.

Burden, R. (2006), 'Introduction: Englishness and spatial practices', in R. Burden and S. Kohl (eds) *Landscape and Englishness*, 13–26, Brill: Amsterdam.

Burt, S. (2000), 'The strategic role of retail brands in British grocery retailing', *European Journal of Marketing*, *34*(8): 875–890.

Burton, R., S. Peoples and M. Cooper (2012), 'Building 'cowshed cultures': a cultural perspective on the promotion of stockmanship and animal welfare on dairy farms', *Journal of Rural Studies*, *28*: 174–187.

Busch, L. (2007), 'Performing the economy, performing science: from neoclassical to supply chain models in the agrifood sector', *Economy and Society*, *36*(3): 437–466.

Busch, L. (2010), 'Can fairy tales come true? The surprising story of neoliberalism and world agriculture', *Sociologia Ruralis*, *50*(4): 331–351.

Busch, L. and A. Juska (1997), 'Beyond political economy: actor networks and the globalization of agriculture', *Review of International Political Economy*, *4*(4): 688–708.

Butterfield, M. E., S. E. Hill and C. G. Lord (2012), 'Mangy mutt or furry friend? Anthropomorphism promotes animal welfare', *Journal of Experimental Social Psychology*, *48*(4): 957–960.

BVA (2010), *Defra call for voluntary food labelling not enough*, Press release, 3 August 2010, London: British Veterinary Association.

Çalışkan, K. and M. Callon (2009), 'Economization, part 1: shifting attention from the economy towards processes of economization', *Economy and Society*, *38*(3): 369–398.

Çalışkan, K. and M. Callon (2010), 'Economization, part 2: a research programme for the study of markets', *Economy and Society*, *39*(1): 1–32.

Callon, M. (1998), *The law of markets*, Oxford: The Sociological Review/Blackwell.

Callon, M., Y. Millo and F. Muniesa (2007), *Market devices*, Chichester: Wiley.

Callon, M. and F. Muniesa (2003), 'Les marchés économiques comme dispositifs collectifs de calcul', *Réseaux*, *6*(122): 189–233.

Campbell, H. (2005), 'The rise and rise of EurepGAP: European (re) invention of colonial food relations', *International Journal of Sociology of Agriculture and Food*, *13*(2), 6–19.

Campbell, M. L. H. (2014), 'Does the current regulation of assisted reproductive techniques in the UK safeguard animal welfare?' *Animal Welfare 23*: 109–118.

Carolan, M. (2011), *Embodied food politics*, Oxford: Routledge.

Carson, R. (1964), 'Forward', in R. Harrison (ed) *Animal machines*, London: Vincent Stuart.

Caswell, J. A., M. E. Bredahl and N. H. Hooker (1998), 'How quality management metasystems are affecting the food industry', *Review of Agricultural Economics*, *20*(2): 547–557.

Chapman, C. and J. Crowden (2005), *Silence at Ramscliffe: foot and mouth in Devon*, Exeter: Bardwell Press.

Chen, M. Y. (2012), *Animacies, biopolitics, racial mattering and queer affect*, Durham, NC: Duke University Press.

China.org.cn (2011), 'Growing concern over school milk program', *China Daily*, 28 April 2011. http://www.china.org.cn/china/2011-04/28/content_22457215.htm, last accessed 21 August 2016.

Cochoy, F. (2007), 'A sociology of market-things: on tending the garden of choices in mass retailing', *The Sociological Review, 55*(s2): 109–129.

Cockcroft, P. and M. Holes (2008), *Handbook of evidence-based veterinary medicine*, Oxford: Wiley.

Codron, J. M., E. Giraud-Héraud and L. G. Soler (2005), 'Minimum quality standards, premium private labels, and European meat and fresh produce retailing', *Food Policy*, *30*(3): 270–283.

Coetzee, J. M. (1999), *Disgrace*, London: Vintage Press.

Cole, M. (2011), 'From "animal machines" to "happy meat"? Foucault's ideas of disciplinary and pastoral power applied to "animal-centred" welfare discourse', *Animals*, *1*(1): 83–101.

Cole, M. and K. Stewart (2014), *Our children and other animals: the cultural construction of human-animal interaction in childhood*, London: Ashgate.

Coleman, G. et al. (2003), 'The relationship between beliefs, attitudes and observed behaviours of abattoir personnel in the pig industry', *Applied Animal Behaviour Science*, *82*: 189–200.

Commission of the European Communities (2009), *Options for animal welfare labelling and the establishment of a European Network of Reference Centres for the protection and welfare of animals Report from the Commission to the European Parliament*. SEC (2009) 1432, Brussels.

Commission of the European Communities (2016), http://ec.europa.eu/food/animals /welfare/international/index_en.htm, last accessed 18 August 2016.

Compassion in World Farming (2012), *Farm assurance schemes and animal welfare*, London: CIWF.

Compassion in World Farming (2013), *EU realizes that labelling matters*. Press Release, 14 June 2013, London, CIWF. https://www.ciwf.org.uk/news/2013/06 /EU-realises-that-Labelling-Matters

Conradson, D. (2003), 'Geographies of care: spaces, practices, experiences', *Social and Cultural Geography*, *4*(4): 451–454.

Cook, I. (2004), 'Follow the thing: Papaya', *Antipode*, *36*(4): 642–664.

Coole, D. and S. Frost (2010), 'Introducing the new materialisms', in D. Coole and S. Frost (eds) *New materialisms: ontology, agency, and politics*, 1–45, Durham, NC: Duke University Press.

Cooper, J. (2015), *RSPCA CEO*, Press release, 10 September 2014, Horsham: RSPCA.

Cox, R. (2012), 'Turning to food: geography, food production/consumption and the cultural turn', in S. Roseneil and S. Frosh (eds) *Social research after the cultural turn*, 160–177, Basingstoke: Palgrave Macmillan.

Craddock, S. and S. Hinchliffe (2015), 'One world, one health? Social science engagements with the one health agenda', *Social Science and Medicine*, *129*: 1–4.

Crossick, S. and E. Reuter (2008) (eds), *China-EU. A common future*, New York: World Scientific.

Da Silva, J. (2006), 'Adverse impact of industrial animal agriculture on the health and welfare of farmed animals', *Integrative Zoology*, *1*: 53–58.

Daily Mail (2007), 'Bernard Matthews worker caught playing football with turkeys', *Daily Mail*. http://www.dailymail.co.uk/news/article-462909/Bernard-Matthews-worker-caught -playing-football-turkeys.html, last accessed 20 September 2016.

Dann, L. (2017), 'RSPCA awarded grant to improve animal welfare in China'. *Farmers Weekly*, 5 April 2017. http://www.fwi.co.uk/news/rspca-awarded-grant-improve -animal-welfare-china.htm, last accessed 30 July 2017.

Davies, A. C., C. J. Nicol and A. N. Radford (2015), 'Effect of reward downshift on the behaviour and physiology of chickens', *Animal Behaviour*, *105*: 21–28.

Dawkins, M. S. (1980), *Animal suffering: the science of animal welfare*, London: Chapman and Hall.

Dawkins, M. S. (1983), 'Battery hens name their price: consumer demand theory and the measurement of ethological "needs"', *Animal Behaviour*, *31*(4): 1195–1205.

Dawkins, M. S. (1990), 'From an animal's point of view: motivation, fitness and animal welfare', *Behavioural and Brain Sciences*, *13*(1): 1–9.

Dawkins, M. S. (2006), 'Through animal eyes: what behaviour tells us', *Applied Animal Behaviour Science*, *100*(1): 4–10.

Dawkins, M. S. (2012), *Why animals matter: animal consciousness, animal welfare, and human well-being*, Oxford: Oxford University Press.

De Bakker, E. and H. Dagevos (2012) 'Reducing meat consumption in today's consumer society: questioning the citizen-consumer gap', *Journal of Agriculture and Environmental Ethics*, 25(6): 877–894.

de Boer, J.H. Schosler and H. Aiking (2014), '"Meatless days" or "less but better"? Exploring strategies to adapt Western mead consumption to health and sustainability challenges', *Appetite*, 76: 120–128.

De Vroom, B. (1985), 'Quality regulation in the Dutch pharmaceutical industry: conditions for private regulation by business interest associations', in P.C. Schmitter (ed) *Private Interest Government: beyond market and state*, 128–149, London: Sage.

Dear, M. (1988), 'The postmodern challenge: reconstructing human geography', *Transactions of the Institute of British Geographers*, 13(3): 262–274.

Defra (2017), *United Kingdom egg statistics – Quarter 1, 2017*, London: Office of National Statistics.

Deleuze, G. (1988), *l'Abecedaire de Gilles Deleuze*, TV film by Pierre-André Boutang, Paris: Editions Montparnasse.

Demeritt, D. (2006), 'Science studies, climate change and the prospects for constructivist critique', *Economy and Society*, 35(3): 453–479.

Department for Environment Food & Rural Affairs (2014), United Kingdom Poultry and Poultry meat Statistics – July 2014. https://www.gov.uk/government/uploads/system/uploads/attachment_data/file/358116/poultry-statsnotice-28aug14.pdf, last accessed 20 September 2016.

Department for Environment Food & Rural Affairs (2016), United Kingdom Egg Statistics – Quarter 1. https://www.gov.uk/government/uploads/system/uploads/attachment_data/file/543468/eggs-statsnotice-05may2016.pdf, last accessed 20 September 2016.

Department of Food Law, University of Reading (1996), UK 'Food Law Cases' at http://www.foodlaw.rdg.ac.uk/uk/cases.htm, last accessed 16 August 2013.

Désiré, L., A. Boissy and I. Veissier (2002), 'Emotions in farm animals: a new approach to animal welfare in applied ethology', *Behavioural Processes*, 60(2): 165–180.

Despret, V. (2006), 'Sheep do have opinions', in B. Latour and P. Weibel (eds) *Making things public. Atmospheres of democracy*, 360–370, Cambridge: MIT Press.

Despret, V. (2016), *What would animals say if we asked the right questions*, Minneapolis: Minnesota University Press.

Despret, V. and J. Porcher (2007), *Être bête*, Arles: Actes Sud.

Dickinson, C. (2014), *State of the Poultry Industry*, Unpublished presentation to AHDB Outlook Conference.

Dixon, J. (2002), *The changing chicken,* Sydney: University of South Wales Press.

Dockes, A. C. and F. Kling Eveillard (2006), 'Farmers and advisors representations of animals and animal welfare', *Livestock Science*, 103: 243–249.

Dolan, C. and J. Humphrey (2000), 'Governance and trade in fresh vegetables: the impact of UK supermarkets on the African horticulture industry', *Journal of Development Studies*, *37*(2): 147–176.

Donaldson, A. and D. Wood (2004), 'Surveilling strange materialities: categorisation in the evolving geographies of FMD biosecurity', *Environment and Planning D: Society and Space*, *22*(3): 373–391.

Douglas, M. (1970), *Natural symbols*, London: Barrie and Rockliffe.

Duncan, I. J. H. (1993), 'Welfare is to do with what animals feel', *Journal of Agricultural and Environmental Ethics*, *6*(Suppl. 2): 8–14.

Duncan, I. J. H. (2005), 'Science-based assessment of animal welfare: farm animals', *Revue scientifique et technique-Office international des epizooties*, *24*(2): 483.

Duncan, I. J. H. (2006), 'The changing concept of animal sentience', *Applied Animal Behaviour Science*, *100*(1): 11–19.

Duncan, I. J. H. and D. Fraser (1997), 'Understanding animal welfare', in M. C. Appleby and B. O. Hughes (eds) *Animal welfare*, 19–31, Wallingford: CAB International.

Edgar, J. et al. (2016), 'Use of conditioned place preference to investigate emotion transfer in domestic hens', in C. Dwyer et al. (eds) *Proceedings of the 50th Congress of the International Society for Applied Ethology*, 3821–3822, Wageningen: Wageningen Academic Publishers.

Eisenman, R. (2013), *Maccabees, Zadokites, Christians, and Qumran*, Nashville, NT: Grave Distractions.

Eisnitz, G. A. (1997), *Slaughterhouse: the shocking story of greed, neglect and inhuman treatment inside the U.S. Meat industry*, London: Prometheus.

Elzen, B. et al. (2011), 'Normative contestation in transitions "in the making": animal welfare concerns and system innovation in pig husbandry', *Research Policy*, *40*(2): 263–275.

Emel, J. and H. Neo eds (2015), *Political Ecologies of Meat*, London: Routledge.

Enticott, G. (2001), 'Calculating nature: the case of badgers, bovine tuberculosis and cattle', *Journal of Rural Studies*, *17*(2): 149–164.

Eurobarometer (2005), *Attitudes of consumers towards animal welfare*, Brussels: Eurobarometer.

Eurobarometer (2007), *Attitudes of EU citizens towards animal welfare*, Brussels: Eurobarometer.

Eurobarometer (2014), *Attitudes of EU citizens towards animal welfare. Special Eurobarometer Report 270*, Brussels: Eurobarmeter.

EU Commission website (2017), https://ec.europa.eu/food/animals/welfare/international_en, last accessed 26 October 2017.

Evans, A. and M. Miele (2008), 'Consumers views about farm animal welfare', Welfare Quality Report 5, Cardiff University.

Evans, A and M. Miele (2012), 'Between food and flesh: how animals are made to matter (and not matter) within Food consumption practices', *Environment and Planning D Society and Space*, *30*(2): 298–314.

FAO (2006), *Livestock's long shadow: environmental issues and options*, Rome: FAO.

FAO (2013), *The state of food insecurity in the world*, Rome: FAO.

FAO (2016), *International year of pulses. Nutritious seeds for a sustainable future*, Rome: FAO.

FAO and Slow Food (2012), *Animal welfare: a win-win opportunity for animals, farmers and consumers*. A conference held at the Salone Internazionale del Gusto and Terra Madre, Turin Italy, 29 October 2012.

FAWC (1979), *Press statement December 5th 1979*, Surbiton: Farm Animal Welfare Council.

FAWC (2005), *Report on the animal welfare implications of farm assurance schemes*, London: Farm Animal Welfare Council.

FAWC (2006), *Report on welfare labelling*, London: Farm Animal Welfare Council.

FAWC (2007), *Report on stockmanship and farm animal welfare*, London: Farm Animal Welfare Council.

FAWC (2009), *Farm animal welfare in Great Britain: past, present and future*, London: Farm Animal Welfare Council.

FAWC (2011), *Report on economics and farm animal welfare*, London: Farm Animal Welfare Council.

FAWC (2012a), *Report on farm animal welfare and disease*, London: Farm Animal Welfare Committee.

FAWC (2012b), *Opinion on the welfare implications of breeding and breeding technologies in commercial livestock agriculture*, London: Farm Animal Welfare Committee.

FAWC (2014), *Report on evidence and farm animal welfare*, London: Farm Animal Welfare Committee.

FAWC (2017), *Sustainable agriculture and farm animal welfare*, London: Farm Animal Welfare Committee.

FAWF (2011), *Labelling food from farm animals*, London: Farm Animal Welfare Forum.

Fearne, A. and R. Walters (2004), *The costs and benefits of farm assurance to livestock producers in England*, Final Report for the Meat and Livestock Commission, Centre for Food Chain Research, Imperial College London.

Ferguson, D. M. and R. D. Warner (2008), 'Have we underestimated the impact of pre-slaughter stress on meat quality in ruminants?' *Meat Science*, 80(1): 12–19.

Fitzgerald, A. J. (2010), 'A social history of the slaughterhouse: from inception to contemporary implications'. *Human Ecology Review*, 17(1): 58–69.

Fitzgerald, A. J. (2015), *Animals as food: (Re)connecting production, processing, consumption, and impacts*, Ann Arbor, MI: Michigan State University Press.

Fitzsimmons, M. (1989), 'The matter of nature', *Antipode*, 21: 106–120.

Foer, J. S. (2010), *Eating animals*, London: Penguin.

Food Chain Evaluation Consortium (2009), *Feasibility study on animal welfare labelling and establishing a Community Reference Centre for Animal Protection and Welfare Part 1: Animal Welfare Labelling*. Final Report to the European Commission, Brussels: European Commission DG Sanco.

Food Chain Evaluation Consortium (2015), *Study on information to consumers on the stunning of animals*, Report to the European Commission, Brussels: European Commission.

Food Policy Evaluation Consortium (2011), 'Executive Summary', *Evaluation of the EU Policy on Animal Welfare & Possible Options for the Future*. GHK consulting in association with ADAS UK. http://ec.europa.eu/food/animals/docs/aw_arch_122010 _summary_report_en.pdf, last accessed 21 August 2016.

Food Standards Agency (2009), *The food safety act: a guide for food businesses*, London: FSA.

Foucault, M. (1979), *Discipline and punish: the birth of the prison*, New York: Vintage Books.

Franklin, A. (1999), *Animals and modern cultures*, London: Routledge.

Fraser, D. (1999), 'Animal ethics and animal welfare science: bridging the two cultures', *Applied Animal Behaviour Science*, 65(3): 171–189.

Fraser, D. (2001), 'The "new perception" of animal agriculture: legless cows, featherless chickens, and a need for genuine analysis', *Journal of Animal Science*, 79: 634–641.

Fraser, D. (2003), 'Assessing animal welfare at the farm and group level: the interplay of science and values', *Animal Welfare*, 12: 433–443.

Fraser, D. (2008a), *Understanding animal welfare: the science in its cultural context*, Oxford: Wiley/Blackwell.

Fraser, D. (2008b), 'Towards a global perspective on farm animal welfare', *Applied Animal Behaviour Science*, 113: 634–641.

Fraser, D. (2014), 'The globalization of farm animal welfare', *Revue Scientifique Et Technique (International Office of Epizootics)*, 33(1): 33–38.

Fraser, D. (2016), *What do we mean by 'One Welfare'*, Paper to the OIE Conference, Mexico City, December 2016.

Fraser, D. et al. (1997), 'A scientific conception of animal welfare that reflects ethical concerns', *Animal Welfare*, 6: 187–205.

Freidberg, S. (2003a), 'Not all sweetness and light: new cultural geographies of food', *Social and Cultural Geography*, 4(1): 3–6.

Freidberg, S. (2003b), '"Cleaning up down South: supermarkets", ethical trade and African horticulture', Social and Cultural Geography, 4(1): 27–43.

Freidberg, S. (2004), 'The ethical complex of corporate food power', *Environment and Planning D: Society and Space*, 22: 513–531.

Friel, S. et al. (2009), 'Public health benefits of strategies to reduce greenhouse-gas emissions: food and agriculture', *The Lancet*, 374(9706): 2016–2025.

Fudge, E. (2002), 'A left-handed blow: writing the history of animals', in N. Rothfels (ed) *Representing animals*, 3–18, Bloomington: Indiana University Press.

Fudge, E. (2010), 'Why it's easy being a vegetarian', *Textual Practice*, 24: 149–166.

Fulponi, L. (2007), 'Private voluntary standards in the food system', *Food Policy*, 31(1): 1–13.

Garner, R. et al. (2016), *How to protect animal welfare*, Sheffield: Centre for Animals and Social Justice.

Gatward, G. (2001), *Livestock ethics*, Devon: Old Pond Publishing.

Geyhalter, N. (2005), *Our Daily Bread* (Film).

Gibbs, P. (2014), 'The evolution of One Health', *Veterinary Record*, *174*(4): 85–91.

Gillespie, K and R. C. Collard eds (2015), *Critical animal geographies*, London: Routledge.

Goldenberg, M. J. (2006), 'On evidence and evidence-based medicine: lessons from the philosophy of science', *Social Science and Medicine*, *62*(11): 2621–2632.

Goldenberg, J. et al. (2001), 'I am NOT an animal: mortality salience, disgust, and the denial of human creatureliness', *Journal of Experimental Psychology*, *130*: 427–435.

Goodman, D. (1999), 'Agro-food studies in the 'age of ecology': nature, corporeality, bio-politics', *Sociologia Ruralis*, *39*(1): 17–38.

Goodman, D. (2001), 'Ontology matters: the relational materiality of nature and agro-food studies', *Sociologia Ruralis*, *41*(2): 182–200.

Goodman, D. (2002), 'Rethinking food production–consumption: integrative perspectives', *Sociologia Ruralis*, *42*(4): 271–277.

Goodman, D. and E. M. DuPuis (2002), 'Knowing food and growing food: beyond the production–consumption debate in the sociology of agriculture', *Sociologia Ruralis*, *42*(1): 5–22.

Goodman, D., E. M. DuPuis and M. K. Goodman (2012), *Alternative food networks: knowledge, practice, and politics*, London: Routledge.

Greenhough, B. and E. J. Roe (2011), 'Ethics, space, and somatic sensibilities: comparing relationships between scientific researchers and their human and animal experimental subjects', *Environment and Planning D: Society and Space*, *29*(1): 47–66.

Greenhough, B. and E. J. Roe (2017), Exploring the role of animal technologists in implementing the 3 Rs. An ethnographic investigation of the UK University Sector. Science, Technology & Human Values Online.

Grunert, K. G. (2005), 'Food quality and safety: consumer perception and demand', *European Review of Agricultural Economics*, *32*(3): 369–391.

Grunert, K. G. (2011), 'Sustainability in the food sector: a consumer behaviour perspective', *International Journal on Food System Dynamics*, *2*: 207–218.

Grunert, K. G., S. Hieke and J. Wills (2014), 'Sustainability labels on food products: consumer motivation, understanding and use', *Food Policy*, *44*: 177–189.

Grusin, R. ed (2015), *The non-human turn*, Minneapolis: Minnesota University Press.

Guy, C., G. Clarke and H. Eyre (2004), 'Food retail change and the growth of food deserts: a case study of Cardiff', *International Journal of Retail & Distribution Management*, *32*(2): 72–88.

Guzman, M. A. and U. Kjaernes (1998), *Humans and animals: a qualitative study*. SIFO report number 6, Lysaker, Norway: The National Institute for Consumer Research.

Hann, C. ed (2007), *Postsocialism: ideas, ideologies and practices in Eurasia*, London: Routledge.

Haraway, D. (2003), *The companion species manifesto*, Chicago: Prickly Paradigm Press.

Haraway, D. (2008), *When species meet*, Minneapolis: Minnesota Press.

Haraway, D. (2015), 'Cosmopolitan critters', in K. Nagai et al. (eds) *Cosmopolitan animals*, London: Palgrave.

Hardy, T. (1895), *Jude the obscure (Penguin Classics 2003 edition)*, London: Penguin.

Harman, G. (2010), *Towards speculative realism*, Ropley: Zero Books.

Harper, G. and S. Henson (2001), 'Consumer concerns about animal welfare and the impact on food choice', EU FAIR CT98–3678. www.londonpressservice.org.uk /haeu/20131031020146/, http://ec.europa.eu/food/animal/welfare/research/fair_project .pdf, last accessed 30 October 2015.

Harper, G. C. and A. Makatouni (2002), 'Consumer perception of organic food production and farm animal welfare', *British Food Journal*, *104*(3/4/5): 287–299.

Harrison, P. (2008), 'Corporeal remains: vulnerability, proximity and living on after the end of the world', *Environment and Planning A*, *40*: 423–445.

Harrison, R. (1964), *Animal machines*, London: Vincent Stuart.

Harvey, F. et al. (2017), 'Rise of mega farms: how the US model of intensive farming is invading the world', *The Guardian*, 18 July 2017.

Hatanaka, M., C. Bain and L. Busch (2005), 'Third-party certification in the global agrifood system', *Food Policy*, *30*(3): 354–369.

Heath, C. A. E. et al. (2014), 'Navigating the iceberg: reducing the number of parameters within the Welfare Quality assessment protocol for dairy cows', *Animals*, *8*(12): 1978–1986.

Heerwagen, L. R., M. R. Morkbak, S. Denver, P. Sandoe and T. Christensen (2015), 'The role of quality labels in market-driven animal welfare', *Journal of Agriculture and Environmental Ethics*, *28*(1): 67–84.

Hemsworth, P. (2003), 'Human–animal interactions in livestock production', *Applied Animal Behaviour Science*, *81*(3): 185–198.

Hemsworth, P. and G. Coleman (1998), *Human–livestock interactions: the stockperson and the productivity and welfare of intensively farmed animals*, Wallingford: CAB International.

Henson, S. (2008), 'The role of public and private standards in regulating international food markets', *Journal of International Agricultural Trade and Development*, *4*(1): 63–81.

Henson, S. and T. Reardon (2005), 'Private agri-food standards: implications for food policy and the agri-food system', *Food Policy*, *30*(3): 241–253.

Hinchliffe, S. (2015), 'More than one world, more than one health: reconfiguring interspecies health', *Social Science and Medicine*, *129*: 28–35.

HMSO (1990), *Food Safety Act*, London: HMSO.

Hoek, A. et al. (2011), 'Replacement of meat by meat substitutes', *Appetite*, *56*: 662–763.

Hollands, C. (1985), 'Animal rights in the political arena', in P. Singer (ed) *In Defense of animals*, 168–178, New York: Blackwell.

Holloway, L. (2002), 'Smallholding, hobby-farming, and commercial farming: ethical identities and the production of farming spaces', *Environment and Planning A*, *34*(11): 2055–2070.

Holloway, L. (2007), 'Subjecting cows to robots: farming technologies and the making of animal subjects', *Environment and Planning D: Society and Space*, *25*(6): 1041–1060.

Holloway, L. and C. Morris (2008), 'Boosted bodies: genetic techniques, domestic livestock bodies and complex representations of life', *Geoforum*, *39*(5): 1709–1720.

Holmes, M. and P. Cockcroft (2004). 'Evidence-based veterinary medicine 1. Why is it important and what skills are needed?', *In Practice*, *26*(1): 28–33.

Hoogland, C. T., J. de Boer and J. J. Boersema (2007), 'Food and sustainability: do consumers recognize, understand and value on-package information on production standards?', *Appetite*, *49*(1): 47–57.

Horseman, S. V. et al. (2014), 'The use of in-depth interviews to understand the process of treating lame dairy cows from the farmers' perspective', *Animal Welfare*, *23*: 157–165.

House of Commons, Environment, Food and Rural Affairs Committee (2008), *The English pig industry*. First Report, HC96, London, House of Commons.

Hovi, M., A. Sundrum and S. M. Thamsborg (2003), 'Animal health and welfare in organic livestock production in Europe: current state and future challenges', *Livestock Production Science*, *80*(1): 41–53.

Howkins, A. and L. Merricks (2000), '"Dewy-Eyed Veal Calves". Live Animal Exports and Middle-Class Opinion, 1980–1995', *The Agricultural History Review*, *48*(1): 85–103.

Hubbard, M. C., M. Bourlakis and G. Garrod (2007), 'Pig in the middle: farmers and the delivery of farm animal welfare standards', *British Food Journal*, *109*(11): 919–931.

Hughes, A. (1996), 'Retail restructuring and the strategic significance of food retailers' own-labels: A UK—USA comparison', *Environment and Planning A*, *28*(12): 2201–2226.

Hughes, A. (2001), 'Multi-stakeholder approaches to ethical trade: towards a reorganisation of UK retailers' global supply chains?' *Journal of Economic Geography*, *1*(4): 421–437.

Hulme, M. (2008), *Why we disagree about climate change*, Cambridge: Cambridge University Press.

Humphrey, J. and H. Schmitz (2008), 'Inter-firm relationships in global value chains: trends in chain governance and their policy implications', *International Journal of Technological Learning, Innovation and Development*, *1*(3): 258–282.

Hutter, M. (2011), 'Lucien Karpik: valuing the unique. The economies of singularities', *Journal of Cultural Economics*, *34*(1): 1–5.

Hvorka, A. (2008), 'Transpecies urban theory: chickens in an African city', *Cultural Geographies*, *15*(1): 95–117.

IGD (2009), *Consumer attitudes to animal welfare: a report for freedom food*, Watford: IGD.

Iovino, S. (2012), 'Material ecocriticism: matter, rext and posthuman ethics', in T. Muller and M. Sauter (eds) *Literature, ecology, ethics: recent trends in ecocritcism*, 51–68, Heidelberg: University of Heidelberg Press.

Jackson, P. (2013), *Food words*, London: Bloomsbury.

Jackson, P., N. Ward and P. Russell (2006), 'Mobilising the commodity chain concept in the politics of food and farming', *Journal of Rural Studies*, *22*: 129–141.

Jackson, P., N. Ward and P. Russell (2009), 'Moral economies of food and geographies of responsibility', *Transactions of the Institute of British Geographers*, *34*(1): 12–24.

Jackson, P., P. Russell and N. Ward (2011), 'Brands in the making: a life history approach', in A. Pike (ed) *Brands and branding geographies*, 59–74, Cheltenham: Elgar.

Jasanoff, S. ed (2004), *States of knowledge: the co-production of science and social order*, London: Routledge.

Jensen, M. B. and L. J. Pedersen (2008), 'Using motivation tests to assess ethological needs and preferences', *Applied Animal Behaviour Science*, *113*: 340–356.

Jensen, M. B. et al. (2008), 'Genetics and genomics of animal behavior and welfare – challenges and possibilities', *Applied Animal Behaviour Science*, *113*: 383–403.

Jensen, P. (2014), 'Behaviour epigenetics – the connection between environment, stress and welfare', *Applied Animal Behaviour Science*, *157*: 1–7.

Jensen, P. and L. Andersson (2005), 'Genomics meets ethology: a new route to understanding domestication, behaviour and sustainability in animal breeding', *Ambio*, *34*: 320–324.

Jerolmack, C. (2009), 'Humans, animals, and play: theorizing interaction when intersubjectivity is problematic', *Sociological Theory*, *27*(4): 371–389.

Johnson, C. L. (2015), 'The political science of farm animal welfare in the US and EU', in J. Emel and H. Neo (eds) *The political economic of meat*, London: Earthscan.

Karel, K. H., J. De Greef and A. P. Bram (2007), 'Can the science meet expectations in the animal welfare debate', in European Society of Agriculture and Food Ethics (ed) *Sustainable food production and ethics*, 293–299, Wageningen: Wageningen Academic Publishers.

Karpik, L. (2010), *The economics of singularities*, Princeton, NJ: Princeton University Press.

Keene, B. W. (2000), 'Towards evidence-based veterinary medicine', *Journal of Veterinary Internal Medicine*, *14*(2): 118–119.

Keping, Y. and T. Herberer (2008), 'Developing a Chinese civil society', in S. Crossick and E. Reuter (eds) *China-EU. A common future*, New York: World Scientific.

Key, B. (2016), 'Why fish do not feel pain,' *Animal Sentience*, *1*(3): 1–34. Online journal at http://animalstudiesrepository.org/animsent/vol1/iss3/1/.

Kielland, C. et al. (2010), 'Dairy farmer attitudes and empathy toward animals are associated with animal welfare indicators', *Journal of Dairy Science*, *93*(7): 2998–3006.

Kirk, R. (2014), 'The invention of the "Stressed Animal" and the development of a science of animal welfare, 1947–86', in D. Cantor and E. Ramsden (eds) *Stress, shock, and adaptation in the twentieth century,* 241–263, Rochester: University of Rochester Press.

Kjaernes, U. and R. Lavik (2008), 'Opinions on animal welfare and food consumption in seven European countries', in U. Kjærnes, B. Bock, E. Roe and J. Roex (eds) *Welfare quality reports no 7. Consumption, distribution and production of farm animal welfare*, Cardiff: Cardiff University/Welfare Quality.

Kjaernes, U., B. Bock, M. Higgin and J. Roex eds (2009), *Welfare quality reports no. 8: farm animal welfare within the supply chain: regulation, agriculture, and geography*, Cardiff: Cardiff University/Welfare Quality.

Kjellberg, H. and C.-F. Helgesson (2007), 'On the nature of markets and their practices', *Marketing Theory*, *7*(2): 137–162.

Korte, S. M., O. Berend and J. M. Koolhaas (2007), 'A new animal welfare concept based on allostasis', *Physiology & Behavior*, *92*(3): 422–428.

Kreilkamp, I. (2005), 'Petted things: wuthering heights and the animal', *The Yale Journal of Criticism*, *18*(1): 87–110.

Labatut, J. et al. (2009), 'The active role of instruments in articulating knowing and knowledge', *The Learning Organization*, *16*(5): 371–385.

Landbouwraad (2005), *Beschrijving van de landbouw in Hongarije*, Ministerie van de Vlaamse Gemeenschap, Administratie Land- en Tuinbouw (ALT), Afdeling Monitoring en Studie (AM&S), Budapest: Ministerie.

Larsen, J. (2012), *Meat consumption in China is now double that in the United States*, Plan B Updates. Earth Policy Institute, 24 April 2012. http://www.earth-policy.org/plan_b _updates/2012/update102, last accessed 21 August 2016.

Latour, B. (1993), *We have never been modern*, Boston, MA: Harvard University Press.

Latour, B. (2004), 'Why has critique run out of steam? from matters of fact to matters of concern', *Critical Enquiry*, *30*: 225–248.

Latour, B. (2005), *Reassembling the social, an introduction to actor-network-theory*, Oxford: Oxford University Press.

Latour, B. (2016), Forward: the scientific fables of an empirical La Fontaine. Forward to V. Despret *What would animals say if we asked the right questions*, Minneapolis: Minnesota University Press, vii–xiv.

Law, J. (1994), *Organizing modernity*, Oxford: Blackwell.

Law, J. (2004), *After method: mess in social science research*, London: Routledge.

Law, J. (2008), 'Culling, catastrophe and collectivity', *Distinktion*, *16*: 61–77.

Law, J. (2010), 'Care and killing: tensions in veterinary practice', in A. Mol, I. Moser and J. Pols (eds) *Care in practice: on tinkering in clinics, homes and farms*, 57–69, Bielefeld: Transcript Publishers.

Lawrence, A. B. (2008), 'Applied animal behaviour science: past, present and future prospects', *Applied Animal Behaviour Science*, *115*(1): 1–24.

Lay, D. C. et al. (2011), 'Hen welfare in different housing systems', *Poultry Science*, *90*(1): 278–294.

LEAF (2015), *The generation that hasn't heard a cow moo*, Press release, 'Farm Sunday'.

Leitch, S. and S. Davenport (2007), 'Corporate brands and social brands: co-branding GM-free and UK supermarkets', *International Studies of Management & Organization*, *37*(4): 45–63.

Levi-Strauss, C. (1964), *Le Cru et le Cuit*, Paris: Plon.

Li, P. J (2006), 'The evolving animal rights and welfare debate in China: Political and social input analysis', in J. Turner and J. D'Silva (eds) *Animal, ethics and trade*, 111–128, London: Earthscan.

Li, P. J. (2009), 'Exponential growth, animal welfare, environmental and food safety impact: the case of China's Livestock Production', *Journal of Agriculture and Environmental Ethics*, *22*: 217–240.

Li, P. J. (undated), *The development of School Milk Programme in China*. Presented at the fourth International School Milk Conference, South Africa. http://www.fao.org /fileadmin/templates/est/COMM_MARKETS_MONITORING/Dairy/Documents/12 _Jien_Li___China_country_report_paper.pdf, last accessed 21 August 2016.

Li, P. J. and G. Davey (2013), 'Culture, reform politics and future directions: a review of China's animal protection challenge', *Society & Animals*, *21*: 34–53.

Lloyd, T. et al. (2004), *Food scares, market power and relative price adjustment in the UK*. Nottingham Discussion Papers in Economics, Paper 04/10, Nottingham: University of Nottingham.

Low, L. (2004), *Developmental states: relevancy, redundancy or reconfiguration?* New York: Nova Science Publishers Inc.

Lowe, P., J. Clark, S. Seymour and N. Ward (1997), *Moralizing the environment: countryside change, farming and pollution*, London: UCL Press.

Lu, P. J., K. Bayne and J. Wang (2013), 'Current status of animal welfare and animal rights in China', *Alternatives to Laboratory Animals*, *41*: 351–357.

Lund, V., R. Anthony and H. Röcklinsberg (2004), 'The ethical contract as a tool in organic animal husbandry', *Journal of Agricultural and Environmental Ethics*, *17*(1): 23–49.

Lund, V., G. Coleman, S. Gunnarsson, M. C. Appleby and K. Karkinen (2006), 'Animal welfare science—working at the interface between the natural and social sciences', *Applied Animal Behaviour Science*, *97*(1): 37–49.

Lymbery, P. (2014), *Farmageddon: the true cost of cheap meat*, London: Bloomsbury Publishing.

Lyons, C. A. P., J. M. Bruce, V. R. Fowler and P. R. English (1995), 'A comparison of productivity and welfare of growing pigs in four intensive systems', *Livestock Production Science*, *43*(3): 265–274.

Ma, Q. (2008), *Non-governmental organisations in contemporary China. Paving the way to civil society?* Abingdon, Oxon: Routledge Contemporary China Series.

Main, D. et al. (2000), 'Animal welfare assessment in farm assurance schemes', *Acta Agriculturae Scandinavica*, *51*: 108–113.

Main, D. C. J., A. J. F. Webster and L. K. E. Green (2001), 'Animal welfare assessment in farm assurance schemes', *Acta Agriculturea Scandinavica*, *51*: 108–113.

Main, D. C. J., H. R. Whay, C. Leeb and A. J. F. Webster (2007), 'Formal animal-based welfare assessment in UK certification schemes', *Animal Welfare*, *16*(2): 233–236.

Main, D. C. J., Z. E. Barker, K. A. Leach, N. J. Bell, H. R. Whay and W. J. Browne (2010), 'Sampling strategies for monitoring lameness in dairy cattle', *Journal of Dairy Science*, *93*(5): 1970–1978.

Main, D. C. J., S. M. Mullan, C. Atkinson, A. Bond, M. Cooper, A. Fraser and W. J. Browne (2012), 'Welfare outcome assessments in laying hen farm assurance schemes', *Animal welfare*, *21*: 389–396.

Manning, L., R. N. Baines and S. A. Chadd (2006), 'Quality assurance models in the food supply chain', *British Food Journal*, *108*(2): 91–104.

Marsden, T. and N. Wrigley (1995), 'Regulation, retailing, and consumption', *Environment and Planning A*, *27*(12): 1899–1912.

Marsden, T., J. Banks and G. Bristow (2000), 'Food supply chain approaches: exploring their role in rural development', *Sociologia Ruralis*, *40*(4): 424–438.

Marsden, T., M. Harrison and A. Flynn (1998), 'Creating competitive space: exploring the social and political maintenance of retail power', *Environment and Planning A*, *30*(3): 481–498.

Marsden, T., R. Munton, S. Whatmore and J. Little (1986), 'Towards a political economy of capitalist agriculture: a British perspective', *International Journal of Urban and Regional Research*, *10*(4): 498–521.

Marsden, T., R. Munton, N. Ward and S. Whatmore (1996), 'Agricultural geography and the political economy approach: a review', *Economic Geography*, *72*(4): 361–375.

Mason, G. and M. Mendl (1993), 'Why is there no simple way of measuring animal welfare?' *Animal Welfare*, *2*: 301–319.

Matheny, G. and C. Leahy (2007), 'Farm-animal welfare, legislation, and trade', *Law and Contemporary Problems*, *70*(1): 325–358.

Maye, D., L. Holloway and M. Kneafsey (2007), *Alternative food geographies: representation and practice*, Bingley: Emerald Group Publishing.

McCulloch, S. P. (2013), 'A critique of FAWC's five freedoms as a framework for the analysis of animal welfare', *Journal of Agricultural and Environmental Ethics*, *26*(5): 959–975.

McEachern, M. and G. Warnaby (2008), 'Exploring the relationship between consumer knowledge and purchase behaviour of value-based labels', *International Journal of Consumer Studies*, *32*: 414–426.

McInerney, J. (2004), *Animal welfare, economics and policy*. Report on a study undertaken for the farm & animal health economics, London: Division of Defra.

Mellor, D. J. (2016a), 'Moving beyond the "Five Freedoms: by updating the "Five Provisions" and Introducing Aligned "Animal Welfare Aims"', *Animals*, *6*(10): 59.

Mellor, D. J. (2016b), 'Updating animal welfare thinking: moving beyond the "Five Freedoms" to "A Life worth Living"', *Animals*, *6*(3): 21.

Mendl, M., O. Burman, R. M. A. Parker and E. Paul (2009), 'Cognitive bias as an indicator of animal emotion and welfare: emerging evidence and underlying mechanisms', *Applied Animal Welfare Science*, *118*: 161–181.

Mennell, S., A. Murcott and A. H. Van Otterloo (1992), *The sociology of food: eating, diet, and culture*, *40*(2), London: Sage.

Miele, M. (2012), 'The taste of happiness: free-range chicken', *Environment and Planning A*, *43*: 2076–2090.

Miele, M. (2013), 'Economisation of animals: the case of marketization of halal foods', in H. Rocklinsberg and P. Sadin (eds) *The ethics of consumption*, 21–24, Wageningen: Wageningen Academic Publishers.

Miele, M. and A. Evans (2010), 'When foods become animals: ruminations on ethics and responsibility in Care-*full* practices of consumption', *Ethics, Place & Environment*, *13*(2): 171–190.

Miele, M. and J. Lever (2013), 'Civilizing the market for welfare friendly products in Europe? The techno-ethics of the Welfare Quality assessment', *Geoforum*, *48*: 63–72.

Miele, M. and K. Rucinska (2015), 'Producing halal meat: the case of halal slaughter practices in Wales, UK', in J. Emel and H. Neo (eds) *Political ecologies of meat production*, Vol. *54*. Routledge Studies in Political Ecology, 253–277, London: Routledge.

Miele, M. et al. (2013), 'Changes in farming and in stakeholder concern for animal welfare', in H. Blokhuis et al. (eds) *Improving farm animal welfare*, 19–48, Wageningen: Wageningen University Press.

Milman, O. and S. Leavenworth (2016), 'China's plan to cut meat consumption by 50% cheered by climate campaigners', *The Guardian,* 20 June 2016.

Mitchell, R. W. and N. S. Thompson eds (1997), *Anthropomorphism, anecdotes, and animals*, Albany, NY: SUNY Press.

Mol, A. (2003), *The body multiple: ontology in medical practice*, Durham, NC: Duke University Press.

Mol, A. (2008), *The logic of care*, Oxford: Routledge.

Mol, A., I. Moser and J. Pols eds (2010), *Care in practice: on tinkering in clinics, homes and farms*, Bielefeld: Transcript Publishers.

Monath, T. P, L. Kahn and B. Kaplan (2010), 'One health perspective', *Journal Institute of Laboratory Animal Resources*, *51*(3): 195–198.

Montaigne, M. (1993), *De la Cruauté. from the essays*, Harmondsworth: Penguin.

More, T. (1516 [1965]), *Utopia*, transl. Paul Turner, London: Penguin Books.

Morelli, C. (1997), 'Britain's most dynamic sector? Competitive advantage in multiple food retailing', *Business and Economic History*, *26*(2): 770–781.

Morris, P. (2012), *Blue juice. Euthanasia in veterinary medicine*, Philadelphia, PA: Temple University Press.

Muhlhausler B. S., F. H. Bloomfield and M. W. Gillman (2013), 'Whole animal experiments should be more like human randomized controlled trials', *PLoS Biology*, *11*(2): 1–6.

Muniesa, F., Y. Millo and M. Callon (2007), 'An introduction to market devices', *The Sociological Review*, *55* (Suppl. 2): 1–12.

Murdoch, J. (2006), *Post-structuralist geography*, London: Sage.

Nagel, T. (1974), 'What is it like to be a bat?' *The Philosophical Review*, *LXXXIII*(4): 435–50.

Napolitano, F., A. Girolami and A. Braghieri (2010), 'Consumer liking and willingness to pay for high welfare animal-based products', *Trends in Food Science & Technology*, *21*(11): 537–543.

Neo, H. and L.-H. Chen (2009), 'Household income diversification and the production of local meat: the prospect of small-scale pig farming in Southern Yunnan, China', *Area*, *41*(3): 300–309.

Nicol, C. (2015), *The behavioural biology of chickens*, Wallingford: CABI.

Nimmo, R. (2011), 'Actor-network theory and methodology: social research in a more-than-human world', *Methodological Innovations Online*, 6(3): 108–119.

Nocellall, A. J et al. (2014), *Defining critical animal studies – an intersectional social justice approach for liberation*, New York: Peter Lang.

Northen, J. (2000), 'Quality attributes and quality cues. Effective communication in the UK meat supply chain', *British Food Journal*, 102(3): 230–245.

Norwood, F. B. and J. L. Lusk (2011), *Compassion, by the pound: the economics of farm animal welfare*, Oxford: Oxford University Press.

Noske, B. (1997), *Beyond boundaries: humans and animals*, Buffalo: Black Rose Books.

Novek, J. (2005), 'Pigs and people: Sociological perspectives on the discipline of nonhuman animals in intensive confinement', *Society & Animals*, 13(3): 221–244.

O'Neill, J. (2016), *Tackling drug-resistant infections globally: Final report and recommendations. The Review on Antimicrobial Resistance Chaired by Jim O'Neill.* London: HM Government & Wellcome Trust.

Office of National Statistics (2017), *Family spending in the UK*, London: ONS.

OIE (2016), 'Introduction for the recommendations for animal welfare'. *Terrestrial Animal Health Code.* http://web.oie.int/eng/normes/mcode/en_chapitre_1.7.1.htm, last accessed 21 August 2016.

Olesen, I., F. Alfnes, M. B. Røra and K. Kolstad (2010), 'Eliciting consumers' willingness to pay for organic and welfare-labelled salmon in a non-hypothetical choice experiment', *Livestock Science*, 127(2): 218–226.

Ophuis, P. A. O. and H. C. Van Trijp (1995), 'Perceived quality: a market driven and consumer oriented approach', *Food Quality and Preference*, 6(3): 177–183.

Osburn, B., C. Scott and P. Gibbs (2009), 'One World – One Medicine – One Health: emerging veterinary challenges and opportunities', *Revue Scientifique Et Technique (International Office of Epizootics)*, 28(2): 481–486.

Pachirat, T. (2013), *Every twelve seconds. Industrialised slaughter and the politics of sight*, New Haven: Yale University Press.

Palczynski, L. et al. (2016), 'Farmer attitudes to injurious pecking in laying hens and to potential control strategies', *Animal Welfare*, 25: 29–38.

Parr, H. and C. Philo (2003), 'Rural mental health and social geographies of care', *Social and Cultural Geography*, 4(4): 471–88.

Paul, E. S., E. J. Harding and M. Mendl (2005), 'Measuring emotional processes in animals: the utility of a cognitive approach', *Neuroscience and Biobehavioural Reviews*, 29: 469–491.

Peggs, K. (2012), *Animals and sociology*, London: Palgrave-Macmillan.

Pettersson, I. C., C. A. Weeks, L. R. M. Wilson and C. J. Nicol (2016), 'Consumer perceptions of free-range laying hen welfare', *British Food Journal*, 118(8): 1999–2013.

Phillips, C. J. C., S. Izmirli, S. J. Aldavood, M. Alonso, B. I. Choe, A. Hanlon, A. Handziska, G. Illmann, L. Keeling, M. Kennedy and G. H. Lee (2012), 'Students' attitudes to animal welfare and rights in Europe and Asia', *Animal Welfare-The UFAW Journal*, 21(1): 87.

Philo, C. (1995), 'Animals, geography, and the city: Notes on inclusions and exclusions', *Environment and planning D: Society and Space*, *13*(6): 655–681.

Philo, C. and C. Wilbert (2000), *Animal spaces, beastly places: new geographies of human-animal relations*, London: Routledge.

Philo, C. and J. Wolch (1998), 'Through the geographical looking glass: space, place, and society-animal relations', *Society and Animals*, 6(2): 103–118.

Pi, C. with Z. Rou and S. Horowitz (2014), 'Fair or Fowl? Industrialisation of poultry production in China', *Global meat complex: the China Series*, February 2014, Institute of Agriculture and Trade Policy.

Pinillos, R. G et al. (2016), 'One welfare – a platform for improving human and animal welfare', *Veterinary Record*, *22*, 412–415.

Policy Commission on the Future of Farming and Food (2002), *Farming and food: a sustainable future*, Curry Report, London: Cabinet Office.

Pollan, M. (2006), *The omnivore's dilemma: a natural history of four meals*, Harmondsworth: Penguin.

Pollan, M. (2009), *The Omnivores Dilemma*, London: Bloomsbury.

Porcher, J. (2002), *Eleveurs et animaux: reinventer le lien*, Paris: PUF.

Porcher, J. (2006), 'Well-being and suffering in livestock farming: living conditions at work for people and animals', *Sociologie Du Travail*, *48*: e56–e70.

Porcher, J. (2009), 'Le challenge des Cochons d'Or. Un pilier défensif et un maître étalon de la filière porcine industrielle', *Économie rurale. Agricultures, alimentations, territoires*, *313/314*: 163–170.

Porcher, J. (2011), 'The relationship between workers and animals in the pork industry: a shared suffering', *Journal of Agricultural and Environmental Ethics*, *24*(1): 3–17.

Porcher, J. (2016), 'Quant les vaches auront des cornes', in P. Busser, C. Thoyer and J. Porcher (eds) *Le yin et la yang*, 1–32, Montvicq: Editions du mirroir.

Porcher, J. and T. Schmitt (2012), 'Dairy cows: workers in the shadows?' *Society & Animals*, *20*(1): 39–60.

Power, M. (1994), *The Audit Explosion*, Demons Paper No. 7, London: Demos.

Probyn, E. (1999), 'Beyond food/sex: eating and an ethics of existence', *Theory Culture Society*, *16*: 215–228.

Proctor, H. (2012), 'Animal sentience: where are we and where are we heading?' *Animals*, 2(4): 628–639.

Proulx, A (2002), *That old ace in the hole*, New York: Fourth Estate.

Pugh, R. F. (1990), 'Food safety and the retail industry', *International Journal of Retail & Distribution Management*, *18*(6): 3–7.

Puig de la Bellacasa, M. (2017), *Matters of care*, Minneapolis: University of Minnesota Press.

QA Research (2013), *Method of production labelling of meat and dairy products – report*, York: QA Research.

QA Research (2014), *The European product labels research*. Report for Labelling Matters. York: QA Research.

Radford, M. (2001), *Animal welfare law in Britain*, Oxford: Oxford University Press.

Ransom, E. (2007), 'The rise of agricultural animal welfare standards as understood through a neo-institutional lens', *International Journal of Sociology of Agriculture and Food*, *15*(3): 26.

Rauch, A. and J. S. Sharp (2005), *Ohioans attitudes about animal welfare: a topical report from the 2004 Ohio Survey of Food, Agriculture and Environmental Issues*, Columbus, OH: The Ohio State University.

Reducetarian (2017), https://reducetarian.org, last accessed 26th July 2017.

Regan, T. (2004 [1983]), *The case for animal rights*, Berkeley: University of California.

Renard, M. C. (2005), 'Quality certification, regulation and power in fair trade', *Journal of Rural Studies*, *21*(4): 419–431.

Richardson, P. S., A. K. Jain and A. Dick (1996), 'Household store brand proneness: a framework', *Journal of Retailing*, *72*(2): 159–185.

Risan, L. C. (2005), 'The boundary of animality', *Environment and Planning D: Society and Space*, *23*(5): 787–793.

Ritvo, H. (1987), *The animal estate: the English and other creatures in the Victorian Age*, Cambridge, MA: Harvard University Press.

Rocklinsberg, H., C. Gamborg and M. Gjerris (2014), 'A case for integrity', *Laboratory Animals*, *48*(1): 61–71.

Roe, E. and B. Greenhough (2014), 'Experimental partnering: interpreting improvisatory habits in the research field', *International Journal of Social Research Methodology*, *17*(1): 45–57.

Roe, E. and M. Higgin (2008), 'European meat and dairy retail distribution and supply networks: a comparative study of the current and potential markets for welfare-friendly foodstuffs in six European countries', in Unni Kjaernes, Bettina Bock, Marc Higgin and Joek Roex (eds) *Farm animal welfare within the supply chain. Regulation, agriculture and geography*, 215–280 (Welfare Quality Reports, 8 Part IV: Chapter), Cardiff: Cardiff University.

Roe, E., H. Buller and J. Bull (2011), 'The performance of farm animal welfare assessment', *Animal Welfare*, *20*(1): 69–78.

Roe, E., U. Kjaernes, B. Bock, M. Higgin, M. Van Huik and C. Cowan (2007), *Farm animal welfare in Hungary: a study of Hungarian producers, its food retail market and of Hungarian Consumers*, Welfare Quality Reports, Lelystad, The Netherlands: Welfare Quality.

Roe, E. J. (2006), 'Things becoming food and the embodied, material practices of an organic food consumer', *Sociologia Ruralis*, *46*(2): 104–121.

Roe, E. J. (2010), 'Ethics and the non-human: the matterings of sentience in the meat industry', in B. Anderson and P. Harrison (eds) *Taking-place: non-representational theories and geography*, 261–280, Farnham, GB: Ashgate.

Rohrmann, S. et al. (2013), 'Meat consumption and mortality – results from the European Prospective Investigation into Cancer and Nutrition', *BMC Medicine*, Mar 7, *11*: 63.

Rollin, B. et al. (2011), 'Defining agricultural animal welfare: varying viewpoints and approaches', in W. G. Pond et al. (eds) *Animal welfare in animal agriculture*, 75–120, Boca Raton: CRC Press.

Rollin, B. E. (1990), *The unheeded cry*, Oxford, UK: Oxford University Press.

Rollin, B. E. (1993), 'Animal welfare, science, and value', *Journal of Agricultural and Environmental Ethics*, 6(Supp. 2): 44–50.

Rollin, B. E. (1995), *Farm animal welfare: social, bioethical, and research issues*, Ames: Iowa State University Press.

Rollin, B. E. (2013), *An introduction to veterinary medical ethics: theory and cases*. London: John Wiley & Sons.

Royal College of Veterinary Surgeons (2012), *Position paper on evidence based veterinary medicine*, London: RCVS.

RSPCA (2014), *Trustees report and accounts*, Horsham: RSPCA.

Rushen, J. (1991), 'Problems associated with the interpretation of physiological data in the assessment of animal welfare', *Applied Animal Behaviour Science*, 28(4): 381–386.

Rushen, J. (2008), 'Farm animal welfare since the Brambell report', *Applied Animal Behaviour Science*, 113(4): 277–278.

Rushen, J. et al. (2014), 'Farm animal welfare assurance: science and application', *Journal of Animal Science*, 89: 1219–1228.

Rutgers, B. and R. Heeger (1999), 'Inherent worth and respect for animal integrity', in M. Dol et al. (eds) *Recognising the intrinsic value of nature*, 41–53, Assen: Van Gorcum.

Sabel, C. F. and J. Zeitlin (2008), 'Learning from difference: the new architecture of experimentalist governance in the EU', *European Law Journal*, 14(3): 271–327.

Sandøe, P., S. B. Christiansen and M. C. Appleby (2003), 'Farm animal welfare: the interaction of ethical questions and animal welfare science', *Animal Welfare*, 12(4): 469–478.

Sandøe, P., B. Forkman and S. B. Christiansen (2004). 'Scientific uncertainty—how should it be handled in relation to scientific advice regarding animal welfare issues?', *Animal Welfare*, 13(1): 121–126.

Sainsbury.co.uk (2014), *20/20 Factsheet Sourcing with Integrity*, London: Sainsburys PLC.

Sayer, K. (2013), 'The public response to intensification in Great Britain, c. 1960–c. 1973', *Agricultural History*, 87(4): 473–501.

Schmid, O. and R. Kilchsperger (2010), *Overview of animal welfare standards and initiatives in selected EU and third countries*, Final report deliverable, 1. 2. Lelystad, The Netherlands: Econwelfare.eu.

Schneider, M. with S. Sharma (2014), 'China's Pork Miracle? agribusiness and development in China's Pork Industry', *Global Meat complex: The China Series*. Institute for Agriculture and Trade Policy. February 2014.

Schroder, M. J. A. and M. G. McEachern (2004), 'Consumer value conflicts surrounding ethical food purchase decisions. a focus on animal welfare', *International Journal of Consumer Studies*, 28(2): 168–177.

Scott, C. (2003), 'Regulation in the age of governance: the rise of the post regulatory state'. *National Europe Centre Paper No. 100*, Australian National University.

Sexton, A. (2016), 'Alternative proteins and the (non) stuff of "meat"', *Gastronomica. The Journal of Critical Food Studies*, *16*(3): 66–78.

Sharma, S. (2014), 'The need for feed. China's demand for industrialised meat and its impact'. *Global Meat Complex: The China Series*. Institute for Agriculture and Trade Policy.

Sharma, S. and Z. Rou (2014), 'China's Dairy Dilemma. The evolution and future trends of China's Dairy industry'. *Global Meat Complex: The China Series*. Institute of Agriculture and Trade Policy. February 2014.

Sherwin, C., G. Richards and C. Nicol (2010), 'A comparison of the welfare of layer hens in four housing systems used in the UK', *British Poultry Science*, *51*(4): 488–499.

Shukin, N. (2009), *Animal capital*, Minneapolis: Minnesota University Press.

Sinclair, U. (2002 [1914]), *The jungle*, California: Chelsea House.

Singer, P. (1974), 'All animals are equal. Philosophical Exchange 1', Reprinted in H. LaFollette (ed) (2007), *Ethics in practice: third edition*, 171–180, Malden, MA: Blackwell.

Singer, P. (1995 [1974]), *Animal liberation* (2nd ed), Pimlico: London.

Singer, P. (2008), 'Forward', in M. Dawkins and R. Bonney (eds) *The Future of Farm Animal Welfare*, Oxford: Wiley-Blackwell.

Singer, P. and J. Mason (2008), *The ethics of what we eat*, New York: Rodale.

Skarstad, G. A., L. Terragni and H. Torjusen (2007), 'Animal welfare according to Norwegian consumers and producers: definitions and implications', *International Journal of Sociology of Food and Agriculture*, *15*(3): 74–90.

Smith, J. et al. (2014), 'The traditional food market and place: new insights into fresh food provisioning in England', *Area*, *46*(2): 122–128.

Sorensen, J. T. and D. Fraser (2010), 'On farm welfare assessment for regulatory purposes: issues and possible solutions', *Livestock Science*, *131*(1): 1–7.

Špinka, M. (2006), 'How important is natural behaviour in animal farming systems?' *Applied Animal Behaviour Science*, *100*(1): 117–128.

Stassart, P. and S. J. Whatmore (2003), 'Metabolising risk: food scares and the un/re-making of Belgian beef', *Environment and Planning A*, *35*(3): 449–462.

Stassart, P. M. (2003), *Produit Fermier: entre Qualification et Identité*, Bruxelles, Belgique: Presses Interuniversitaires Européennes.

Stassart, P. M and D. Jamar (2005), 'Equiper des filières durables? L'élevage Bio en Belgique', *Natures Sciences Sociétés*, *13*(4): 413–420.

Steeves, H. P. (1999), *Animal others: On ethics, ontology, and animal life*, New York: SUNY Press.

Sterchi, B. (1988), *The cow*, trans. Michael Hofmann, Oxford: Faber and Faber.

Sylvander, B. (1995), 'Conventions de qualité, marchés et institutions: le cas des produits de qualité spécifique', in *Agro-alimentaire: une économie de la qualité*, 167–183, Paris: INRA-Economica.

Sylvander, B., G. Belletti, A. Marescotti and E. Thévenod-Mottet (2006), 'Establishing a quality convention, certifying and promoting the quality of animal products: the case of beef', *Publication-European Association for Animal Production*, *118*: 61.

Symes, D. and T. Marsden (1985), 'Industrialisation of agriculture: intensive livestock farming in Humberside', *The industrialisation of the countryside*, Norwich: Geobooks.

Tawse, J. (2010), 'Consumer attitudes towards farm animals and their welfare: a pig production case study', *Bioscience Horizons*, *3*(2): 156–165.

Taylor, N. and R. Twine (2014), *The rise of critical animal studies: from the margins to the centre* (Vol. *125*), London: Routledge.

Tesco (2017), 'Home on the range', unpaginated. https://realfood.tesco.com/our-food /home-on-the-range.html, last accessed 12 January 2015.

The Meatrix (2017), 'The Meatrix relaunched', unpaginated. http://www.themeatrix.com, last accessed 29 July 2017.

Thevenot, L. (1995), 'Des marchés aux normes', in G. Allaire and R. Boyer (eds) *La grande transformation de l'agriculture: lectures conventionnalistes et régulationnistes*, 33–51, Paris: Economica & INRA.

Thiermann, A. and S. Babcock (2005), 'Animal welfare and international trade', *Revue Scientifique Et Technique (International Office of Epizootics)*, *24*(2): 747–755.

Thomas, K. (1984), *Man and the natural world*, Harmondsworth: Penguin.

Thrift, N. (2008), *Non-representational theory: space, politics, affect*, London: Routledge.

Torsonnen, S. (2015), 'Sellfare: a history of livestock welfare commodification as governance', *Humanimalia: A Journal of Human/Animal Interface Studies*, 7(1) Fall 2015: 23–58.

Tovey, H. (2003), 'Theorising nature and society in sociology: the invisibility of animals', *Sociologia Ruralis*, *43*(3): 196–215.

Turner, J. and J. D'Silva (2005), *Animals, ethics and trade: the challenge of animal sentience*, London: Earthscan.

Twigg, J. (1979), 'Food for thought: purity and vegetarianism', *Religion*, 9(1): 13–35.

Twigg, J. (1983), 'Vegetarianism and the meanings of meat', in A Murcott (ed) *The sociology of food and eating: essays in the sociological significance of food*, 18–30, Aldershot: Gower.

Twine, R. (2010), *Animals as biotechnology: ethics, sustainability and critical animal studies*, London: Routledge.

United Nations (2016), *High level panel on food security and nutrition, sustainable agricultural development for food security and nutrition, including the role of livestock*, Rome: FAO.

Van Der Weele, C. and C. Driessen (2013), 'Emerging profiles for cultured meat: ethics through and as design', *Animals*, *3*: 648–662.

Van Huik, M. M. and B. B. Bock (2007), 'Attitudes of Dutch pig farmers towards animal welfare', *British Food Journal*, *109*(11): 879–890.

Van Langenhove, L. (2003), 'Rethinking the social sciences', in OECD (ed) *The social sciences at a turning point*, 43–52, Paris: OECD.

Vanhonacker, F., W. Verbeke, W. Van Poucke and F. Tuyttens (2007), 'Segmentation based on consumers' perceived importance and attitude toward farm animal welfare', *International Journal of Sociology of Agriculture and Food*, *15*(3): 91–107.

Veale, R., P. Quester and A. Karunaratna (2006), 'The role of intrinsic (sensory) cues and the extrinsic cues of country of origin and price on food product evaluation.' In *3rd International Wine Business and Marketing Research Conference, Refereed Paper, Montpellier, July 2006*, 6–8.

Vegetarian Society (2014), *Fact Sheet 8/11/14, public attitudes and consumer behaviour*, Altrincham: Vegetarian Society.

Veissier, I., A. Butterworth, B. Bock and E. Roe (2008), 'European approaches to ensure good animal welfare', *Applied Animal Behaviour Science*, *113*(4): 279–297.

Vialles, N. (1994), *Animal to edible*, Cambridge: Cambridge University Press.

Von Keyserlingk, M. A. G., J. Rushen, A. M. De Passillé and D. M. Weary (2009), 'Invited review: the welfare of dairy cattle – key concepts and the role of science', *Journal of Dairy Science*, *92*(9): 4101–4111.

Von Keyserlingk, M. A. G. and M. J. Hotzel (2015), 'The ticking clock: addressing farm animal welfare in emerging countries', *Journal of Agriculture and Environmental Ethics*, *28*: 179–195.

Vorley, B. (2007), 'Supermarkets and agri-food supply chains in Europe: partnership and protest', in D. Burch and G. Lawrence (eds) *Supermarkets and agri-food supply chains: transformations in the production and consumption of foods*, Cheltenham: Edward Elgar.

Waiblinger, S., X. Boivin, V. Pedersen, M. V. Tosi, A. M. Janczak, E. K. Visser and R. B. Jones (2006), 'Assessing the human–animal relationship in farmed species: a critical review', *Applied Animal Behaviour Science*, *101*(3): 185–242.

Wasley, A. et al. (2017), 'UK has nearly 800 livestock mega farms, investigation reveals', *The Guardian*, 17 July 2017, unpaginated. https://www.theguardian.com /environment/2017/jul/17/uk-has-nearly-800-livestock-mega-farms-investigation -reveals, last accessed 12 July 2017.

Watts, M. (2000), 'Afterword: enclosure', in C. Philo and C. Wilbert (eds) *Animal spaces, beastly places: new geographies of human-animal relations*, 291–301, London: Routledge.

Webster, J. (1994), *A cool eye towards Eden*, Oxford: Blackwell.

Webster, J. (1998), 'What use is science to animal welfare?' *Naturwissenschaften*, *85*(6): 262–269.

Webster, J. (2001), 'Farm animal welfare: the five freedoms and the free market', *The Veterinary Journal*, *161*: 229–237.

Webster, J. (2006), 'Animal sentience and animal welfare: what is it to them and what is it to us?' *Applied Animal Behaviour Science*, *100*(1–2): 1–3.

Webster, J. (2008), *Animal welfare: limping towards Eden*, Oxford: Blackwell Publishing.

Webster, J. (2009), 'The virtuous bicycle: a delivery vehicle for improved farm animal welfare', *Animal Welfare*, *18*(2): 141–147.

Webster, J. (2010), 'Food from the dairy: husbandry regained', in J. D'Silva and J. Webster (eds) *The meat crisis: developing more sustainable production and consumption*, 99–117, London: Earthscan.

Webster, J. (2011), *Management and welfare of farm animals: the UFAW farm handbook* (Vol. 5), Oxford: Wiley-Blackwell.

Webster, J. (2013), 'Ruth Harrison – Tribute to an inspirational friend', in J. Harrison and J. Wilson (eds) *Animal machines*, 5–9, Wallingford: CABI.

Webster, J. (2016), 'Animal welfare: Freedoms, dominions (sic) and "A Life Worth Living"', *Animals*, *6*(6): 35.

Weil, K. (2006), 'Killing them softly: animal death, Linguistic disability and the struggle for ethics', *Configurations*, *14*(1–2): 87–96.

Weil, K. (2010), 'A report on the animal turn', *Differences*, *21*(2): 1–23.

Weil, K. (2012), *Thinking animals: why animal studies now?* New York: Columbia University Press.

Welfare Quality (2009a), *Welfare assessment protocol for dairy cows*, Wageningen: Wagening University.

Welfare Quality (2009b), *Welfare assessment protocol for pigs*, Wageningen: Wagening University.

Welfare Quality (2009c), *Welfare assessment protocol for broilers*, Wageningen: Wagening University.

Welfare Quality (2004–2009), www.welfarequality.net, last accessed 1 August 2017.

Wemelsfelder, F. (1997), 'The scientific validity of subjective concepts in models of animal welfare', *Applied Animal Behaviour Science*, *53*(1): 75–88.

Wemelsfelder, F. (2007), 'How animals communicate quality of life: the qualitative assessment of animal behaviour', *Animal Welfare*, *16*(S): 25–31.

Wemelsfelder, F. and A. B. Lawrence (2001), 'Qualitative assessment of animal behaviour as an on-farm welfare monitoring tool', *Acta Agriculturae Scandinavica*, suppl, *30*: 21–25.

Wemelsfelder, F. and S. Mullan (2014), 'Applying ethological and health indicators to practical animal welfare assessment', *Scientific Technical Review, Office International des Epizooties*, *33*: 111–20.

Wemelsfelder, F., E. A. Hunter, M. T. Mendl and A. B. Lawrence (2000), 'The spontaneous qualitative assessment of behavioural expressions in pigs: first explorations of a novel methodology for integrative animal welfare measurement', *Applied Animal Behaviour Science*, *67*(3): 193–215.

Wemelsfelder, F., T. E. Hunter, M. T. Mendl and A. B. Lawrence (2001), 'Assessing the "whole animal": a free choice profiling approach', *Animal Behaviour*, *62*(2): 209–220.

Westhoek, H. et al. (2011), *The Protein puzzle: the consumption and production of meat, dairy and fish in the European Union*, The Hague: Netherlands Environmental Assessment Agency.

Whatmore, S. (1997), 'Dissecting the autonomous self: hybrid cartographies for a relational ethics', *Environment and planning D: Society and Space*, *15*(1): 37–53.

Whatmore, S. (2006), 'Materialist returns: practising cultural geography in and for a more-than-human world', *Cultural Geographies*, *13*(4): 600–609.

Whatmore, S. and L. Thorne (1997), 'Alternative geographies of food', in D. Goodman and M. J. Watts (eds) *Globalising food: agrarian questions and global restructuring*, 287–304, London: Routledge.

Whay, B. (2007), 'The journey to animal welfare improvement', *Animal Welfare*, *16*: 117–122.

Whay, H. R., D. C. J. Main, L. E. Green and A. J. F. Webster (2003), 'Assessment of the welfare of dairy cattle using animal-based measurements: direct observations and investigation on farm', *The Veterinary Record*, *153*(7): 197–202.

Wheeler, W. and L. Williams (2012), 'Editorial: the animal turn', *New Formations*, *76*: 5–7.

White, R. (2015), 'Animal geographies, anarchist practice and critical animal studies', in K. Gillespie and R.-C. Collard (eds) *Critical animal geographies*, 19–34, London: Routledge.

Whitmore, C. (2015), 'Bovine Urbanism: the ecological corpulence of Bos urbanus', in Bruce Clarke (ed) *Earth, life, and system: evolution and ecology on a gaian planet*, 225–249, New York: Fordham University Press.

Wilkie, R. M. (2005), 'Sentient commodities and productive paradoxes: the ambiguous nature of human-livestock relations in Northeast Scotland', *Journal of Rural Studies*, *21*(2): 213–230.

Wilkie, R. (2010), *Livestock/Deadstock: working with farm animals from birth to slaughter*, Philadelphia, PA: Temple University Press.

Wilkins, D. B. et al. (2005), 'Animal welfare: the role of non-governmental organisations', *Revue Scientifique Et Technique (International Office of Epizootics)*, *24*(2): 625–638.

Wilkinson, J. (2002), 'The final foods industry and the changing face of the global agro-food system', *Sociologia Ruralis*, *42*(4): 329–346.

Winter, M. (2003), 'Geographies of food: agro-food geographies making reconnections', *Progress in Human Geography*, *27*(4): 505–513.

Witmore, C. (2015), 'Bovine Urbanism: the ecological corpulence of Bos urbanus', in Bruce Clarke (ed) *Earth, life, and system: evolution and ecology on a gaian planet*, 225–249, New York: Fordham University Press.

Wolch, J. R. and J. Emel (1998), *Animal geographies: place, politics and identity in the nature-culture borderlands*, London: Verso.

Wolfe, C. (2008), 'Flesh and finitude: thinking animals in (post)humanist philosophy', *SubStance*, *37*(3): 8–36.

Wolfe, C. (2010), *What is posthumanism?* (Vol. *8*). Minneapolis: University of Minnesota Press.

Wolfe, C. (2013), *Before the Law: Humans and other animals in a biopolitical frame*, Chicago: University of Chicago Press.

Wood-Gush, D. G. and K. Vestergaard (1989), 'Exploratory behavior and the welfare of intensively kept animals', *Journal of Agricultural Ethics*, *2*(2): 161–169.

Woods, A. (2010) *Domination or accommodation? Rethinking the history of intensive farming through the nature, sentience, and production of the pig, c1910-64*. Paper to the 'Sentient Creatures' conference. Transforming biopolitics and life matters. Thorbjørnrud Hotel, outside Oslo, 16–17 September 2010.

Woods, A. (2011), 'A historical synopsis of farm animal disease and public policy in twentieth century Britain', *Philosophical Transactions of the Royal Society of London B: Biological Sciences*, *366*(1573): 1943–1954.

Woods, A. (2012), 'The history of veterinary ethics in Britain 1870–2000', in C. Wathes et al. (eds) *Veterinary and animal ethics*, Wiley: Chichester.

Woods, A. (2013), *A manufactured plague: the history of foot-and-mouth disease in Britain*, London: Earthscan.

Woods, A. (2014), 'One Health, many histories', *Veterinary Record*, *2014*: 650–654.

World Animal Protection (2014), 'People's Republic of China', *Animal Protection Index 2014*.

Wypkema, P. R., D. M. Broom, I. J. H. Duncan and G. V. Putten (1983), *Abnormal behaviours in farm animals*, Brussels: Commission of the European Communities.

Xiao, X. (2014), '*Animal Welfare Focal Point P.R.China*'. Seminar for OIE Focal Point on Animal Welfare, Canberra, Australia, 12–14 November 2014. http://www.rr-asia.oie.int/fileadmin /Regional_Representation/Programme/I_Welfare/2014_AWFP_Canberra/06_Dr_Xiao _Achievements_and_Challenges_on_Implementation_of_OIE_AW_Standards.pdf, last accessed 30 July 2017.

Xiuxiang, M., R. Hamer, W. Meng, P. Wang, F. Meng, H. Li, J. Feng, D. Xue and Y. Zhou (2012), 'Animal welfare development in China', *Science*, *338*(6111): 1150–1151.

Yeates, J. W. and D. Main (2008), 'Assessment of positive welfare: a review', *The Veterinary Journal*, *175*(3): 293–300.

Yeates, J. W. et al. (2011), 'Is welfare all that matters? A discussion of what should be included in policy-making regarding animals', *Animal Welfare*, *20*(3): 423–432.

You, X., Y. Li, M. Zhang, H. Yan and R. Zhao (2014), 'A survey of Chinese citizens' perception on farm animal welfare', *PLoS ONE*, *9*(10): e109177.

Index